A CULTURAL HISTORY OF THE HOME

VOLUME 2

A Cultural History of the Home
General Editor: Amanda Flather

Volume 1
A Cultural History of the Home in Antiquity
Edited by Andrew Wallace-Hadrill and Joanne Berry

Volume 2
A Cultural History of the Home in the Medieval Age
Edited by Katherine L. French

Volume 3
A Cultural History of the Home in the Renaissance
Edited by Amanda Flather

Volume 4
A Cultural History of the Home in the Age of Enlightenment
Edited by Clive Edwards

Volume 5
A Cultural History of the Home in the Age of Empire
Edited by Jane Hamlett

Volume 6
A Cultural History of the Home in the Modern Age
Edited by Despina Stratigakos

A CULTURAL HISTORY OF THE HOME

IN THE MEDIEVAL AGE

Edited by Katherine L. French

BLOOMSBURY ACADEMIC
LONDON • NEW YORK • OXFORD • NEW DELHI • SYDNEY

BLOOMSBURY ACADEMIC
Bloomsbury Publishing Plc
50 Bedford Square, London, WC1B 3DP, UK
1385 Broadway, New York, NY 10018, USA
29 Earlsfort Terrace, Dublin 2, Ireland

BLOOMSBURY, BLOOMSBURY ACADEMIC and the Diana logo are trademarks of
Bloomsbury Publishing Plc

First published in Great Britain 2021
This edition published in Great Britain, 2024

Copyright © Bloomsbury Publishing, 2021

Katherine L. French has asserted her right under the Copyright, Designs and Patents Act, 1988, to be identified as Editor of this work.

Cover image © Heritage Images /Getty Images

All rights reserved. No part of this publication may be reproduced or transmitted in any form or by any means, electronic or mechanical, including photocopying, recording, or any information storage or retrieval system, without prior permission in writing from the publishers.

Bloomsbury Publishing Plc does not have any control over, or responsibility for, any third-party websites referred to or in this book. All internet addresses given in this book were correct at the time of going to press. The author and publisher regret any inconvenience caused if addresses have changed or sites have ceased to exist, but can accept no responsibility for any such changes.

A catalogue record for this book is available from the British Library.

A catalog record for this book is available from the Library of Congress.

ISBN: HB: 978-1-4725-8423-6
       Set: 978-1-4725-8441-0
       PB: 978-1-3504-1223-1
       Set: 978-1-3504-1235-4

Series: The Cultural Histories Series

Typeset by RefineCatch Limited, Bungay, Suffolk
Printed and bound in Great Britain

To find out more about our authors and books visit www.bloomsbury.com
and sign up for our newsletters..

CONTENTS

LIST OF ILLUSTRATIONS — vii

GENERAL EDITOR'S PREFACE — x
Amanda Flather

Introduction — 1
Katherine L. French

1 The Meaning of Home in the Middle Ages — 11
   Roisin Cossar

2 The Family and the Household — 31
   Tovah Bender

3 The House in Europe, 800–1450 — 49
   Mark Gardiner

4 Furniture and Furnishings in the Medieval House — 71
   Katherine L. French

5 Work and the Home — 91
   Tanya Stabler Miller

6 Gender and the Home: Archaeological Perspectives — 117
   Eva Svensson

7 Hospitality and the Home — 139
   Jennifer Kolpacoff Deane

8	Religion and the Home: Jewish and Christian Experiences *Elisheva Baumgarten and Katherine L. French*	163
NOTES		185
BIBLIOGRAPHY		193
NOTES ON CONTRIBUTORS		219
INDEX		221

ILLUSTRATIONS

CHAPTER 1

1.1	Detail from the Bayeux Tapestry of a woman and child fleeing a burning house	12
1.2	St Anne teaching the Virgin to read. Master of Sir John Fastolf	18
1.3	Margherita Datini	20
1.4	Letter written by Margherita Datini to Franceso Datini	21
1.5	Washing facilities, Sicily	29

CHAPTER 3

3.1	Reconstruction of the exterior view, and the interior plan and view of a ninth-century sunken hut at Březno, Czech Republic	52
3.2	Distribution of building types and materials in Europe in the early and high Middle Ages	54
3.3	Reconstruction of Complex 4 at Pergamon, Greece	60
3.4	Plan and reconstruction of the mid-thirteenth-century House 1B at Saltés (Huelva), Spain	61
3.5	Section, elevation and plan of the later thirteenth- or fourteenth-century House I/60 at Pfaffenschlag, Czech Republic	63
3.6	Reconstruction of the original form of fifteenth-century urban buildings in Sandwich (Kent), England	67

CHAPTER 4

4.1	Oseburg chest, ninth century	76
4.2	Shoveling chairs, fifteenth century	79

4.3	Reconstruction of an Oseburg bed	80
4.4	'Blind Tobit', 1470–9	83
4.5	French or south Netherlandish chest, fifteenth century	85
4.6	Presentation copy of John Lydgate's *Lives of SS Edmund and Fremund*	87
4.7	'Feast of Herod and the Beheading of John the Baptist', *c.* 1330	89

CHAPTER 5

5.1	Winter Work from *The Golf Book*	94
5.2	Pig Slaughtering from *The Golf Book*	96
5.3	Woman Weaving on a Horizontal Loom from *The Egerton Genesis Picture Book*	98
5.4	Silk Shop from *Tacuinum Sanitatis*	99
5.5	Market Scene from *Livre du gouvernement des princes* by Gilles Romain	100
5.6	Cloth Dyeing from *De proprietatibus rerum*	102
5.7	Gaia, Caecilia, or Tanaquil Spinning, Combing, and Weaving from anonymous French translation of *Des cleres et nobles*	110

CHAPTER 6

6.1	The forest farmer's year in Offerdal parish, Sweden	120
6.2	Dice, chessmen and sherds of a stoneware jug from Edsholm	124
6.3	Dress accessories and jewellery from Saxholmen	125
6.4	Alt-Wartburg	127
6.5	Reconstruction of Lelekovice	128
6.6	Spindle whorl with runic inscription	129
6.7	Reconstruction of farms and fields in the medieval hamlet of Skramle	134

CHAPTER 7

7.1	Hospitality of Abraham. *The Golden Haggadah*	141
7.2	St Martin of Tours Dividing his Cloak with the Beggar from the Sacramentary of Warmund d'Ivrea	145
7.3	Pilgrim from *The Luttrell Psalter*	147
7.4	Kings and queens feasting, while servants below the table serve them with two large pitchers from *Omne Bonum*	152
7.5	January: The Feast of the Duke of Berry from *Les Tres Riches Heures de Duc de Berry*	154
7.6	'A Strange Guest' from *Sir Gawain and the Green Knight*	156

CHAPTER 8

8.1	Middleham Jewel	168
8.2	Lighting Sabbath lamp	171
8.3	Mazer with the inscription '*Potvm et nos benedicat agyos*'	175
8.4	Jewish family meal	176
8.5	Birthing girdle	178
8.6	Early-modern depiction of a birthing chamber and rituals	180

GENERAL EDITOR'S PREFACE

AMANDA FLATHER

A Cultural History of the Home is an authoritative, interdisciplinary, six-volume series investigating the changing meaning of home, both as an idea and as a place to live, from ancient times until the present. Each volume follows the same basic structure and begins with an overview of the cultural, social, political and economic factors that shaped ideas and requirements of home in the period under consideration. Experts examine important aspects of the cultural history of home under eight main headings: the meaning of home; house and home; family and home; gender and home; work and home; furniture and furnishings; religion and home; hospitality and home. A single volume can be read to obtain a thorough knowledge of the period or one of the eight themes can be followed through history by reading the relevant chapter in each of the six volumes, providing an understanding of developments over the longer term.

Individual volumes in the series will cover six historical periods:

Volume 1: *A Cultural History of the Home in Antiquity* (500BCE–800CE)
Volume 2: *A Cultural History of the Home in the Medieval Age* (800–1450)
Volume 3: *A Cultural History of the Home in the Renaissance* (1450–1650)
Volume 4: *A Cultural History of the Home in the Age of Enlightenment* (1650–1800)
Volume 5: *A Cultural History of the Home in the Age of Empire* (1800–1920)
Volume 6: *A Cultural History of the Home in the Modern Age* (1920–2000+)

Introduction

KATHERINE L. FRENCH

In 1387, in an effort to quell London's rebellion against him, King Richard II (r. 1377–99) of England proposed commandeering the houses of elite Londoners, as he moved from Windsor to the Tower. Kings and their retinues across medieval Europe would routinely expect to move into one of their noble's residences when they were in the vicinity; it was both a way of controlling their nobles and a way for nobles to support their king. While Richard's behaviour was not unusual, the power base of most nobles was rural, and London was a city. The mayor and aldermen, the very men whose houses were in danger of being appropriated, had to explain why this would not work for London.

> the allotment of accommodation in this way was quite out of the question in London . . . without their wares the merchants could not make their living here and without their houses they had no means of showing them to purchasers, since they had no means of keeping them elsewhere.
>
> —Riddy 2008: 26

The mayor and aldermen were arguing that they, urban merchants, used their houses very differently from the rural nobility. To be sure, both merchant and noble houses provided shelter from the elements, but crucially, the urban houses in question were places of commerce, unlike the nobles' rural counterparts. Customers came to a merchant's house to purchase goods. Without the sale of merchandise, the merchant could not feed his household (or the king and his retinue), unlike a castle or manor house, which could and did store food for household use. As both Richard and the city officials understood, houses were much more than places to shelter from the rain, sun and snow, but places of labour, social control, government, piety, play and rest.

This volume looks at medieval European houses as both physical spaces and moral units. The chapters focus largely on the western portion of Europe and Christian households receive the bulk of the focus. As such, the authors in this collection address the ways in which houses were symbolic, economic, gendered and social, and how occupants created, sustained and understood the relationship between houses and their many functions. Medieval houses could be grand castles, humble thatched huts, or anything in between. As Mark Gardiner's chapter 'The House in Europe, 800–1450' shows, the construction, size and layout of houses varied not only by wealth, but by region, and across time.

Regardless of construction or size, houses are most commonly thought of as places where families lived, but this was only one part of medieval people's experience with them. Most basically, houses contained households, which, as Tovah Bender's chapter 'The Family and the Household' shows, comprised both individuals related by blood and people connected by economics and politics. These relationships varied across time and space as well. Families living together could comprise two or three generations, married siblings and their spouses' children, or just one married sibling and (usually) his wife, children and unmarried siblings. Household members bound by economic and political affiliations included masters, lords, servants, apprentices, retainers and the enslaved. A household often started with a married couple, but it did not have to. Households might include unrelated individuals of the same or different sexes living together for emotional, spiritual or economic reasons. Whether related by blood or economics, the household living within the walls of a house evolved over time as members aged and fortunes changed.

Houses and households had economic, religious, political and social meanings. These consequences are not only interesting to scholars but were debated over the course of the Middle Ages. In the twelfth century, the renowned French abbess, Heloise (d. 1164), famously ventriloquized by her former husband and philosopher Abelard (1079–1142) in his 'History of My Calamities', described domestic life as busy, noisy, and crowded with children and visitors.

> Consider . . . the true conditions for a dignified way of life. What harmony can there be between pupils and nursemaids, desks and cradles, books or tablets and distaffs, pen or stylus and spindles? Who can concentrate on thoughts of Scripture or philosophy and be able to endure babies crying, nurses soothing them with lullabies, and all the noisy coming and going of men and women about the house? Will he put up with the constant muddle and squalor which small children bring into the home? The wealthy can do so, you will say, for their mansions and large houses can provide privacy, and

being rich, they do not have to count the cost nor be tormented by daily cares.

—Abelard 2003: 14

Heloise's critique comes at a point in Abelard's narrative when he is trying to convince her to marry him, now that she is pregnant with their child. Heloise resists his proposal because, for her, children and their requirements were incompatible with intellectual pursuits. Her critique picks up on early Christian tropes that privileged a monastic or an ascetic life over a secular life, which to the monastic mind naturally and inevitably included women and babies and therefore sex (Salih 2001: 6).[1] Heloise's commentary brings together a number of assumptions about houses, the activities conducted within them, and their significance. Perhaps most profoundly, she connects houses and households to women. Childbirth, which in the Middle Ages happened at home, solidified the connection between houses and women, even if this was not true of all households. Yet this is an ancient but socially contingent connection, which helps deny as households those domestic arrangements that did not produce babies, did not have women, or both. The Hebrew Bible provides but one starting place for connecting women to houses. Proverbs 14:1 states: 'A wise woman builds her house: but a foolish one will pull down with her hands that also which is built.' Here the house is as much a moral object as a physical one, and the behaviour of the women it contains has implications for the wider community, which underscores the patriarchal nature of the association of women with houses.

Modern scholars have perpetuated this unquestioned gendering of the house as female by ascribing to it the concept of 'private'. Distinctions of 'private', and its implied antithesis, 'public', developed in the nineteenth century, when the Victorians also developed an idea of the 'Angel in the Household' as a way of legitimizing and further moralizing women's ties to the house. As many scholars have noted, the idea of women staying at home and not working, while men went out in the world and worked, was attainable by only some classes, which further distinguished work from labour.[2] Yet, none of these assumptions can be applied to the Middle Ages (if indeed they worked for the nineteenth century), making public and private deeply anachronistic concepts. Nonetheless, many medievalists, most notably Georges Duby (1919–96) in his five-volume series *A History of Private Life*, found 'private' to be a useful analytic. In the preface to his volume on the Middle Ages, Duby askes:

Is it legitimate (not merely pertinent) to speak of private life in the Middle Ages, to transfer to such a remote era the idea of *privacy*, which first emerged in the nineteenth century in England, at the time the society that had progressed furthest in the establishment of a 'bourgeois culture'?

—1988: ix

Duby answers in the affirmative and the chapter headings he included in *A History of Private Life* revolved around various kinds of domicile. The activities he discussed include childbirth, food and self-control, or that lack thereof, all of which involved women, were performed by women, or required women. In this way, he continued the close connection between privacy, the house and women.

Many medievalists pushed back against the use of public and private analytical categories, at least in the ways that Duby used them. They argue that the behaviour and activities that happened within houses had larger social and political significance, making private and public the wrong concepts for discussing them.³ As such, the activities conducted in beds and at tables were heavily regulated and controlled. For example, the sex life of a king had international consequences and was carefully monitored, while guilds regulated and enforced the work schedule of member artisans who worked within their homes. Whether or not we accept the argument that medieval notions of private, if they existed, were different from modern ones, unpacking assumptions about what we in the twenty-first century mean by private and what medieval people might have meant by private helps further to historicize women's connections with the house, showing it not to be inevitable or necessarily natural in the Middle Ages (Riddy 2008).

As with so many assumptions, once we historicize them, they start to unravel; the connection between women and houses is no different. As Eva Svensson shows in her chapter in this volume, 'Gender and the Home: Archaeological Perspectives', houses in and of themselves are – not unproblematically – gendered female. Castles, which are technically defined as fortified residences, housed many more men than women. Consequently, many of the so-called housekeeping tasks necessary to their functioning were carried out by men.

Heloise's description of a busy, noisy house full of babies and women's work, however, underlies another important medieval expectation of households: they were sites of production, whether they are producing babies, chaos, or knowledge, as Heloise expects, or items for sale, as in the case of merchants' and artisans' houses. The medieval household and its dwelling was an economic unit, and therefore, a place of a great deal of labour. As Svensson points out, labour is the easiest place to see gender in a house, because most of it was gendered in some fashion. But as she and Tanya Sabler Miller, in her chapter 'Work and the Home', both discuss, the gendering of labour was not universally the same across medieval Europe. The changing status of certain occupations along with evolving technology and environment all played a role in determining who performed which activities. Medieval society prioritized this labour, with the labour of male householders valued above that of wives, which was valued above that of servants and the enslaved. Moreover, because men performed much of the labour conducted within the confines of a house, the house could not be universally viewed as a female space.

Heloise is also acutely aware of the role that wealth played in shaping the experience of house and household. As all the chapters show, wealth allowed for the construction of different kinds of houses that served different purposes or fulfilled the same purposes differently. Castles housed a noble family and its military retinue. Thus, shelter, military functions and domestic provisioning all combined within their walls. While some urban houses were built of stone possibly to withstand attack, urban houses, as the mayor and aldermen of London noted, were more readily market places rather than military spaces. Peasant huts, with and without foundations, protected not only humans and food supplies from the elements, but also housed animals. Their material precariousness made them vulnerable to extreme weather and military predation. My chapter 'Furniture and Furnishings in the Medieval House' demonstrates that the level of comfort afforded by wealth was tremendous, but also a choice; householders did not automatically choose to spend resources on comfort. Wealth not only determined comfort within a house, but also the tasks assigned to members of the household and how they experienced the house. As Heloise notes, the wealthy could hire help to care for children and to contain dirt and chaos, the poor could not. In a poor house, women did any number of tasks that would be distributed to servants and the enslaved of either sex when there were resources.

Heloise's complaint also underscores the belief that the house was a moral, symbolic and emotional space. As she denounces the noise, chaos and dirt of a busy household, she implicitly invokes peace, quiet and cleanliness – ideas that not only draw to mind a monastic cell, but had, as Rossin Cossar shows in her chapter 'The Meaning of Home in the Middle Ages', moral and symbolic import in the Middle Ages. While medieval people had many different associations wrapped up with the buildings in which they lived, law, religion and social expectation distinguished the behaviours carried out inside a house and those outside, making it possible for Cossar to argue that medieval people had a concept of 'home'. As we might then expect, the boundaries that demarcated the perimeter of a house carried great legal and moral weight. How one entered its confines was significant. Uninvited, one is an intruder; invited, one is a guest. Yet, as Jennifer Kolpacoff Deane shows us in her chapter 'Hospitality and the Home', hospitality was a fraught concept, where the host and the visitor needed to negotiate a series of concerns that included not only the safety of each, but also their reputations. If the house belonged to a king or lord, then the behaviour of the host and guest had larger political consequences. If the host or guest was poor, then there were spiritual ones, as sharing what one had with a stranger was charity for Christians, Muslims and Jews. Because life so often began and ended within the walls of a house, houses were also spiritual units, regulated by the religious proscriptions, as Elisheva Baumgarten and my chapter 'Religion and the Home: Jewish and Christian Experiences' shows. Religious practices shaped daily life and could imbue quotidian household items with spiritual significance, even if only temporarily. How household residents observed religious strictures added to the morality of living in a medieval house.

The chapters in this volume draw on a long historiographical tradition, but one that lies more with anthropologists and archaeologists than historians. Houses, and the activities they contain, have long been of interest to anthropologists and archaeologists, because they were some of the earliest scholars to argue that houses shaped behaviour and world view. It would take many more words than I am allowed for this introduction to trace anthropological interest in houses, but one important figure is Pierre Bourdieu (1930–2002). His work on North Africa and Berber houses ultimately led to his concept of *habitus*, which he understood as a system of habit or disposition, coming from one's repeated experiences of place, space and conditions (Bourdieu 1977). Bourdieu's influence has been profound on archaeologists excavating and interpreting houses. House design, whether 'organic' or 'intentional', tells us a great deal about the social attitudes and material conditions of those building and living in the house. Habitus remains an important concept for scholars of many disciplines interested in the relationship between individuals and behaviour and spaces and structures.

Despite the pregnant meanings of space represented by Heloise's comments and in the work of archaeologists, historians, in contrast, have a long tradition of ignoring houses, households, and household concerns. This is in part because of unexamined assumptions about houses and their connection to women and the seeming ahistoricity of the activities conducted in them. Great men might have slept in houses, but their important historical contributions happened elsewhere: on battlefields, or in government buildings, religious structures and universities. Marxists' attention to labour and the changing means of production put households, if not houses, on the historical agenda, as the household was the unit of 'feudal' production. As Duby's series, *A History of Private Life*, discussed earlier, shows, the rise of interest in social history, women's history and material culture further promoted studies of the house, households, and the residents and activities conducted within its confines. While not accepting the connection of women to houses as natural or inevitable, houses were still often where medieval women were to be found, and their activities, whether described by contemporaries or modern scholars, are usually cast in the context of household contributions, so questions of women's experiences often encompass the household.

This overly brief historiography implies greater division among disciplines interested in houses and housing than there really is. Archaeologists ask questions about the relationship between building style and prevailing economic or intellectual systems; historians are interested in how the concept of habitus can illuminate, among other things, gender roles; and both archaeologists and historians are interested in change over time. As the chapters by historians and archaeologists in this collection show, we all borrow freely from each other to answer the questions we have.

The period covered by this volume, roughly 800–1450, is more symbolic than anything else, but it does define a meaningful time period conventionally known as the Middle Ages. The year 800 marks Pope Leo III's (r. 795–816) coronation of Charlemagne (742–814) as the Holy Roman Emperor. Through a combination of inheritance and conquest, Charlemagne's vast territory came to include all of modern-day France and Germany, northern Italy, and a bit of northern Spain. While historians debate the political significance of this achievement, it marks the first time since the Roman Empire that this much European territory had been under one rule. Even though historians debate the quality and depth of Charlemagne's territorial unification and it did not last beyond the reign of his son Louis the Pious (r. 814–40), western Europe enjoyed economic expansion during his reign. At the same time, Norse, Magyar and Muslim expansion between the eighth and eleventh centuries made life difficult for many individuals in Europe, but also spread goods from the Middle East across Europe. Charlemagne's shroud, for example, was made of Byzantine silk.

The year 1450 is even more symbolic as an end point for the Middle Ages, although many things that medieval people took for granted were ending. In 1453, the Ottoman Turks finalized their conquest of Byzantium by taking over Constantinople. The same year, the English, who had been fighting the French for far longer than one hundred years, would decisively lose the Battle of Castillon, thereby ending their current military engagement, the so-called Hundred Years' War (1337–1453), although no treaty would be signed for another twenty-two years. Lastly, in 1455, Johannes Gutenberg (c.1398–1468) would introduce to Europe his 42-line Bible created by moveable type. Although it would be a while before the significance of all these changes would become apparent, they mark profound shifts in orientation, expectation and practice that had been fundamental to living in the medieval world.

The movement of people, goods and ideas all had an impact on how and where people lived. To fend off the Vikings and other military threats, Frankish lords built castles. With surplus resources, householders bought items that provided comfort and colour, or aided devotion. Technological changes, such as the horizontal loom, the waterwheel and beer brewing, to name only three, altered how people laboured within their houses and who performed which tasks. The codification of laws shaped how people understood the physical integrity of their homes, the reception they should give to those who wanted to enter, and their identification with the house itself.

Many of these changes were the result of economic expansion that accelerated in the twelfth century. The slowing pace of migration and invasion and increasing political consolidation boosted trade and introduced broad shared trends that diminished local isolation and thus localized cultures. Conventionally, historians talk about the twelfth century as a time of urban expansion; old Roman cities such as Paris and Florence were revitalized and new cities such as Ghent developed. To protect and aid their businesses, merchants and artisans – men (and some women) whose livelihoods depended solely on manufacturing and trading rather than agriculture or military engagement – began to assert their interests by seeking charters for their trade associations and the cities that fostered them. Those living in cities, whether well-off and connected to city governance or poor and dependent on piece work or charity, lived substantially differently from those in the countryside, although the prosperity of one affected the other. As all the chapters in this collection note, urban houses, household composition, furnishings, work routines and attitudes towards strangers all differed from their rural counterparts. Cities were also more diverse. By 1200, cities across Europe had Jewish populations and cities in southern Italy and Iberia also included Muslims. Their needs, aesthetics and concerns shaped not only their own housing and households, but those of their Christian neighbours.

The textual sources employed by the authors of these chapters further reflect these historical changes. The differences between the sources used before and after 1200 reflect growth in both royal and civic bureaucracies, as well as the ending of migrations and invasions, where books and other documents were often collateral damage in raids. For the earlier period, literature, most notably *Beowulf*, an epic poem referenced by many of the authors, but also saints' lives, sermons and law codes offer glimpses into living conditions and concerns. Given the patterns of medieval source survival, we have many more administrative records for the later Middle Ages. The Florentine Catasto helps us see household composition, wills and inventories show us the contents of houses, and civic ordinances regulated interactions among neighbours, often over issues brought on by close proximity and economic competition. Other sources, such as letter collections, open up the emotional entanglements of families, and self-help manuals, such as *The Good Wife's Guide*, also used by many contributors, lay out moral expectations and hopes. Textual sources thus offer uneven coverage of the issues pertinent to medieval houses.

Material culture, whether the remarkable and unique Bayeux Tapestry, artworks or archaeological finds, offers a different vision of the medieval home. While archaeological finds present their own challenges of recovery and interpretation, they are able to offer a more even coverage of the periods in question. Thus, from archaeology we know about the broad localization of housing styles, something that is difficult to see in texts. Archaeology also shows us how male-dominated castles were in practice, while romances would have us believe women were numerous and ever-present.

Taken together, the eight chapters in this volume address a variety of issues that impact houses and their residents. This is an interdisciplinary volume, although art historians and literary scholars are missing. In part this is a consequence of people's busy schedules, but it is also in part due to the questions different disciplines ask. For many, houses and households are still a backdrop for other issues rather than a direct focus. All contributors here hope that this collection will start more conversations and produce more scholarship related to the places and spaces in which medieval people lived and died and worked and played. Houses, whatever their composition, size and location, are fundamental to the human experience, providing much more than shelter, but framing world view and social expectations.

CHAPTER ONE

The Meaning of Home in the Middle Ages

ROISIN COSSAR

INTRODUCTION

Midway through the Bayeux Tapestry, with its depiction of the 1066 Norman invasion of England, there is a brief scene of an attack on a house or cottage (Figure 1.1). In the scene there are two figures: a woman with her hair covered wearing a long dress, and a smaller person, likely a child. The two flee from the flames that rise from the roof of the house, which has been set alight by Norman soldiers carrying torches. The woman leads the child by her right hand while gesturing to the fire with her upturned left hand, her eyes seemingly focused on the flames consuming the house above their heads (Wilson 2004: Fig. 50).[1] The Latin inscription above the fleeing pair simply states that 'a house (*domus*) is on fire', but the identities of the figures, their responses as seen in their gestures, and their inclusion at this pivotal moment in the text suggest that the designer of the tapestry was trying to evoke the effect of the invasion not only on the political institutions of the kingdom, but also on its domestic world.[2] The medieval audience for the tapestry would have understood that this scene depicted not only a location, but also a feeling of attachment and obligation to a place and a group of people – that is, a 'home'.[3] The designer of the tapestry seems to have believed, as the American poet Robert Frost wrote centuries later, that 'home' was 'the place where, when you have to go there, they have to take you in' (1915: 20).

This chapter surveys the medieval idea of home, examining how it was defined in two ways: first, as emotional bonds among members of a household

FIGURE 1.1: Detail from the Bayeux Tapestry of a Woman and Child Fleeing a Burning House (11th century). © City of Bayeux Museum.

and second, as behaviours within domestic space. I have restricted my examination to a Christian context. In Christian theology, home and family existed in tension with the concept of salvation, as seen in scriptural instructions to the faithful to leave their homes in order to follow Jesus.[4] As such, medieval legal, ecclesiastical and literary sources from a Christian perspective contain evidence of ambivalence about the place of the home and the household in the Christian world. As written sources increasingly described and discussed domestic culture over the course of the Middle Ages, such concerns were more often articulated. For medieval Christians, the idea of 'home' was anchored by a spectrum of feelings ranging from security and intimacy to tension and even unease.

PROBLEMS AND SOURCES

'Home' is a concept with a history, but for some scholars, the pre-modern period did not participate in that history. For instance, a long tradition of seeing people in the Middle Ages as controlled by a monolithic religious culture and unable to understand themselves as individuals has led some to deny the possibility of a medieval notion of domesticity, defined by modern commentators as 'family, intimacy, and a devotion to the home' (Riddy 2008: 14). Another commonplace, that medieval people did not make a distinction between work space and domestic space, might lead some to question whether people in the Middle Ages shared an idea of 'home' as separate from the rest of their world. It is certainly true that artisans' workshops could often be located within their dwellings, professors taught their students in their residences, and some English peasant houses incorporated taverns into their living spaces (Hanawalt 1986: 28; Goldberg 2008: 135). Furthermore, in some medieval law or custom, the house was seen as a space that public officials could enter and search if they suspected any untoward sexual behaviour, including consensual acts such as fornication or adultery, was occurring there (McSheffrey 2004: 987–8). But just because in the Middle Ages the culture of 'home' had a different relationship to the world outside the walls of a residence than it does today does not mean that the period entirely lacked such a culture.[5] The medieval idea of home was more flexible than the modern concept in some ways, but it was also structured around fairly rigid legal and social expectations of relationships and behaviours. We will begin tracking these expectations by examining the types of sources where they can be found.

Texts written in the Middle Ages that establish the expectations of domestic culture include a range of prescriptive sources, explicitly designed as teaching tools or to shape behaviour, such as conduct literature and civic statutes and other legislation. Others appear descriptive but contain prescriptive elements, such as biographies of saints (hagiography) and literary texts. All of these sources yield understandings of the ideal behaviours, relationships and organization of space within medieval dwelling places. But the moral meaning of home can also be found in texts normally considered 'descriptive', such as the visual depictions found in the Bayeux Tapestry, records of court cases, legal contracts, inventories of household objects, and personal letters. The normative aspects of these texts have sometimes been ignored by historians, but many are underpinned by implicit ideals of home life, such as inventories that describe certain prized objects in detail while neglecting others.[6] In this chapter I examine how many of those sources have been employed by other historians who study the idea of home in the Middle Ages. I also trace those ideas as found in texts written by or on behalf of several medieval women: the *Life* of the twelfth-century English mystic Christina of Markyate; the letters dictated in Italy by a fourteenth-century merchant's wife, Margherita Datini; the book detailing the religious and domestic life of the early fifteenth-century Englishwoman Margery Kempe; and finally the letters of the Florentine widow Alessandra Strozzi to her sons Filippo and Lorenzo.

The Latin terms used to refer to residences or dwellings were particularly flexible in the Middle Ages. While moderns make distinctions between terms such as 'house' and 'building', in the Middle Ages the Latin words *domus* (house), *cella* (cell), *hospitium* (hospice, tavern) and *edificium* (building) all referred to spaces where people ate, slept, had sex, raised children and possibly worked. The reasons behind the choice to use certain terms in given contexts were not always clear. For instance, *domus* could be used to refer to a freestanding dwelling or one part of a larger structure. This fluidity is evident in the *Life* of Christina of Markyate, a twelfth-century English girl raised in comfortable circumstances who eventually became an anchoress and then abbess of a monastery. The author of the text describes Christina's childhood in the lavishly decorated and spacious *domus* belonging to her parents. When she left her parents' house for a tiny room attached to the chapel of an anchorite named Roger, the writer similarly refers to this enclosure, which he also calls a 'prison', as a *domus* (Talbot 1987: 102–3). In some other contexts the term *domus* was closely associated with the secular realm. For instance, while in twelfth-century England it could be used in both secular and religious contexts, by contrast, in early medieval Italy, *domus* was closely linked to secular life. For instance, when the Italian bishops of the early medieval period used the term *domus* to refer to their residences, they were making an architectural, ecclesiastical and cultural break with the Roman name for similar structures (*episcopia*) that had previously been their dwelling places. Their choice of *domus* instead of *episcopia* to describe their residences made a linguistic link between themselves and the laity (Miller 2004: 14; 2017: 35, 40). Maureen Miller further traces how bishops then ceased to employ *domus* to describe their residences around the time of episcopal reforms of the eleventh and twelfth centuries, choosing instead to describe them as 'palaces' (*palatia*), thus marking the higher power to which they now aspired in Italian cities.

But while *domus* shifted in meaning across geographic areas, everywhere it remained largely a word for a structure, and so it does not easily map onto the concept of 'home', with its evocation of both place and emotional bonds. Unitary terms for this concept were rare in the Middle Ages. The closest we come to it could be the term *lar*, formerly used to refer to Roman household gods and employed in some medieval legal records to refer to households. Its reference to both place and spiritual context is close to the modern understanding of 'home'.[7] For example, in the early fourteenth century, a widow living with her brother-in-law in northern Italy argued that she was too poor to pay taxes to her local neighbourhood association, shown by the fact that she was legally a member of her brother-in-law's household, as they shared 'bread, wine, a hearth and a *larem* (Bergamo 1316: #420). Here the best translation for *larem* might be 'home'. But this type of statement is rare for the period; for the most part we have to understand an idea of home in medieval records from descriptions of shared activities. For instance, as in the above example, acts of commensality were typical in legal records concerned with home life. Similarly, in another example from a legal record, a group of unrelated residents in a twelfth-century Italian hospital was described before a court as householders because they shared 'bread, wine, and a hearth' (Saccomani 2000: 151). Such descriptions indicate that in the moral universe of the Middle Ages, definitions of 'home' were based in part on the shared activities of those who lived under the same roof, rather than on the blood relationship among those people.[8] These definitions thus suggest that medieval ideas of 'home' were in part founded on notions of reciprocity and even equitable relations.

The shared activities that ideally defined the household were only part of the definition of 'home'. The legal relationships between residents that constituted ideal home life in the Middle Ages were also powerfully hierarchical. Several important legal relationships delineated the legal rights of a male head of household over his dependents, including both his children and, in some places, his wife. For instance, in England, the concept of *coverture* established the rights of a husband to 'cover' his wife, safeguarding her (and her property) and denying her any legal personality of her own. This legal ideal had far-reaching effects for married women's ability to act for themselves in public, although Margery McIntosh (2005) argues that it may have had benefits as well as drawbacks for women who worked.[9] In other parts of the West, the Roman-law category of the household head or patriarch (*paterfamilias*), who exercised the authority of paternal control (*patria potestas*) over his dependents, underpinned domestic life. According to this model, the patriarch did not have to share a residence with all of his dependents. As Leon Battista Alberti wrote in his treatise on the family in the fifteenth century, families might not all share the same dwelling, but 'let them place themselves under the shadow of a single will' (Herlihy and Klapisch-Zuber 1985: 324). Patriarchs could even exercise control over their married sons and daughters who might live elsewhere (Kuehn 1994: 201–3). The ideals of *patria potestas* applied only to some individuals in medieval communities, notably lay men. But the concept could also be claimed and performed by those who did not necessarily have a legal right to it. For instance, clergy could adopt roles as *patres familiares* in their households, despite the fact that they were legally prohibited from marrying and their children were not legitimate (Cossar 2017). Similarly, Lucie Laumonier has shown that in Montpellier, in the south of France, the concept of *patria potestas* was rarely, if ever, explicitly used in that city's legal records, but many laws in the city used it as an implicit organizing principle (2015: 653–4).

The language used to refer to dwelling places and to the relationships within those places might be elastic, but the ideal home was not necessarily a flexible place. Instead, a potentially uneasy mix of social hierarchies and shared activities defined home for medieval people. That tension within the definition of home extended to encompass the state of homelessness, which might be deployed both to threaten and to gain spiritual reward. We have already seen that the concept of home in the Middle Ages extended beyond the idea of an intimate space to include the emotional and social bonds among its members. Both as a space and a set of relationships, the idea of home thus acted as a means of organizing the members of a community, making them accountable to political, social and religious authority. Consequently, homelessness could be deployed as a social threat, and those whose homes were not ordered according to expected ideals were increasingly of concern to both secular and ecclesiastical authorities over the course of the period.[10]

A lack of home reflected and shaped marginal legal status across Europe in the Middle Ages. William Ian Miller notes that in Iceland, the spectre of homelessness was the source of much anxiety within the island's political culture, and those who had no specific home were particularly vulnerable. Their attackers were not liable to punishment and sexual attacks on homeless women were not legally defined as rape (Miller 2004: 126). The imposition of homelessness could also be wielded as a weapon by authorities against individuals. Across the West in the twelfth and thirteenth centuries, papal and imperial laws stated that those convicted of heresy, political crimes, or who were excommunicated were to have their property confiscated or even demolished (Sutherland 1984: 15; Vodola 1986: 166). The practice was widespread – seen, for instance, when the twelfth-century count, Charles of Flanders burned down the house of his enemy Borsiard, who was involved in a private war within Charles' domain (Galbert of Bruges 1982: 105). Similarly, priests who continued to live in sexual relationships with women after the papal reform movement of the twelfth century might be subject to the loss of their benefices, while their female partners could be threatened with expulsion from their homes (Cossar 2017: 56). Home, then, was ideally founded on a stable location and set of relationships. It thus reflected and established the social order in medieval communities, and so the destruction of a residence and the homelessness that resulted could be used as a weapon against those who rejected that order.

While in the secular realm a stable and secure home was held up as a social ideal, in the medieval Christian world the idea of home provoked more unease. Despite scriptural calls for individuals to leave home and follow Christ, within the early medieval Christian church, religious figures advocated for the ideal of fixed residences for ecclesiastics and religious. By contrast, centuries later, some medieval Christian thinkers embraced homelessness as an ideal. For instance, in his influential early medieval rule for monasteries, Benedict of Nursia (2016: 138) defined co-residence and physical stability for monks as an important feature of legitimate religious life, while he criticized homeless religious wanderers as a destabilizing force. He wrote that wandering monks 'are always on the move and never settle down', and noted that 'of their wretched way of life it is better to be silent than to speak'. Benedict's strict statements about the need for monks to remain enclosed within their religious homes or monasteries became the foundation of a monastic movement that spread across the medieval West.[11] But while that ideal of the paramount importance of stability within monasticism was highly influential, it found a challenge in the early thirteenth-century ideas of Francis of Assisi. Francis made wandering and homelessness the core of his new religious movement, which was founded on the idea of emulating the poverty of Christ and his followers. Although the Franciscans eventually did settle into their own churches and religious houses, the ideal of apostolic poverty lived as rootlessness remained an appealing aspect of the movement for many (Burr 2001). These conflicting ideas suggest that a stable domestic culture was not the only ideal of medieval Christian experience, and transcending stability for a more precarious existence could provide spiritual benefits as well.

While most people did not become monks or friars, they could temporarily give up their stable homes in search of Christian salvation by embarking on a pilgrimage to holy places – perhaps the cathedral dedicated to St James the Apostle in north-western Spain, or to the churches of Rome, or the Holy Land itself. The armies who set out to recapture Jerusalem and other sites in the eastern Mediterranean, too, described themselves as pilgrims throughout the Middle Ages. Those who wrote about their experiences as pilgrims often reflected on the anxiety and fear that accompanied leaving home. For instance, as she thought about a planned pilgrimage to Jerusalem, Margery Kempe (2015: 43) worried, 'what shall I do when I am far from home, and in strange lands, and my manservant is against me? Then my physical comfort will be gone . . .' Margery was right about the physical and emotional privations she would endure while on pilgrimage – for instance, when her fellow pilgrims left her alone and sick in Venice, and she was forced to eat by herself and her servant refused to cook or clean for her (Kempe 2015: 62–3). Although he did not experience the same social isolation as Margery when he accompanied the French king Louis IX on crusade in the mid-thirteenth century, Jean de Joinville, seneschal to Louis, also described the experience of dislocation that leaving home could bring. He wrote that he forced himself to not look back as he departed, 'fearful that my heart would melt for the fine castle and two children I was leaving behind' (de Joinville 2008: 176).

Leaving the comforts and security of home voluntarily, on pilgrimage or as part of a commitment to enter the religious life, demonstrated the importance of an individual's personal spiritual goals. The fact that such goals were often sought outside the physical confines of the home points once again to ambivalence about domestic culture in medieval Christian society. 'Home' was a powerful concept that could reinforce but also challenge the social and religious order. Its double-edged aspect was particularly evident when we examine the role of women within a home. Women were responsible for many aspects of home life, and as such they had arguably more authority at home than they did in the world outside the household walls. For example, women were commonly expected to serve as their children's spiritual teachers, a role that medieval people believed traced back to St Anne's teaching of her daughter

Mary, memorialized in art of the later Middle Ages (Sheingorn 2003) (Figure 1.2). As Pamela Sheingorn (2003: 134) argues, 'through the pictorial arts, Anne empowers her daughter and encourages other mothers to follow her example'. As caregivers to all members of their households, women also occupied positions of authority within the home. Felicity Riddy (2003: 222) argues that women's tasks within the household, and in particular their care for the bodies of their family members, allowed them an authority that 'work[ed] against the hierarchical structures that were assumed by urban and national lawmakers'. But the home could also be a place where women were silenced or controlled, as we shall see in the second section of this chapter.

The medieval definition of home was further marked by the development of new forms of domestic language during the later Middle Ages. Riddy (2002: 222) has described how 'homely' words associated with the feelings and

FIGURE 1.2: St. Anne Teaching the Virgin to Read. Master of Sir John Fastolf (French, active c. 1450). Via Wikimedia Commons (public domain).

obligations of 'home' became more common in England by the fourteenth century, reinforcing her view that the home was a place where social barriers common in the outside world relaxed (Erler 2008: 275–6). As Jennifer Deane's chapter in this volume shows us, the linguistic form of transactions between residents and guests in the home reflected or shaped the close relationships expected in that space. But the language used with and by visitors illustrated the complicated nature of the home, which both mitigated social barriers and reinforced some hierarchical distinctions. For instance, when the parishioners and clients of a Venetian notary-priest and moneylender came to his house asking to borrow small amounts of cash or have him write up a legal document, they employed a version of 'homely' language to approach him, calling him their 'intimate friend' (*intimo mio*). But social hierarchies remained a part of this domestic world, as well. The would-be clients of the Venetian moneylender knew this, as some also appealed to his 'fatherly' nature in their requests for assistance (Cossar 2017: 150). Such language indicates the existence of a medieval domestic culture which mingled social hierarchies and shared intimacies, with both based on an unspoken understanding of the potentially disruptive power of the affective bonds within the household.

DOMESTICITY AND INTIMACY

The ideal home for many people in the Middle Ages was a place where intimate bonds abounded. Intimacies linked couples, parents and children, residents and visitors, and masters and their apprentices or servants. Intimacies can also be complicated, encompassing both love (or at least affection) and more fraught emotions; they can also exist between people of different rank or status. The moral universe of the medieval home reflected these realities. Many sources from the period point to a common expectation of bonds of affection or at least familiarity among medieval household members. For example, in her letters to her Italian merchant husband Francesco Datini as he followed his business interests to Avignon, Florence and Barcelona, Margherita Datini (2012: 58) often wrote about her feelings, including her frustration, anger and concern for him (Figure 1.3). She also noted her familiarity with his habits, writing in 1387 that 'having lived with you for ten years, it would be a disgrace if I didn't know your ways' (Figure 1.4). Admiration and respect, more than love, were understood to be the bedrock of a stable domestic life in the medieval West. Margery Kempe, who lived around the same time as Margherita Datini, tried to follow a Christian life apart from her husband, who was not eager to separate from her. But even during the couple's times of difficulty, Margery noted her husband's 'tenderness and compassion' for her (2015: 12).

Although she was reluctant to do so, prodded by her visions of Jesus and by her flesh-and-blood neighbours, Margery (2015: 162) gave up living separately

FIGURE 1.3: Margherita Datini (c. 1400). From *La Trinità*, Niccolò di Pietro Gerini, Musei Capitolini Rome. Sailko (own work) via Wikimedia Commons (public domain).

from her husband to care for him in his old age out of concern for his wellbeing after he had fallen at home. Care for the aging was an important expectation of home life across the medieval West. Alessandra Strozzi (1997: 140–1) told her son Filippo that above all else, she hoped to come and live with him in her older age, since 'in that natural course of things I love you and feel much more tenderness for you than you do for me. And the reason is that I can only do badly without you, but you can do everything without me.' The expectation that people would care for each other in times of illness and upheaval was a common feature of the culture of home in the Middle Ages. Much of that care fell to women, and in some cases treatises and other didactic texts encouraged caregivers to consider the spiritual benefits of their work. In her *Book*, Margery Kempe drew on her experience of returning home to care for her husband to

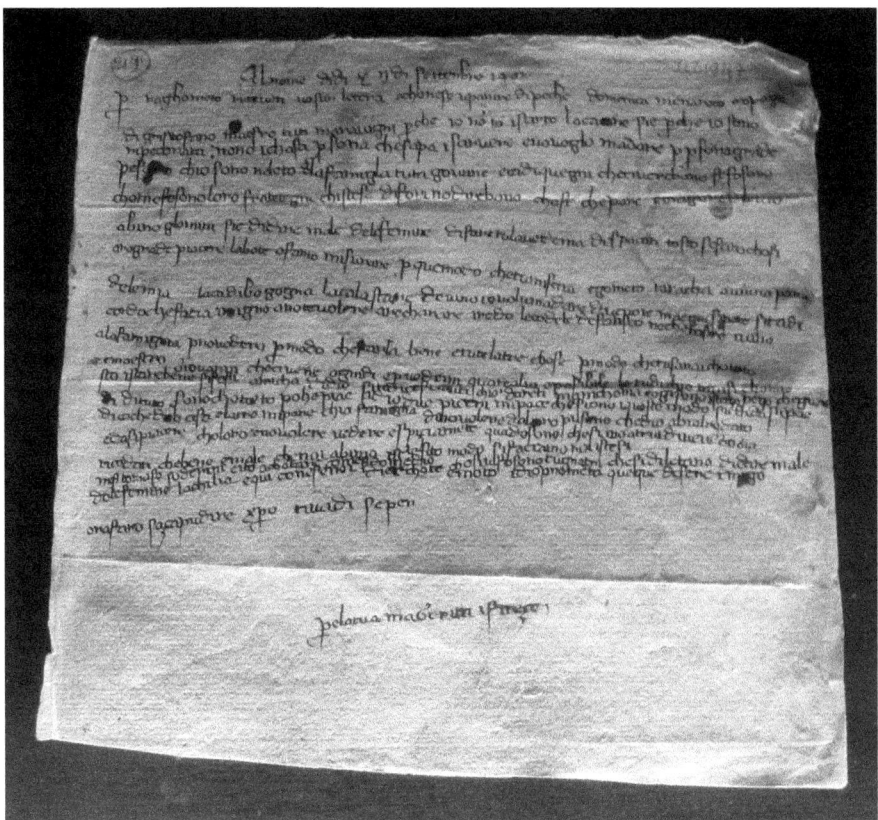

FIGURE 1.4: Letter written by Margherita Datini to Franceso Datini (1387). Sailko (Own work) [CC BY-SA 3.0 via Wikimedia Commons (public domain).

reflect on her relationship with Christ. She perhaps enhanced that experience to an extent when she noted that she 'served [her husband] and helped him . . . as she would have done Christ Himself' (Kempe 2015: 162). Margery's reluctant assistance of her husband might also have been driven by the spectre of the social opprobrium she would likely have faced if she abandoned him completely. Certainly tales of those who did not fulfil their obligations to their aged parents were common in the medieval period. The famous story of the man who turned his ailing father outside wrapped in a blanket, only to find his own son setting aside a blanket for his father for the time when he would grow old and sick, was one cautionary story that made the rounds in the Middle Ages (Murray 2001: 444).

The expectation that intimate care for those living in one's home should serve as the foundation of domestic life can also be found in literary sources from the period. The fourteenth-century writer Giovanni Boccaccio famously described the breakdown of relations between family members during the first terrible outbreak of plague in mid-fourteenth-century Florence. He wrote that the plague was so devastating that each individual acted only for themselves, and that 'brothers abandoned their brothers, uncles their nephews, sisters their brothers, and in many cases wives deserted their husbands. But even worse, and almost incredible, was the fact that fathers and mothers refused to nurse and assist their own children, as though they did not belong to them' (Boccaccio 1972: 54). While Boccaccio's descriptions of family members, even those most closely connected, forgetting their obligations to each other have often been read as a chronicle of lived experience during the Black Death, scholars today tend to argue that his words should be read as a moralizing statement about the need to preserve the stability of home and family bonds even in challenging times (Wray 2004).

Boccaccio's emphasis on the terrible shame of parents who neglected their obligations to their children found echoes in many other texts, both descriptive and prescriptive, about the need to care for the most vulnerable within the home across the medieval period. Just as the woman fleeing the burning house in the Bayeux Tapestry pulled the smaller child along by the hand, so did Alessandra Strozzi (1997: 38–9) hesitate to send her youngest son Matteo to join his brothers outside Florence in the winter of 1448 because, as she wrote, 'he's little and still needs me to look after him'. In another text recognizing the conventional ideal that adults should safeguard small children in their care, Piero di Strenna, the 'milk father' (that is, husband of the wet nurse) of Francesco Datini's young daughter Ginevra, wrote to Francesco to tell him that Piero would be accompanying four-year-old Ginevra to Florence, where the little girl would rejoin her father's household. Piero planned to make the trip 'because [Ginevra] is a good child and it makes her very frightened that you do not wish her to bring those things she finds dear [from her wet nurse's house]' (Congdon 2009: 443–4). The implicit criticism of Francesco, the father who was oblivious to the needs of his vulnerable daughter, was particularly evident in this missive.

While home life conventionally included expectations about responsibilities of care, especially for vulnerable children or the elderly, the relationships that made up the emotional side of domestic life were not always permanent. Piero di Strenna's solicitous concern for Ginevra would come to an end when he delivered her back to her birth family. Similarly, some individuals living within the home had only a temporary role to play there. Apprentices and servants, in particular, were expected to come and go from the household. In her letters to her husband, Margherita Datini described several relationships with household servants and slaves. Those relationships could involve significant emotional labour for both parties, as when the servant Monna Giuliva implored Margherita to be allowed to leave their household over some unspecified 'sorrow' that she was ashamed about when Francesco found out about it (Datini 2012: 146–7). In Valencia, even slaves might inhabit their masters' houses only temporarily, with some contracts specifying the period of time an individual could be held by an owner before being freed (Blumenthal 2009: 194).

Just as the idea of home included servants or slaves with only temporary ties to their masters, wives and mothers too were sometimes expected to be short-term inhabitants of the household. Christiane Klapisch-Zuber argues that the late medieval Italian *casa* was both the residential structure and the 'entire agnatic kinship group', meaning that theoretically women were excluded from the idea of the home in Florence.[12] In the moral universe of the Florentine household, 'women were passing guests', since they arrived at the house upon their marriages and left again to remarry once they had been widowed, often leaving young children behind. Such disruptions to home life could be emotionally difficult, but Klapisch-Zuber (1985) has argued that it was the economic difficulties that departing mothers created for families who had to provide the women with their dowries that were especially challenging.

HOME AS PLACE

To this point we have focused on the medieval idea of home as a series of emotional and legal attachments, tracing the tensions within those bonds in the period and considering the problem of home as an idea in a Christian context. Now we turn to the meanings ascribed to the spaces associated with home in the Middle Ages, and to some of the approaches and debates among scholars studying those spaces. Domestic spaces, like relationships, include a moral component that cannot be overlooked. As Mark Gardiner (2008: 39) argues, 'buildings must be viewed as the realization of ideas about domestic space'. Denaturalizing the layout and uses of spaces and examining the ideas that lay behind their production is a crucial aspect of thinking about the home. Here, too, Christian sources articulate unease about the meaning of the home, particularly the potential moral challenges that domestic spaces posed to young, unmarried women.

How can we assess what the physical place called 'home' meant to its inhabitants? Some scholars assert that we can look at sources in novel ways to make them speak about the way spaces were conceived. Medieval historians are often challenged by the fragmentary survival of evidence from the period, and those who study domestic life, both in its written and material forms, have even less to work with than their counterparts working on religious or political history. Discussions of the ideal use of the spaces within domestic interiors and the moral meaning of home itself have been shaped by these constraints. Using methods such as 'access analysis', which traces movement through domestic spaces, and reading prescriptive literary sources, some scholars argue that there were both ideal and real gendered divisions of space in medieval houses.[13] This method of interpreting the evidence can provide valuable perspectives on the understanding of home space in the Middle Ages. For instance, access analysis of plans of royal residences show that rooms set aside for queens were more secluded than those for male members of royal families (Richardson 2003). Employed alongside written materials, scholars argue, access analysis can clarify some of the otherwise murky aspects of medieval domestic organization (Richardson 2003: 131).

The problem with this type of analysis is that it often relies on no-longer-extant materials, and thus has to anticipate the movements of long-dead people. For instance, tracing movement through doorways – a key feature of access analysis – can be impossible when doorways are no longer evident in floor plans. Scholars then have to guess at their placement, and as P. J. P. Goldberg (2011: 207 n.11) argues, the analysis based on these guesses is thus open to question. Even when materials survive, they may not tell us the whole story of how they were used. Jane Grenville (1997: 20) points out that similar access patterns, such as movement along hallways, can veil or obscure different ways of ordering social relations within a household. A servant might walk along a corridor for very different reasons and in different ways than her employer, for instance. And in some cases the materials that remain may not preserve the meanings that were present for inhabitants (Kristiansen 2014: 154). The conventional idea of 'home' as defined along gender lines has increasingly been challenged by historians, who posit that perhaps other forms of division, such as that between safe work and dangerous work in the household, might have applied.[14] Increasingly scholars remind us as well that even when gender divisions were an ideal aspect of home life, they were not always possible to maintain in practice (Kristiansen 2014: 154).

Another significant scholarly debate around medieval ideas about home focuses on the significance of building materials and methods of construction during the Middle Ages. Traditional scholarly convention holds that fragility and impermanence marked some residential structures throughout the Middle Ages. In England, structures built of grass, wattle and daub, and wood could be flimsy and might not have been expected to survive their inhabitants' lifetimes.[15] Even in late medieval Italian cities, which we tend to identify with sturdier buildings built increasingly with stone, inhabitants expected fires to destroy houses quite regularly (Goldthwaite 1972: 981). A vivid picture of the impermanence of some dwellings is found in a court record from the northern Italian city of Verona during the thirteenth century, when a group of lepers who had been living together in a hospital outside the city were required to move from their original area to a new location. In doing so, they moved not only the smaller items within their homes, such as cooking pots and clothing, but their houses themselves. One of the inhabitants of this community, questioned about the events of the move, described how the walls and beams (*cupeis et lignamen*) of their houses were taken down (*disfacta et discoperta*) and moved from one site to another (Saccomani 2000: 148).

These striking examples stand out in the sources and seem to suggest that medieval domestic culture was characterized by a state of impermanence and, perhaps, insecurity. However, the extent and the meaning of fragility in medieval structures has been a contentious subject of debate among scholars, especially historians and archaeologists, for several decades. Medieval archaeologists in particular sustain that there was more solidly built housing in the period than some social historians have had us believe.[16] Furthermore, while some historians argue that impermanent dwellings did not engender strong feelings of attachment to place, others disagree, arguing that there was sometimes a distinction between the fragility of the actual structures people lived in and their more robust idea of 'home' as a place that provided a sense of identity to people.[17] A dwelling that had to be rebuilt often might not be considered a 'new' dwelling each time.

The solidity of dwelling places may not have changed as dramatically as we once believed, but it is likely that by the end of the Middle Ages there was more variety of residences across Europe than at the beginning of the period. From the twelfth century onwards, throughout western Europe historians and archaeologists have documented a rise in house building and renovating across the economic spectrum. Some historians see a close connection between this development of a more permanent sense of houses as structures and the cultural development of a stable idea of 'home' in the later Middle Ages, in particular.[18] Some have also mapped the growth and development of structures that people called home onto changing ideas of the social significance of domestic life. As Sarah Rees Jones (2008: 71) has shown, by the end of the Middle Ages in English cities such as Coventry and Bristol, differences in house size and construction had come to indicate differences in social status, so that record makers used the labels 'hallholder' and 'cottager' to describe members of different social ranks.

While an entire structure could readily convey status and power to the world, the spaces inside a dwelling also expressed domestic values, both to its inhabitants and to outsiders. One question about the interior spaces of medieval residences across Europe is the medieval custom of assigning several different functions to individual rooms, so that the same room within a residence could serve as a space for eating and working during the day and for sleeping at night. Some might see the multifunctionality of medieval spaces as evidence of a chaotic or simplistic medieval idea of domesticity. Others argue that multifunctionality deserves to be studied for its contributions to the understanding of those spaces, and not merely as a simplistic or primitive domestic feature. For example, in England across many centuries, high-status dwelling places were built around a hall, a truly multifunctional space, where people met, ate and – especially in the case of lower-status people and servants – slept.[19] In the view of some scholars, the features and uses of the hall trickled down from the highest ranks of the nobility and royalty to the less well-off, so that versions of halls can be found in much smaller and less elaborate houses (Emery 2005: 145). The hall was a physical structure with significant influence over its cultural milieu. As Matthew Johnson (2013: 386) sustains, the hall 'derived its cultural authority, in part, from the mixing and the resonance between . . . [its] different functions'. Furthermore, recent scholarship has linked the architectural features of medieval halls with changing ideals in attitudes and behaviours during the central Middle Ages, especially those that travelled from the ecclesiastical realm into the lay world. Matthew Reeve (2011: 106) argues that halls such as that constructed at the palace of the archbishop of Canterbury in the early thirteenth century articulated 'a new mode of corporeal splendor and elegance – a new refined style of living and being'. Reeve notes that the hall at Canterbury was used as a template for other halls similarly built for both bishops and members of royalty in the thirteenth century. While the hall largely reflected the domestic aspirations of those building in rural areas, some work on urban housing also suggests that in England the urban elite may have sought to build halls in their homes in order to articulate and reinforce their authority in the community (King 2009: 475, 485).

Not all spaces within the medieval residence were entirely flexible. Certain aspects of buildings, such as their entrances and exits, some of their interior rooms, and their openings to the outside, were assigned quite specific purposes and values. Details about those values can provide suggestions about changing expectations of domestic behaviour across the Middle Ages, with important connections made between women's morality and their domestic activities in many texts. Windows and balconies were potentially problematic domestic spaces, and we have evidence of strongly articulated ideas about their use, especially for women. In late medieval Italy, didactic texts for women instructed female readers to stay away from the open windows of their houses, lest they be thought to be flirting (or worse!) with strangers (Bell 1999). We can see an echo of this same instruction in the letters written by Alessandra Strozzi in the same period. As Alessandra sought a wife for her son Filippo, she remarked that one candidate was acceptable since 'you don't see her all day at the window, which seems to me a good sign' (Strozzi 1997: 159).[20] In Venice artists often depicted balconies used for such morally acceptable female tasks as sewing, but other sources depict concern about the moral meaning of women sitting out on balconies, where they could be observed by and even converse with strange men. Women in Venice and elsewhere in Italy were encouraged to demonstrate the concept of *ritiratezza*, showing themselves to be morally upright by withdrawing from public scrutiny that could occur if they appeared on balconies (Cowan 2011: 727).

The ideal of women's reserve within spaces that were potentially open to the outside world was thus a common feature of late medieval society. Such ideals of control over women's use of space are also found in texts that describe women's access to the interior spaces of their houses. For instance, the relationship between women and the 'service spaces' of the house in medieval England articulates an ideal of women's self-regulation within English domestic culture. In middling and upper-status English residences, valuable domestic items, including cookware, food and drink, were kept within specialized rooms, the buttery and the pantry. Mark Gardiner (2008: 48) argues that these rooms were 'an embodiment of domestic order'. This assertion is reinforced by the fact that during her bouts of mental illness Margery Kempe was denied the keys to the buttery in her own house (Kempe 2015: 12). Her lack of control, as she describes it, led to her being locked out of a space within her own house, a situation that would have emphasized for her medieval readers the extreme disorder of her domestic circumstances at that moment and which conveys to modern readers the value that was placed on the regulation of women within domestic settings.

The spectrum of meanings associated with the interior spaces of a residence is further evidenced by descriptions of the multiple functions of the bedchamber, or *cubiculum*, in sources from the twelfth century onwards. In some sources these small chambers were presented as sites for spiritual contemplation, just as they had been in the Roman period.[21] In other accounts, the *cubiculum* was a more complex entity, a moral microcosm of the home itself. References to 'chambers' in some texts suggest that these spaces could act as both a refuge from the world outside and a place where intimate words and deeds could be used to deceive, trap, or abuse.[22] In her search to live a religious life and in her rejection of her parents' plans to organize a socially and economically beneficial marriage for her, Christina of Markyate triumphed over several threatening situations within bedchambers. The first time she evaded a near-rape by a bishop, when her parents had forced her into the bishop's chamber. Once there, Christina pretended to acquiesce to the bishop's overtures and got up to lock the door of his chamber, telling him 'allow me to bolt the door: for even if we have no fear of God, at least we should take precautions that no man should catch us in this act'. Having said this, she slipped out of the room and did indeed bolt the door, but from the outside, locking the bishop within (Talbot 1987: 43). Sometime later, Christina kept her newly engaged fiancé busy in her chamber sitting on the bed talking about God rather than having sex, as he had hoped (Talbot 1987: 51). Finally, when Christina's parents told the young man to rape her in her chamber so that their marriage would be consummated, Christina hid herself behind one of the tapestries hanging on the wall. She dangled there from a nail and kept quiet, even when someone trod on her foot as they searched for her (Talbot 1987: 53). Clearly for the writer of this text, the chamber was a dangerous site, a place of potential sexual and spiritual threat, and only Christina's unusual intellect and enviable upper-body strength saved her from some real dangers within it.

The beds that stood in chambers such as Christina's were often the largest and most valuable items many individuals owned. As a costly piece of furniture, a bed and its coverings might be used to display an individual's power and privilege, and it could be handed on to heirs with this value in mind. Even bedcoverings could communicate power and privilege. Goldberg (2008: 133) has argued that bourgeois households owned many more cushions than their peasant counterparts in later medieval England, and he attributes the preponderance of these objects not only to a need for more people to find comfort within the house, but to a greater need on the part of the householders of that rank to communicate their 'wealth and leisure' to those outsiders who commonly came into their houses. The bed's importance as reflection of household wealth was probably outweighed by its role as symbol of the 'honest' sexual and domestic relationship at the foundation of many households.[23] Sharing a bed was an indication of a marital relationship (or a marital-like one), and so an individual's 'bedfellow' was also one who had a right to a share of their property (Korpiola 2011: 2). The bed was also the place where offspring were conceived, and expressions such as 'children of the marriage bed' were common in legal texts (Warner 1999: 104).

Ideals about the moral regulation of the home increasingly emphasized order and regulation during the medieval period. As such, cleanliness of household items, especially linens and clothing, was highly valued as a sign of moral rectitude. Many institutions, such as the monastery of Corpus Domini in Venice, had their own wash houses and servants to undertake the task of washing (Bornstein 2000). And yet despite the importance of cleanliness to showcasing the moral virtue of the home, the people who cleaned and washed for the household were often its most vulnerable and morally denigrated members (Biow 2006: 103). Studying the organization and idea of cleaning reinforces the presence of moral hierarchies within the medieval idea of home, with those in power able to enjoy moral rectitude because of the less honourable status of those below them.

Cleaning and especially laundry were demanding tasks in the Middle Ages. Their physical challenges are easy to imagine: soiled household linens needed to be soaked, beaten with a paddle or trampled underfoot, and then rinsed, wrung out by hand, and hung or draped to dry (Rawcliffe 2009: 152–4). Many of these tasks took place in dangerous conditions on the banks of muddy, insect-ridden waterways (Rinne 2001: 42; Rawcliffe 2009: 154; Henderson 2006: 209–10). In other places, public fountains were set aside for washing; these were safer than riverbanks but they did not make the work of washing less onerous[24] (Figure 1.5). On top of its physical challenges, washing had a fraught moral dimension – that is, cleanliness signalled virtue, but the act of getting

FIGURE 1.5: Washing facilities, Sicily (thirteenth century). Leodekri (Own work) via Wikimedia Commons (public domain).

things clean was not the province of the virtuous. Instead, since it was marked with the traces of bodily emissions, laundry itself was associated with filth and equated with other 'disgusting' but necessary tasks such as tanning leather and butchery. Unlike leather tanners or butchers, however, those who did the laundry were themselves associated with filth by their contemporaries; they were also not protected by guild status. In fact, washerwomen were often associated with prostitutes, and vice versa. For centuries, women who washed clothes supplemented their wages by selling sex, a cycle of marginality, poverty and deprivation that carried down from one generation to the next (Rinne 2001: 35).[25] Preachers also worried about the morality of the laundress, perhaps because she moved freely around her community and worked half-clothed (Rinne 2001: 46). These examples suggest that housewives would likely have sought to evade the work of washing if they could. Even servants in several late medieval cities negotiated contracts that ensured they would not be required to do the laundry – probably a reflection of both the moral and physical burdens of the task.[26] The work of doing the laundry within the medieval home was thus another arena for the tensions within the ideals of medieval domesticity.

CONCLUSION

The idea of home in the Christian Middle Ages could envelop and threaten, comfort and coerce. It provided rare opportunities and set strict limits. Ideals of home were characterized by attachments and intimacies that were particularly comfortable and appealing for those in positions of power, but often regulatory and exploitative for those under them. The ideal spaces of the home were similarly morally charged, with all aspects of the construction and layout of a dwelling imbued with meaning. We might think that this was especially true for the women and lower-status members of the household. But men and high-status figures were also shaped by this system, since they were expected to adopt the authoritative postures of the head of household regardless of their actual status. Changes to the shape, size and (possibly) solidity of residences and the gradually increasing complexity of the functions of domestic interiors over the course of the Middle Ages also reflect and helped shape the ideas about home that permeated the medieval world. The medieval idea of home, then, was hardly a refuge from the outside world. Instead, it duplicated many of the assumptions prevalent in that world.

CHAPTER TWO

The Family and the Household

TOVAH BENDER

INTRODUCTION

In a peasant house in southern France in the early 1300s lived Bernard and Guillemette Maurs, their two children, Bernard's widowed mother, and two servants to herd the livestock and plough the fields (Ladurie 1984: 41). The servants, Jean and Bernard Pellissier, were themselves brothers. Individuals in this household are numerous and their relationships to one another complicated. Some are related by biology, others through ties of employment or marriage. Some of these individuals considered themselves family while others did not.

Household and family are inextricably linked in medieval life because they had a great deal in common. Mutual obligations as dictated by social convention, economics, laws, or emotion bound both households and families together. Further, both families and households had a hierarchical organization and were headed by a patriarch. The patriarch – usually the eldest male, but occasionally a younger man or a woman, usually a widow – was the symbolic, legal and – usually – practical head of the family or household, with both control over and obligations towards those under him. Finally, the behaviour of all members and the functioning of the unit as a whole influenced the reputation and status of all members of the unit. Both household and family were basic units of medieval life.

While families and households have a great deal in common, they are not synonymous. Families were groups of individuals, who were not defined by physical space but by a variety of lasting interpersonal bonds. While some of these bonds were biological, many were not, and it is the lasting nature of these bonds that is important rather than the basis of the bonds. These familial relationships were maintained as people moved in and out of households. Bonds were often hierarchical and certain obligations – particularly economic – were enshrined in law. However, there were also more fluid ties based on emotion, a broad category that might include loyalty, a sense of responsibility, concern for a shared reputation, and affection. Absence did not diminish these relationships. In the Maurs family, Bernard shared a close relationship with his widowed mother, who lived in the household, and with his brother, who headed a separate household next door. Although living separately, they shared the same heretical religious beliefs, indicating spiritual closeness, frequent communication and trust that transcended physical walls.

The household, by contrast, was defined by physical space; it consisted of all those individuals living under one roof at any moment. It was, first and foremost, an economic unit; all members contributed labour so that the house could operate and, ideally, prosper. Households resembled the family in organization, but were more fixed and hierarchical, with the patriarch at the top, followed by the family, and then a strict ranking of employees. There were certainly many households – both efficient and inefficient – that did not conform to the ideals. Because household members interacted closely and daily, their relationships could become tense or affectionate, end abruptly, or become long-lasting and family-like. Wills from across Europe include bequests from masters to servants, including those who had left the household long ago, demonstrating ties that went far beyond contractual obligations (McKee 1995: 54; Hanawalt 2007: 187). Nonetheless, what differentiates a household from a family is change; households were in constant flux and, unlike families, did not necessarily maintain emotional connections or obligations to one another when they stopped sharing the same roof. Jean Pellissier had worked in several households before and after the Maurs' (Ladurie 1984: 73–4). When Bernard Maurs and his mother were in trouble with the inquisition, Jean stressed that he was not family but only briefly a member of the household.

This chapter explores the nature and variety of family and household bonds. It argues for the permanence and affective nature of the family, on the one hand, and the mutability and hierarchical, functional nature of the household on the other. But while this chapter works to define and differentiate households and families, it is important to keep in mind that diversity in form was a hallmark of both. This is true across the geographic spread of western Europe, the chronological span of the Middle Ages, but also between neighbouring households and families, or even within individual households and families over time.

SOURCES

Lack of appropriate sources makes it difficult to answer the basic question of who was a member of a medieval household or family. There are few census-like sources, particularly for the early centuries of the Middle Ages. Of those that do survive, the most fully studied are the English poll tax of 1377 and the 1429 catasto survey, which covers Florentine-controlled Tuscany. Earlier sources include the Domesday Book, which covers Norman England in 1086, and smaller, more localized documents, such as the Carolingian Polyptiques, but they are few and far between.

While each of these documents is valuable to the demographic study of its time and place, they also present challenges. First, the documents describe not physical households or affective families but taxable or fiscal units (Herlihy and Klapisch-Zuber 1985: 303). Fiscal 'households' might be quite different in shape from actual co-residential units. Second, those who could not or did not pay taxes were less accurately documented or intentionally omitted. These factors combine to make demographic comparison across time and place very difficult.

The historical record is not limited to these census-type documents. There are household expense accounts, instruction books, treatises, literature, court cases and other sources from which scholars can determine the roles and relationships among household members. These sources go beyond the structure to contemporary ideas of the household. Law codes detail legal responsibilities between individuals, while documents of practice such as contracts, wills, court cases and notarial records demonstrate actual ties between individuals. Sermons reveal what the clergy believed to be people's obligations to one another and warned against practices they saw as problematic. These documents all privilege the experience of men, the clergy and the elite over those of women, dependents, the laity and the poor. They reflect the authors' concerns with patrilineal inheritance, property, status, and the householder's own reputation. Nonetheless, these sources do allow scholars to glimpse the variety of informal, distant, non-biological and occasionally called-upon relations.

FAMILIES

Long-term and affective ties held medieval families together. Family members moved in and out of each other's homes over the course of their lives, but their interest in each other extended beyond the walls of the household and across the lives of the family members. Members were bound by law, social expectations and co-residence as well as by sentiments. Indeed, the patriarch's obligations to more junior family members were not dissimilar to those towards household members: he had to make sure that family members were fed, clothed and sheltered at a level commensurate with their status, to educate them in their tasks – present and future, worldly and spiritual – and to make sure that their behaviour did not damage the family's or household's reputation. But the family consisted of more than patriarchs and dependents; family ties and the obligations they entailed were diverse and often extended beyond what was required by law. This long-term interest in one another, based on emotional connections, was what defined the family and distinguished it from other social units, including the household.

One way to conceptualize families is as a lineage, and a fascination with lineage stretches across the Middle Ages, especially for the elite. A range of medieval texts such as *Beowulf*, the *Histories of the Franks* and the Icelandic Sagas from the early Middle Ages, to the late medieval *ricordanze*, or family record books, of Florentine merchants, all trace the lineage of the central figure back numerous generations, occasionally to a mythical ancestor. In most cases, the patriline is the main focus, but female ancestors enjoyed varying degrees of prominence based on the importance of the individuals on the matrilineal side and on the specific time and place within medieval Europe.

But while medieval people might trace their lineage in detail, they generally limited their concept of family to kin descended from an ancestor in recent memory (Harney 1993: 24; Worby 2010: 142). Even so, medieval families could be large and complicated with in-laws or step-children.

While extended family networks might be large, nuclear families, as well as patrilines, were small due to infertility and child mortality. The number of children who survived varied with environmental factors as well as wealth and geography. It is difficult to get precise figures, but demographers accept that approximately a third to a half of all pre-modern children did not survive to adulthood (Hanawalt 1993: 55; Haas 1998: 163). In ninth-century Saint-Germain-des-Prés (France), Emily Coleman (1971: 208) calculates that the average number of children per household ranged from slightly more than one to slightly more than three. Jean-Pierre Cuvillier estimates that Germanic families in the eighth and ninth centuries were similarly sized (Boswell 1989: 257). In both cases, these figures represent the number of living children in the household at the moment of the survey. John Boswell (1989: 271) reasons that the number of surviving children must have increased during the high Middle Ages (1000–1200) as the population of Europe grew rapidly, but declined again towards the end of the Middle Ages. This hypothesis is supported by James A. Raftis's (1982: 163) calculation that one town in England in the first half of the fourteenth century, a time of famine, contained just under two children per household.

Of the children that made it to adulthood, not all continued the lineage. Accidents, illnesses, wars and famines were a threat to children and adults alike (Hanawalt 1986: 171–87; Herlihy and Klapisch-Zuber 1985: 276, Table 9.5).

Jack Goody calculated that 10 to 25 per cent of couples produced no children who survived to adulthood (Boswell 1989: 14). Childbirth itself was risky for women, and maternal death not only limited the size of families but also the survival of infants (Shahar 1990: 35). As a result, scholars have found that in several different late medieval English cities, few families survived with an unbroken male patriline for more than two generations, although more continued through the female line (Kermode 2002: 78–9). At the same time, many children grew up without their parents.

The circumstances that broke families apart created new bonds. Widows and widowers remarried, often bringing children to their new marital household. The elderly and the infirm, as well as widows and widowers, might move back in with natal family or adult children, as with Bernard Maurs' co-resident mother. Families took in related and unrelated children. Heloise, the early-twelfth-century abbess and philosopher, was raised by her uncle in Paris. Her parentage is unknown; some suspect her mother might have been a nun, while others posit that she was the illegitimate daughter of this 'uncle' (Abelard and Heloise 2003: xix–xx). His investment in her education, pride in her accomplishments, and anger when he found out she was pregnant do not necessarily mean he was her biological father; it means he acted as a father-figure was expected to act. Even apprentices and servants might be adopted to some extent. In these informal ways, parents gained children, children gained parental figures, and non-family members became family.

Foster-kinship also played a major role in forming an individual's familial network, even when parents were alive and involved. One of the most famous love triangles of the Icelandic Sagas features foster brothers Kjarten Olafsson and Bolli Thorleiksson. Kjarten's father volunteered to foster Bolli, age three, as a sign of humility after offending his brother, Bolli's father. Bolli's foster parents 'loved him no less than their own children' and the foster brothers developed a very close relationship that was broken when they fell in love with the same woman (Kristjansdottir 2008: 55–7). In high medieval romances, numerous knights join the court of their more famous uncles, including Tristan and Gawain. The nephews benefited from the uncles' social networks as they built their own reputations. These fosterage relationships, even when blood ties existed, seemed to be even deeper as they were voluntary, based more on emotion than legal obligations.

While departures and mortality were facts of medieval life, they did not undermine the investment people made in those family members around them; there is ample and abundant evidence that people loved their children and recognized childhood as a distinct and special phase of life.[1] Parents cared for children, missed the absent, searched for the missing, nursed the sick and mourned the dead, as has been demonstrated by numerous medieval scholars for different times and places. Society at large regarded such sentiments and actions as right, proper and natural in literature, sermons and law. And while these strong, affective bonds have been most thoroughly studied in the relationships between parents and their biological children, examples such as the Icelandic foster families or Heloise and her uncle, mentioned above, demonstrate that close bonds existed among a great variety of family members.

Medieval families reinforced these bonds in a number of ways, but one of the most basic was meeting the immediate physical needs of family members, particularly by sharing food. Medieval people believed that an infant imbibed character traits along with food while nursing (Klapisch-Zuber 1985: 161). Eating together would remain a way of fulfilling family obligations and of creating and strengthening familial bonds (Smalley 1981: 146). In his treatise on the family written in the 1430s, Florentine humanist Leon Battista Alberti (1969: 185) describes the ideal family situation as one in which all members 'live under one roof . . . warm themselves at one hearth, and . . . seat themselves at one table'. Such a situation was economical but also promoted the happiness of the family – and especially its patriarch – by keeping everyone together.

This association between eating together and family meant that food could prove the existence of a familial relationship. Debra Blumenthal (2009: 173) cites a case of an enslaved Russian woman in fifteenth-century Valencia, who tried to claim the legal status of a concubine rather than slave, specifically arguing that she shared a table and bed with her master. Conversely, in England, when courts found evidence of marital abandonment, they would require the parties to treat each other with 'marital affection in bed and table'. Eating separately signalled that individuals were not family. Servants and other employees did not eat with the family even though they might live under the same roof. While such a division between staff and family was seen as proper, a denial of food or refusal to eat together by those who should be family signified a very troubled relationship. A failure or inability to support children was grounds for automatic divorce in medieval Iceland (Jochens 1995: 55). The church would not legally end a marriage, but it could grant the equivalent of a legal separation, a *divorcio a mensa et thoro*, a separation of table and bed.

While feeding one another was perhaps the most public way that families cared for the immediate physical needs of each other, caring for other people's bodies was another intimate and familiar task. The author of the *Ménagier* includes an entire chapter on 'The Care of the Husband's Person', with advice on eliminating vermin and minimizing smoke in the house (Greco and Rose 2009: 138–41). Family members were also expected to care for each other in sickness. Sharon Farmer (2002: 152–4) provides numerous examples of poor Parisians whose spouses, children and relatives helped them through illnesses. Others were criticized for not doing so: when John Kempe, over sixty years old, suffered a fall, his neighbours in Lynn, England, told his long-estranged wife, Margery, that she was culpable for his fall through neglect and responsible for nursing her husband. Somewhat reluctantly and only after Jesus appeared to her, she cared for her increasingly senile and incontinent husband (Kempe 2000: 219–21). While Margery seemed to feel that this was an unreasonable burden, her neighbours and even Jesus (in her vision) disagreed; caring for a family member was an admirable act of Christian charity and a reasonable expectation of a Christian wife.

In addition to meeting their immediate needs, family heads also needed to prepare for the long-term future of family members. One of the primary responsibilities of medieval parents was to give their children the tools they needed to establish themselves in the world through appropriate education or training, social connections and economic support. Children themselves often had limited say in the matter; they were limited first by gender, social status, birth order and their parents' circumstances, and then by their parents' choices. Some resisted their parents' choices. Peter Abelard's parents seem to have accepted his request, around 1100, to renounce his inheritance and pursue an education, leaving his brother to assume his father's noble title and military duties (Abelard and Heloise 2003: 3). Catherine of Siena's parents, however, violently fought her desire to pursue the religious life. Nonetheless, no one in medieval society questioned the appropriateness of parents choosing a road for their children.

In addition to their economic security, it was the duty of good parents to settle their children, particularly women, into a suitable marriage. For the vast majority of medieval women, marriage marked a woman's entrance to adulthood and was a public statement about the economic, social and political positions of both spouses' families. While the consent of both partners was required to make a legally valid marriage, the degree of choice each partner had in the marriage varied greatly. Parents, extended families, and even the community weighed in on such an important decision (McSheffrey 2006: 78). Among the elite, marriages were a matter of grave concern and even state decisions. Families planned long in advance, negotiated strenuously, and usually provided very large dowries to their daughters in order to bring these marriages to fruition. Even for those towards the bottom of the social hierarchy, families were concerned about their children's choices. In late medieval Florence, urban-poor women tended to marry within their parish, helping their families form social networks there (Cohn 1980: 81). In other areas, including late medieval England and Valencia, non-elite women often contributed to their own dowries through wage labour, although parents still played a role in this process of selection (Lightfoot 2009: 335; Frances 2005: 48). The narrator in the fourteenth-century Middle English poem *How the Goodwife Taught her Daughter* advises the listener to take any serious suitor 'and schew hym to thy frendys alle' before agreeing to marry (Shuffleton 2008: 29). In the absence of parents, older relatives, neighbours and friends guided the young couple.

The age of first marriage varied greatly over the course of time and place. An individual's status and gender also influenced age at first marriage. Some of the best demographic data for the period comes from fifteenth-century Tuscany. There, women across the social spectrum tended to marry in their mid- to late teens, while men did so from their mid-twenties in the countryside to their mid-thirties in Florence (Herlihy and Klapisch-Zuber 1985: 210, Table 7.1). Non-elite women in north-western Europe at the same time seemed to marry somewhat later, generally in their mid-twenties, and often to men of approximately the same age (McSheffrey 2006: 78). This discrepancy in ages at marriage has led some to argue for a sharp divergence in marriage patterns between north-western and Mediterranean Europe; more recent scholarship has emphasized local and regional variation in marriage patterns rather than a single divide.[2] As difficult as it is to establish age at first marriage for the later Middle Ages, it is even harder for the earlier period, when the documents are sparser. It seems that among the small community of serfs in the ninth-century village of St Victor, France, both men and women married in their late twenties (Herlihy 1985: 76–7). Across medieval Europe, elite brides and grooms were much younger, often in their early teens or younger, and betrothals might occur years earlier (Hajnal 1965: 116; Hartman 2004: 28; Harris 2002: 248–50).

The younger the bride and groom were, the more willingly they might bend to their parents' or guardian's plans and also to the desires of their new spouse and his (rarely her) family. This malleability was likely one factor in the young age of marriage for elite brides and grooms (Schmugge 2012: 103, 123). A large discrepancy in age and a very young age at marriage for women certainly put many women at a disadvantage in terms of asserting themselves within their marriage (Herlihy 1985: 120). A marriage with less of a difference in ages between spouses could give women more power within the relationship. This is particularly true in cases where the wife was older, wealthier, or had time to live independently before marriage while working (Goldberg 1992: 351). In areas of later medieval northern Europe, wealthy widows were very attractive partners for men looking to advance themselves, including younger men (Hanawalt 1993: 7; Howell 1998: 108, 112–13).

At the other end of the spectrum, there were men and women who never married at all. The permanently unmarried people most visible in the medieval record are those who entered the church. These individuals, both men and women, were usually from elite families. Families decided on church careers for very young children for pious reasons, but this was also a common strategy among wealthy families to keep the patrimony intact – goals that were not mutually exclusive. Hildegard of Bingen, for example, was dedicated to the church by her German parents in the early twelfth century; she entered perhaps as young as eight. Perhaps she was a sickly child, one who might not make a good marriage connection, but she was also the tenth and last of her parents' children and it was not unusual to give the tenth child to the church as a form of donation (Hildegard of Bingen 1998: 5). While some of these individuals might not have been well suited to religious life, many others accepted and even embraced their roles, as Hildegard did.

Most adults spent at least part of their lives living separately from their parents, so establishing a son or daughter in the world almost always meant a move from the natal household. In this sense, fulfilling one's duties as family meant the breakup of the household, at least temporarily, but did not break emotional bonds among family members. Parents left moving evidence of the difficulty of these separations and the continued emotional ties to these children. In 841, northern French noblewoman Dhuoda (1998: 1) composed a book of advice for her son William, then fifteen and living in the court of the Charles the Bald. In writing to William, whom she calls her 'beautiful and loveable son', Dhuoda (1998: 69, 43) explains herself thus: 'I have observed that most women in this world take joy in their children. But, my son William, I see myself, Dhuoda, living separated and far from you. For this reason I am somewhat ill at ease and eager to be useful to you.' Much later, a fourteenth-century physician in Valencia wrote a letter to his sons studying in Toulouse, advising them to avoid sleeping with cold feet, prevent fleas by sweeping daily (but not to dampen the floor as fleas generate from damp dust), and not to 'grow used to strong wine without admixture of water' (Thorndike 1944: 154–60). Both letters were likely intended for the absent child and also a wider audience, garnering praise for the author's abilities, but these multiple goals make it clear that the audience would see these parental feelings as normal, acceptable and admirable.

Children, even when adult, were never really disconnected from the family. While some scholars have seen marriage as the termination of a woman's place in her natal family, one of the goals of marriage – especially among the elite – was to establish ties with another family through marriage. Wealhtheow, the Danish queen in *Beowulf*, was described by the text as 'a kindred pledge of peace between peoples' – that is, her marriage likely sought to end a feud between two groups (Wright 1957: 74). The prominent Medici family signalled their rise above the rest of the citizens in the republic of Florence when Lorenzo de Medici married not a local woman, as had long been the custom, but a member of the Roman aristocracy in 1469. In each of these cases and many others, the women left their households and their countries, often with little in the way of consent on the part of the woman or sometimes even of her family; Wealhtheow's very name means 'foreign slave' (Baker 2013: 163). Nonetheless, the woman's descent and continued connection to her natal line made her vital to her husband's family.

Parents and other members of a woman's natal family still had legal and economic ties to her after her marriage. Various early Germanic law codes in place from antiquity to the eleventh century required someone guilty of murder or assault to pay a *wergeld* in exchange for the life taken, as an alternative to a blood feud. Depending on the region, most or all of the money went to the victim's natal family, even in the case of a married woman (Rullkoetter 1990: 32). Later legal codes and economic practices continued to recognize the ties between family members living apart. In high medieval Castille, where inheritance was divided equally between all children, Heath Dillard (1989: 27) has found that married women returned their dowries to the patrimony to be redivided among the siblings when the parents died. In late medieval Florence, a woman had a right to a dowry and, even once married, to shelter and food in the family home for the rest of her life, or the money to support herself elsewhere at an equivalent rate, in the event of widowhood or abandonment (Kuehn 1991: 239–42). In all of these cases, family bonds remained strong through life, regardless of co-residence.

Certainly, there is abundant evidence that these laws were not always observed. Isabelle Chabot and Barbara Hanawalt (1988: 294; 2007: 98) have found numerous complaints in court cases and tax records from Florentine and London widows against their male relatives. The laws suggest that the society at large believed these ties should exist, while the women who brought the suits believed in their rights and anticipated that the court would back their claims.

As much as some relatives tried to shirk their responsibilities, there are also families who supported each other far beyond the bounds of what the law required. In Venice, for example, Stanley Chojnacki (2000: 140) has demonstrated that female relatives were substantial contributors to the dowries of brides in both their husbands' and their own natal families. Hanawalt (1993: 213) has uncovered similar examples in England. These women did not have to contribute to the dowries but felt a tie of obligation and affection towards these young relations.

Although economic help is easiest to see in the historical record, care could also take other forms. The example of the household from Montaillou, at the start of this chapter, showed a spiritual relationship of influence and trust between Bernard Maurs, his mother and his brother, when all three were arrested together for heresy. Later medieval literature, both comic and instructive, features young wives who confide in and seek advice from their mothers (Greco and Rose 2009: 113; Machiavelli 1981: 34-5). And some of the best evidence on medieval women's lives comes from letters or books of advice between mothers and their children, ranging from Dhuoda's early-ninth-century book through to Florentine widow Alessandra Strozzi's mid-fifteenth-century letters to her sons, filled with advice and updates on her management of the household.

Although some relatives were a constant presence in each other's lives, relatives could also be out of touch for years and still provide support, especially at milestones or crises. Peter Abelard, who left his home in Brittany around 1100, returned when he became ill (Abelard and Heloise 2003: 3, 4 n.8). Later, when he found out that his lover, Heloise, was pregnant and her uncle seeking revenge, he again returned to Brittany with Heloise to await the birth of the baby, whom they then left in the care of Abelard's sister (Abelard and Heloise 2003: 12, 16). Both this son and the aunt who raised him later appear in the necrology (list of deaths or obituaries) for the nunnery Paraclete, which Abelard founded, suggesting that the family continued to support one another (Abelard and Heloise 2003: 253 n.28). The ability to find help, support, advice and refuge, to meet immediate needs and to relaunch oneself to a secure future, even after a long period without contact, was the basis of the medieval family.

HOUSEHOLDS

The nucleus of the household was the co-resident family, in whatever shape it took. The head of the family also headed the household and, in the long run, the family was tied to its economic fortunes. But the household was not limited to the family. Servants, enslaved people, apprentices and other individuals were integral to keeping the household functioning and upholding its reputation, but their membership in the household and their ties to the family typically would not last after they left the walls of the house.

Census documents are much more informative about households than families, providing a snapshot rather than a long-term view and focusing on the physical and economic rather than the affective. Based on the early-ninth-century polyptyque of Saint-Germain-des-Prés, Coleman (1971: 208) notes that most households included only the immediate family, although she does not give specific numbers. Using similar documents from early-ninth-century central Italy, Richard Ring calculates an average household size of 4.7, although he finds that while more than half of the households have four or fewer members, more than half of the population lives in households of six or more individuals (Ring 1979: 2–3, 9–10). While both of these data sets focus on rural tenant farmers, later data that includes both urban and rural areas shows remarkable consistency. Maryanne Kowaleski (2014: 581) uses the 1377 English poll tax figures to calculate average household size for a number of different rural and urban communities. Of the thirteen locations she explored, nine have an average household size of between 3.46 and 4.0, while the remaining four have an average of over 4.0 but no more than 6.35. Similarly, Christiane Klapisch-Zuber and David Herlihy (1985: 283) determined that the average household size in the Tuscan catasto of 1427 was 4.42 people, although they are careful to point out that the large number of single-person households keeps this number low and that over 50 per cent of individuals listed in the catasto actually lived in households of six or more individuals. It seems that across the geographic and chronological span of the Middle Ages most households were small.

While households might be numerically small, the different types of members they could contain were great. The author of the *Ménagier* offers a clear description of his wealthy-urban Parisian household in the 1390s. His household included himself as the head and his young wife, as well as potential future children; the housekeeper, Dame Agnes, and Master Jean, the steward; and three types of servant: those hired for a specific job (unskilled labourers hired as porters or for the harvest); those 'hired for a fixed period because of their specific skills (such as tailors, furriers, bakers, butchers, shoemakers and those who do piecework)'; and 'domestic servants [hired] to serve by the year and live in the home' (Greco and Rose 2009: 215). For late medieval Florence, Christiane Klapisch-Zuber (1986: 70–1) discusses a hierarchy of servants based on pay and status within the household, with wet nurses at the top, followed by male servants, skilled adult female servants, elderly skilled servants, young women working for a dowry, and enslaved people, who were outside of this hierarchy entirely. In the Old Norse *Sturlunga Saga*, a father advises his son that he will need to fill seven different positions on his farm (Jochens 1995: 116). In all of these cases, the positions were numerous but well-defined.

Hired help exchanged labour for payment, but others worked in the households of others on different terms. Apprentices – older boys, and less frequently girls – provided their labour and usually a payment in exchange for instruction in a skilled craft. They were bound to their master through a legal contract usually lasting several years, as opposed to the annual contracts of hired help. Apprentices might begin as young as seven or as late as their teens, terms of the contract might last from two or three years to a decade, apprentices might live at home or with their masters, and their prospects for career advancement varied greatly (Goldthwaite 2009: 349; Roux 2009: 124–31; Hanawalt 1993: 129–54). Ideally, the apprentice would become a master of the craft, although that became more difficult towards the end of the Middle Ages, giving rise to large numbers of artisans working for wage labour in a master's workshop (Hartman 2004: 61).

Finally, slavery was a fact of life in most places and periods of the Middle Ages. Common in both ancient Rome and the non-Roman north of Europe, the warfare of the early Middle Ages ensured a continuous flow of prisoners of war to be used as slaves in the homes of their captors or purchasers. Slavery became more rare – although never illegal – in northern Europe later in the Middle Ages, but it continued in the Mediterranean region, where trade with Byzantine and Muslim regions and inter-religious warfare in Spain generated a continuous supply (Phillips 1985, 2014; Blumenthal 2009: 1–8).

This large number and variety of household staff might seem contradictory to the small household numbers found across Europe. There are, however, a few points to keep in mind. First, wealthier households were larger, both in number and variety of members (Blumenthal 2009: 169–70). Royal courts were the extreme and could include hundreds of members. The numbers demonstrated the wealth and power of the ruler. The vast majority of medieval families were much poorer and, naturally, could support fewer hired hands. Second, there were also differences between urban and rural households. Over much of Europe, large families were an asset on farms, but the organization of the family into households varied. In Tuscany, rural families remained under one roof and were consequently very large, whereas in England they lived separately but close together and pooled labour (Kowaleski 2014: 581; Herlihy and Klapisch-Zuber 1985: 283). In both cases, cities attracted young labourers from the rural surroundings and households were dependent on servant labour. But where English servants were more likely to be counted in the homes of their urban masters, Tuscan servants were counted in their familial home, whether or not they were resident with their employer. In both cases, patterns of residence differed between town and country, and they did so for largely similar reasons, but the demographic patterns that resulted were quite different.

Finally, a defining element of all medieval households was movement. Family members joined the house through birth or marriage, but would leave through death, marriage, or for employment, possibly returning following the death of a spouse, after education or travel, or in need of care. Families formed and reformed in the same or different physical locations. Related and unrelated children might move in and out. Servants, apprentices and other non-family all rotated through. Even within a household, an individual might move from being a dependent, to a head, to a dependent again as the rest of the membership changed. While location and social status certainly shaped one's experiences, most individuals lived in households of all sizes and played a number of different roles in the household over the course of their lifetime.

While individuals came and went, consistency came through the fixed hierarchy of positions, beginning with the patriarch and his wife. The author of the *Ménagier* instructs his reader: 'after your husband, you must be mistress of the house, giver of order, inspector, ruler and sovereign administrator over the servants. It is incumbent upon you to require submission and obedience to you and to teach, reprove and punish the staff' (Greco and Rose 2009: 217). As Judith Bennett (2007: 91–2) has demonstrated, a hierarchy headed by the husband, who held the legal responsibilities and rights for the house, followed by a wife or female head, who ran it on a day-to-day basis, supervised the household and acted with the patriarchal authority of her husband, was remarkably consistent across time, place and social status in western Europe in the late medieval and early modern periods. Her statement is just as true for the early Middle Ages.

Children, hired help, apprentices and other dependents fell below the wife. They were subject to discipline and supervision, on the one hand, and entitled to protection and guidance, on the other. The author of the *Ménagier* urges his wife to supervise closely those 'girls or chambermaids from fifteen to twenty years old, who at that age are so foolish and have seen so little of the world' (Greco and Rose 2009: 223). Elsewhere, he advises his wife to watch carefully the reactions of the servants when she reprimands them, advising 'if she blushes and remains quiet and shamefaced when you correct her, love her as your daughter' (Greco and Rose 2009: 217). Those at the bottom of the household hierarchy were treated much as children would be, albeit without as much investment in their long-term future. Although age and skill are factors in this hierarchy, age alone does not determine position. The wife in the *Ménagier* was 'only fifteen years old the week we were married', the age of the younger servants (Greco and Rose 2009: 49). Her authority was instead based on her position in the household and her relation to the head, which was itself based on social status.

The exercise of control over the household sent an important message to the community about its status and character. An individual who could afford to and had the ability to head a large household and run it well was someone who deserved respect and responsibility in the community. This is one reason that the author of the *Ménagier* is so concerned about carefully vetting potential employees: bad ones 'will shout and howl nasty and disrespectful reproaches ... and the worst of it is, they will give you a bad reputation' (Greco and Rose 2009: 216). And just as the hierarchy was consistent across the Middle Ages, so too was this association between householding and respectability, which were tied to controlling the sexuality of women in the home. In his early-ninth-century biography, Einhard is lavish in his praises of the Emperor Charlemagne. But he does admit it 'strange to say' that Charlemagne never arranged marriages for his daughters and that this led to a 'malignity of fortune', alluding to the daughters' numerous and well-known extramarital affairs (Einhard 1998: 29). Even the promiscuity of the enslaved in late medieval Valencia could damage the reputation of the slave owner (Blumenthal 2009: 169–70). In all cases, failure to maintain control of the women's sexuality was a failure to keep order in the home, a failure in patriarchy.

At the same time, the larger and more prominent a household was, the larger the social gap between the household head and those at the bottom, leaving the weakest members vulnerable even though they were theoretically under the protection of a powerful head. In most medieval cultures, people accepted that enslaved people were sexually available, at least to their owners (Jochens 1985: 35; Blumenthal 2009: 172–4; McKee 1995: 61; Stuard 1992: 126). Female servants, particularly those who were far from family and friends, were also sexually vulnerable (Klapisch-Zuber 1985: 177). Nor was it only young women who were at risk. The most common complaints made by late medieval London apprentices was a lack of food and clothing and physical abuse (Hanawalt 1993: 159). In one case, a master beat his apprentice so severely and kept him in such abhorrent conditions that the young man could not wipe the vermin from his body (Hanawalt 1993: 149). When cases such as this ended up in court, employers cited their patriarchal authority and the need to maintain order. While the court or community might judge the individual's actions excessive, no one disputed the rights of the patriarch over his or her household.

The difference in household position of apprentices, servants and the enslaved illustrates both the vulnerability of household members and the difference between household and family. Apprentices tended to fare better than servants and, certainly, the enslaved, because their families would advocate for them. The enslaved, by definition, did not have families or legal rights. Servants did not have the same contractual protections as apprentices. Further, the geographic distance and social gulf between many servants' families and masters meant that the servants' families could not advocate for them. This vermin-covered apprentice's condition came to light when his father attempted to visit him and his case survives because his father took the master to court. The father had long-term, affective ties to his son that the master did not have to his apprentices. It was a parent's concern for his child, rather than a householder's for his household member, that helped this young man.

ALTERNATIVE HOUSEHOLDS

Small households with a nuclear family and a moving assortment of relatives, dependents and other individuals represented most medieval households and the experience of most medieval people at some point in their lives. Two other types of household – single individual households and group households, including male and female religious houses – were also numerically prominent and familiar to medieval people. Alternative households were governed by the same relationship between size and efficiency, on the one hand, and social status, on the other, demonstrating the extent to which the ideal household hierarchy shaped the way that medieval people believed the world should be structured.

Given the prominence of the large households in modern imaginings and in medieval writing, single-individual households were surprisingly numerous, both in the countryside and more often in the cities. Migrants and individuals with no family were often poor, transitory, and badly connected to the larger community. Data from the 1427 Florentine catasto suggest that 20 per cent of all Florentine households consist of only one person, and the catasto data does not including priests, many of whom would also have lived alone.[3] Nonetheless, Herlihy and Klapisch-Zuber (1985: 283) rightly caution that only 5 per cent of the Florentine population lived alone. It is also true, however, that the poorer, lone individuals on the edge of Florentine society were more likely to be overlooked by the catasto officials.

Those living alone in Florence – excluding clergy members – were approximately evenly divided between men and women (46 per cent men; 54 per cent women) but the men had a much lower average age than the women (36.5 years old for men; 58 years old for women). Almost all of the women living alone claimed to be widows, while most men did not list a marital status. This reflects the real effects of early marriage and infrequent remarriage for women, and later marriage and higher remarriage for men. It also reflects the stigma surrounding unmarried women; it was more socially acceptable for lone women to claim to be widows. Immigrants to the city – whether male or female – were also more likely to live alone than were members of the Florentine population more broadly (17 per cent of migrants lived alone versus 13 per cent for the overall population). Especially noteworthy is the fact that 19 per cent of women living alone were migrants to the city, suggesting that widows or unmarried women felt a pull towards Florence, but also perhaps that women who arrived in the city alone had a difficult time integrating.

The unmarried women (including widows) formed an even greater percentage of the population in northern European cities. Based on documents from Coventry, England in 1523, Maryanne Kowaleski (2014: 582) has estimated that 13 per cent of households consisted of a lone individual, and that the vast majority of these individuals were women. Given the high estimates of unmarried women across north-western Europe – calculated at 30 to 40 per cent of the population in many areas – and especially in cities, where they migrated in hope of work, women living on their own were likely a frequent sight in European cities (Kowaleski 1999: 51; Roux 2009: 148).

These households, however, were no more static than any medieval household. All of these lone individuals, of course, had lived with parents or guardians. Most of the Florentine women, it seems, had previously lived with men and perhaps children. Some of these women and many of the men would marry or remarry and perhaps even have more children or stepchildren. Some might move in with family members, especially as the living situations of these other individuals changed.

Individuals living apart from legal or biological kin did not always live by themselves, even when they registered their household as consisting of only one for tax purposes. Better-off individuals might have servants or apprentices, including those who lived in the home. Some – both clergy and laity – lived with partners in unions resembling marriage. Despite the absence of legal marriage and condemnation by the church, these relationships could be long-term, involve children, and be widely accepted by the community (Karras 2012: 7).

Such arrangements were not limited to opposite-sex couples; same-sex individuals shared homes, rooms, and even beds with other unmarried individuals of the same sex who were not related by blood or marriage. Some communal living situations were undoubtedly same-sex partnerships but, whether or not sex was involved, they provided lone individuals with the companionship, financial support and physical help that came from families. Sharon Farmer has found numerous examples of poor, communal households in Paris in the 1200s and early 1300s. One such woman, Amelot, came to Paris from Chaumont – about 150 miles away – with two other women. The three first sought lodgings together with a woman named Marguerite, whom they might have known directly or indirectly. When Marguerite could not accommodate them, she directed them to a neighbour. The women from Chaumont lived with the neighbour and eventually supported Amelot through a debilitating illness (Farmer 1999: 85; 2002: Ch.5). Scholars have identified similar clusters of female and female-headed households in other cities (Goldberg 1992: 314–6; Reyerson 1997: 209; Jones 2003: 210).

There were also more formal households open to lone individuals, particularly women. As Tanya Stabler Miller shows us in this volume, one option was an unenclosed religious house, such as a beguinage, that did not require that women take permanent vows. These houses provided shelter, economic and physical security, community, a degree of respectability, and an opportunity to lead a religious lifestyle for women disinclined or unable to live a life of isolated contemplation (Simons 2001: 94–9; Miller 2014; Deane 2014: 81). Beguines supported themselves through work or occupied their time performing charitable acts and lived in shared spaces. The beguines experienced brief periods of acceptance alternated with strong insistence that they accept enclosure (Deane 2014: 76–7).

As common as these female and female-headed households might have been, religious and civic authorities saw them as deeply problematic. On the one hand, households of widows and fatherless children were often needy and were thus classified among the deserving poor; to ignore them was not only unchristian but an embarrassment for the community.[4] On the other hand, these households were a threat to the hierarchical order of the city, because they lacked a male head. In response to both issues, civic and religious authorities sought to incorporate these women into patriarchal households. Dowries for poor unmarried girls preserved the chastity of these women and placed them into a male-dominated household. Benefactors also established homes for widows. Some of these were quite small; others, like the Orbatello in Florence, housed as many as fifty widow-headed families and provided dowries for their daughters (Trexler 1998: 69, 75). At the other end of the spectrum, some cities set up parameters for legal prostitution. Although religious and secular officials condemned extramarital sex, they saw prostitution as a necessary evil, protecting respectable women from the sexual predation of unmarried men. City officials legalized prostitution within certain areas, and established strict rules to govern both brothels and individual prostitutes (Karras 1996: 32–5). In both cases, female-headed households were legalized, supported and protected in exchange for submitting to the male patriarchal care of the state. Of course, many women – needy widows, prostitutes, and numerous other poor women who occasionally used sex to survive – rejected this protection, along with the restrictions and labels that came with it.

CONCLUSION

The basic structure of both the family and the household was a hierarchical organization of individuals under a patriarch. This was, in fact, the basic structure of medieval society. Individual families and households might not fit this model, but all medieval people's lives were shaped by the idea that an ordered society was made up of households and families run by patriarchs and that members supported and regulated one another. Laws, government surveys, sermons and the community supported such an organization and condemned people and households that deviated too far from this norm.

Households and families both supported and symbolized the solid foundation of medieval society, but movement was essential to defining both institutions. People moved in and out of the household. They interacted daily while they lived together but were bound together only as long as they lived under the same roof. By contrast, family members moved in and out of households and might not interact with each other for an extended period, but the bonds between them remained strong. Families were more stable in the long run than were households. They were the core around which households were built and moved. Nonetheless, households were the basic economic unit at any moment; people interacted most with members of their own household, whether family or not; and households were clearly defined in a way that made them the basic unit of reckoning for medieval governments. Households existed in the short run to support families over the long run.

CHAPTER THREE

The House in Europe, 800–1450

MARK GARDINER

INTRODUCTION

Evidence survives for tens of thousands of excavated buildings and a similar number of standing medieval houses from across Europe. Yet this enormous body of data still remains to be carefully sifted and the broad patterns identified. The quantity of information and the problems of engaging with numerous languages explain in part why there has been no overview of medieval houses since the subject was last tackled in 1980 (Chapelot and Fossier 1980; Donat 1980). This chapter presents the general trends in the structure and form of houses over a period of six centuries and more. It is concerned primarily with vernacular houses – structures occupied by common people and built with local materials in a regional style. Buildings of the elite might also use local materials and make some reference to the regional style, but they were built on a larger scale and in a more elaborate manner, and so must lie outside the scope of this survey.

The study of European houses is divided into two parts: the early and high Middle Ages (800–1150) and the late Middle Ages (1150–1450). The period around 1150 is an important point of transition in methods of house construction. There was a major shift in much of Europe in a form of building, from timber structures made from posts set in the soil to one in which the timberwork was set above the ground surface. This had two implications. For builders and householders, it meant that a structure would last longer, but for the student of buildings, it has had the consequence that an important source of evidence – the traces of the ground-set timbers – disappears; those set on the ground surface leave much less evidence. So, while on the one hand we have a small but growing number of standing buildings that survive from the mid-twelfth century onwards, the archaeological traces of those no longer standing are very ephemeral. Houses from the thirteenth and even fourteenth centuries are particularly difficult to study in many areas of Europe, because the number of still-standing buildings is small and the archaeological evidence diminished. A consequence of the greater survival of upstanding houses is that it is possible to talk more confidently of the appearance of buildings from 1150. Excavation can provide evidence of plan and materials, but all conclusions about the appearance of buildings, the nature of the roof, and the number and size of windows have to be inferred from what remains at ground level. After 1150, there are surviving fragments of houses, and from later centuries we have complete elevations.

The other reason that the mid-twelfth century is significant is that it marks an increase in the pace of commercialization. The number of towns was growing and spreading, even as far north as Norway, where the towns of Bergen and Trondheim were developing (Hansen 2005). The rising population of Europe helped to drive this expansion of commerce. The greater density of people within towns led to the appearance of new, taller buildings on sites within the constrained urban space. The impact of urban life on house forms is discussed towards the end of the chapter.

The study inevitably draws upon work in many European languages, leading to problems in translation. For example, the English language lacks a word to describe buildings with walls constructed of contiguous horizontal logs set one above another, a type known as *Blockbau* in German and *lafteverk* in Norwegian. 'Log cabin' might be appropriate in the United States, but not all such European buildings could be described as cabins. Here, they are simply referred to as log houses (Volmar and Zimmermann 2012). Equally problematic is the continental use of the term 'three-aisled buildings' for those structures with two rows of aisle posts that divide the interior into three parts. In English such buildings are described as having two aisles and a central nave. In German, *das Schiff* is used for both an aisle and nave, as is *la nef* in French. For simplicity and to avoid ambiguity, the continental term 'three-aisled' is adopted here. Another term that needs to be defined here is 'byre-house', sometimes also referred to as a 'long-house'. Paradoxically, this last expression has no implication for the length of the building, but refers to the use of a single building to house both humans and livestock in close proximity. The description of building levels follows English usage, so the floor above the ground is referred to as the first storey; the American practice of calling it the 'second floor' is not used.

THE EARLY AND HIGH MIDDLE AGES (800–1150)

The survey of houses of the first period – the early and high Middle Ages – begins in Greece and continues north and westwards across Europe. The so-called Greek Dark Ages, beginning in the early seventh century with invasion by the Slavs, was marked by a significant change in the design of the house. A courtyard plan was still found in buildings of the ninth and tenth centuries, but its character was very different from that of late antique houses. Instead of a garden at the centre, the courtyard became a place for cooking and craftwork, and even for the disposal of rubbish. It provided a secluded area for the household and served as a central space giving access to the other rooms of the house. Documents describe one of these rooms with the term *triklinion*, the equivalent of the Roman *triclinia* or dining room, but eating was not the only function carried out there (Sigalos 203; Türkoğlu 2004). Rooms served a variety of purposes during the day, and may have been used for sleeping at night. These rooms around the courtyard were not used just for domestic activities, but in towns they were for the storage of commercial products and in the countryside for housing livestock. Only the larger houses had buildings on all sides of the courtyard; away from the centre of towns and in the country, houses often comprised a single room, or sometimes a pair of rooms set in line or at right angles.

Houses in the southern part of the Balkans were generally constructed with stone walls, although the stone was roughly shaped, unless *spolia* from ancient ruins could be obtained. The stone was bonded with clay, but in the east of the Peloponnese mud-brick was used instead, although few buildings of this type have been excavated. The roofs were formed of rafters of oak, poplar or plane on which tiles were set (Kourelis 2003: 180–1).

Further north in the Carpathians the buildings were rather different. The main form was the sunken or pit house, a type which occurred widely across eastern Europe, extending at least as far as Ukraine and north into Poland and south into the northern parts of Croatia and Serbia. Bulgaria had both pit houses and above-ground buildings comparable to those in neighbouring Greece (Borisov 1999: 86). Pit house varied in form, but the greatest number comprise a square-shaped depression, set about half a metre or so below ground surface, with at least two posts supporting a ridge purlin. The interiors were small, with sides only 3 m or so long and an internal floor area of 9–12 m2 (Figure 3.1a). The interpretation of the portion of the building above ground remains problematic. Some archaeologists have suggested that the ridge purlin supported a tent-like thatched roof which came down to the ground. Such an arrangement, however, would provide inadequate headroom at the sides. It is more likely that the pit was surrounded by a horizontal timbers laid on the ground surface providing walls upon which the rafters of the roof rested. The horizontal wall timbers in some cases were set with the lowest layer sitting on

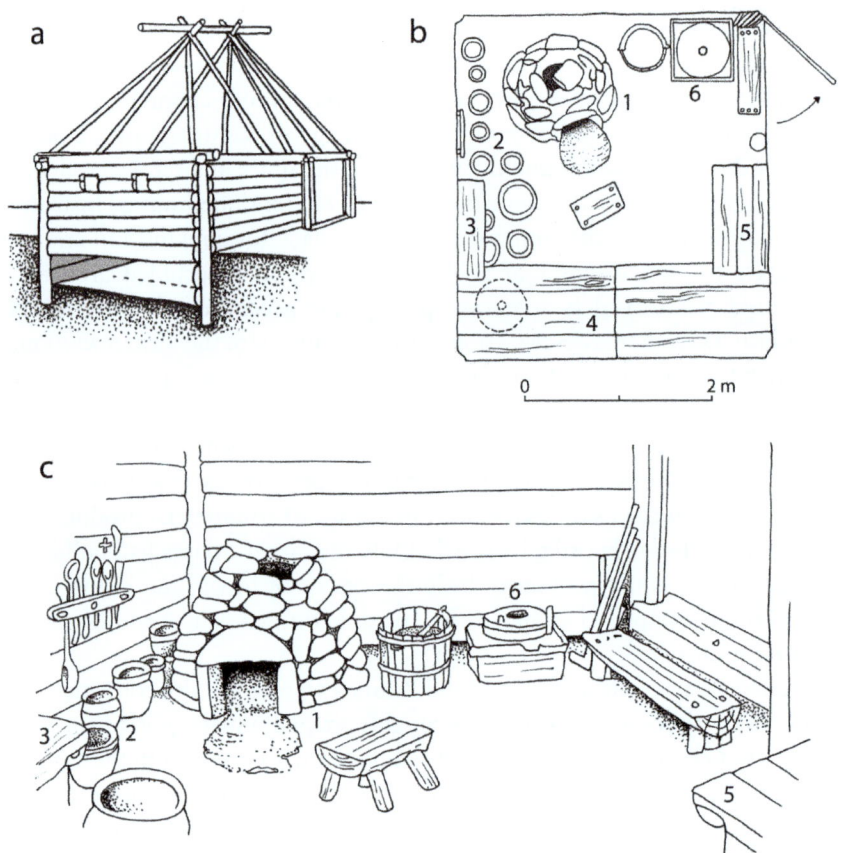

FIGURE 3.1: Reconstruction of the exterior view, and the interior plan and view of a ninth-century sunken hut at Březno, Czech Republic (after Pleinerová, "Pokusy s výstavbou a obýváním staroslovanských domů;") 1. Oven, 2. pots, 3. side bench, 4. bench and main bed, 5. bench and bed, 6. handmill. © Mark Gardiner.

the floor of the pit, but in other examples they rested on the exterior ground surface (Pleinerová 2000: 200–10; Šalkovský 2011: 274–6).

The interiors were modestly furnished (Figures 3.1b, 3.1c). It was common to have a clay and stone stove set in one corner of the building to provide heat and for cooking. Traces of beds or bunks are sometimes found on the wall adjoining the stove. A storage pot was often set into the ground near to the stove, and a grain-storage pit may be found set below the sunken floor. The small size of these buildings suggests that they housed only members of a nuclear family. Buildings of similar form, but without stoves, may have been used for storage or craftwork. The rather limited degree of variation in the form of pit houses suggests a rigid idea of the organization of domestic space, something also found in the same area in the later Middle Ages. Excavations at Roztoky (Czech Republic) showed that the buildings there were orientated to the cardinal directions, a feature unconnected to the local topography. Some 80 per cent of the houses on that site had stoves in the north-west corner (Kuna and Profantová 2011: 423; Cvijanović 2013: 300).

There is, however, a growing suspicion that the settlements of the late first millennium may be rather more complex than has been appreciated. Surface-laid buildings seem to have been more common than had been thought, although they have rarely been recognized by archaeologists (Takaćs 2002: 280; Herold 2007: 78). Excavations at Březno (Czech Republic) uncovered remarkably few pit houses and most of those were from the period before the tenth century. In the succeeding two centuries, the pit dwellings were replaced by a form of above-ground buildings, traces of which have been largely lost through ploughing. There may have been a period of transition with some houses below and some above ground, such as the houses found at Ostrów Lednicki (Poland) (Buko 2010: 204–5; Klápště 2012: 189–90).

Houses in northern Russia were similar in some respects to the pit houses, except that they were always built above ground because of the climate. At the tenth-century site at Minino, the log walls were set on footings of stone and all the buildings had a similar plan. They were typical of the 'five-walled' houses found widely in Russia comprising four outer walls and an interior space divided into two unequal rooms by a cross-wall. The entrance to the house was through the smaller room, and the larger, living room was heated by a stove. The floors were constructed of planks, and in the city of Novgorod were set well above ground level to keep the interior dry. The doors were very small, so that to enter the house you had to crawl in, but it was a practical measure to ensure that little heat was lost when the doors were opened. Similar buildings dating from the tenth century onwards have been found in the towns of Pskov and Novogrudok, suggesting that it was the common house type in this area of Russia, with a distribution extending westwards as far as Estonia and Finland, and south as far as Kiev (Khoroshev and Sorokin 1992; Lavi 2005; Buko 2010: 211–12).

A reasonably clear pattern emerges: surface-built log houses were common in north-eastern Europe, while sunken buildings, possibly with some surface-built houses, are to be found over much of eastern central Europe. In western central Europe the pattern was more complex. Sunken buildings, often referred to by the German term *Grubenhäuser*, were widely found throughout northern Europe, but those in the west were rarely fitted with stoves (Figure 3.2). That, together with the presence of above-ground halls, suggests that they were not used for accommodation, but must have been outbuildings (Donat 1980; Ramqvist 1992: 73–4). There was no sharp dividing line in central Europe between the area of occupied pit houses of eastern central Europe and those further west where they

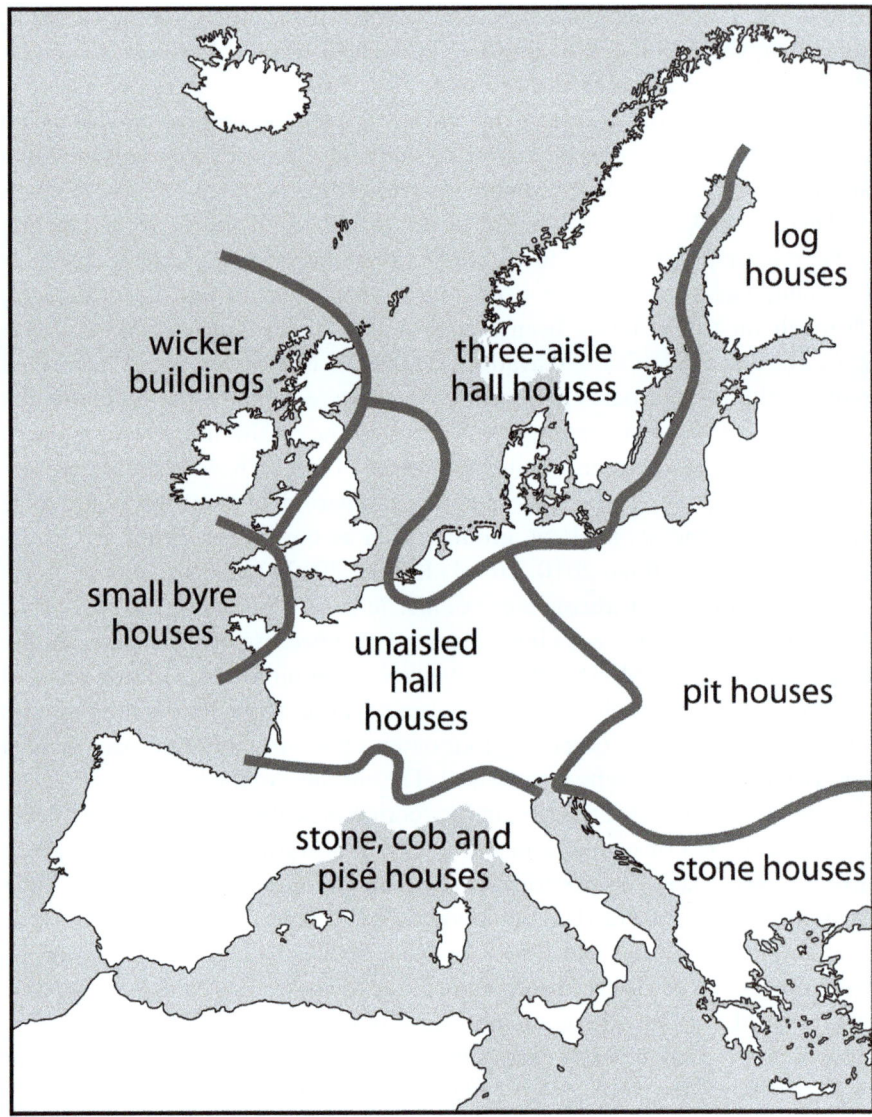

FIGURE 3.2: Distribution of building types and materials in Europe in the early and high Middle Ages. © Mark Gardiner.

were ancillary. Instead, there was intermediate area of mixed house types between the Elbe and Saale on the west and the Oder on the east.

Accommodation in western central Europe and much of Scandinavia and also Finland was, in large, generally rectangular-shaped halls with ground-set posts, a form of building which can be traced back to the prehistoric period

(Viitanen 2001: 96–9). Three-aisled halls were constructed throughout southern Scandinavia during the first half of the first millennium and the house form persisted in Denmark until the eleventh century, when it began to fall out of favour (Skov 2002: 30–3). Elsewhere in northern Europe the aisled building began to disappear earlier as attempts were made to create single internal space. The first step in this process was the movement of the aisle posts to the sides so that they were close to the walls. Alternatively, the posts could be located outside the walls and angled inwards to the wall plate to take the outward thrust of the roof. Buildings of this type appear as early as the eighth century in the Netherlands and in Denmark by around 1000 CE. However, aisled construction continued much longer in western Norway and the North Atlantic islands (Greenland, Iceland and the Faroes) because the outer walls there were constructed with earthen sods, or sod and stone walls, which were less suitable for carrying the weight of the roof. Indeed, in Iceland the aisled building type persisted until the beginning of the fifteenth century (Urbańczyk 1992: 86; Urbańczyk 1999).

The aisle posts served both a structural function and divided the interior space. Within byre-houses, in which cattle were accommodated at one end of the building, the aisle posts usefully served to form the spaces for stalls. At the living end the aisle posts separated the central aisle (or nave) of the building from the outer aisles, which had benches. The accommodation of cattle in one end of the house fell out of favour in much of northern Germany and Scandinavia during the course of the second half of the first millennium, allowing shorter buildings to be constructed, although in the northern parts of Scandinavia the practice of keeping animals with humans seems to have persisted until the twelfth century and beyond. Examples can be found at Kvívik (Faroe Islands), Borg in Lofoten (Norway) and Hvítarhold (Iceland) (Skre 1996: 65; Munch *et al.* 2003: 284–5; Hansen 2013: 190–4).

The interior of the Scandinavian halls was divided not only into the byre (where present) and the heated living room, but also an unheated room or one with only a small fireplace beyond. The living room was used for sleeping, cooking and probably eating. There is also some evidence for metal-working and textile production. The lesser living room was used for various activities: cooking, if this was not done in the main room, and, to judge from the barrel-shaped pits, for the storage of dairy products. The preparation of flour using hand-querns is also suggested on some sites (Myhre 1982; Lucas 2009: 375; Croix 2014).

The use of curving walls for the hall – a type of building sometimes referred to as boat- or bow-shaped – has a long history in Scandinavia, from whence it seems to have spread southwards. Bow-walled buildings appear first in the Netherlands in the late seventh or early eighth century and occur about the same time at Warendorf in northern Germany. The consequence of this form of wall is that the ridge of the roof is unlikely to have been horizontal but, in order to ensure a consistent slope on the thatch, must have risen in height towards the centre. The style persisted alongside rectangular buildings until the twelfth century in Denmark and the Netherlands (Komber 2002: 30–1; van Doesburg 2014: 352).

The western limit of the distribution of three-aisled buildings lay close to the border of France and Belgium. One such apparent structure has been found at Saint-Georges-sur-l'Aa, just on the French side of the border, but it is questionable whether it is in fact an example of the continuing tradition of three-aisled byre-houses, or an example of an aisled hall, a type which was actually newly emerging in northern France and England in the tenth century (Herbin and Oueslati 2011). The earlier three-aisled form did not cross the North Sea and is not found in Britain. In northern France the typical buildings of the ninth to twelfth centuries were commonly divided into two rooms, one with a hearth set against the wall and the other containing storage pits dug into the ground. The two rooms may be set at right angles to one another and in some buildings there was a semi-circular apsidal end. The simplest buildings had no internal posts, but others had a line running down the length of the house, which have thus been described as two-aisled structures. It was imagined that the central line of posts supported a ridge purlin, but more recent work has tended to cast doubt on this view and it has been suggested that the posts were much shorter and supported the joist of a wooden floor (Hamerow 2002: 46–51; Peytremann 2005: 218).

Before turning to southern France, it is useful to look in further detail at buildings in Brittany and Normandy, as well as those from the Channel Islands and south-west of England. The apsidal or curved ends, common in French early medieval buildings, disappear in most areas in the eleventh century, remaining widespread only in the north-west of France where the houses had an oval plan. At the same time, as elsewhere in the northern half of France, buildings increasingly served to accommodate both animals, which were kept at one end, and people, who occupied the other. The division between the two parts of the house was marked by a cross-passage between opposed entrances. It is notable that similar buildings were being constructed at Mawgan Porth on the north coast of Cornwall and a little later at Beere (Devon), which were quite different from others elsewhere in England. We can therefore identify a distinctive type characteristic of both sides of the western end of the English Channel with a form and use of space separate from those to the east (Jope and Threlfall 1958; Bruce-Mitford 1997; Batt 2008).

Cob (clay and straw) and pisé (rammed earth) seems to have been more widely used in the walls of buildings in southern France. These materials have been found particularly near the Mediterranean coast and further north in the Rhône valley, although the full extent of its distribution has yet to be established. Stone was also commonly employed in the south of France, although earth-fast timber structures are also found. Excavation near Baixas in Roussillon identified stone houses of the late ninth and tenth centuries with domestic hearths set against the walls (Catafau and Passarrius (2007: 93–8).

A similar variety of building techniques is found in Italy. Whereas it was once thought that many medieval buildings were constructed in stone, recent work has demonstrated that timber was very widely used as late as the twelfth century, even for churches. Buildings constructed with posts set in the ground have been found in growing numbers as archaeologists become aware of the need to search for evidence of structures of this type. Other buildings were constructed of cob or pisé set in a low base of stone. A systematic survey is in progress, but the preliminary results show that in Italy there was relatively little change in the building materials used in the period 800 to 1150. Timber was used in a little over half of the total of non-stone buildings recorded, while those built of timber with stone footings accounted for between a quarter and a fifth. Earth buildings, which include both cob and pisé, formed a tenth of the total, and the remainder were constructed of uncertain materials.[1]

It would indeed have been surprising if stone, so widely available as *spolia* in the former Roman towns, had not been extensively used. Certainly it was employed, particularly in the construction of high-status two-storey buildings in Brescia, Lucca, Milan, Naples, Ravenna and Rome. The houses built in Nerva's Forum in Rome are the most thoroughly studied in this area. Excavation found two buildings constructed of reused blocks of grey tuff bonded with clay mortar. A portico of four rounded arches was added to the front of one of the buildings, and an exterior timber staircase rose to a first floor. Historical evidence suggests that the ground floor was used for cooking and storage, while the first floor served for living accommodation. A latrine in a projecting balcony was also provided in one of the Nerva's Forum buildings. The complexities of occupation cannot be picked up from excavation alone. Tenth-century documents from Naples show how a two-storey house could be divided up in between two families, each of which had a portion of the cellar and dining room, and separate entrances (Skinner 1994: 286–7; Valenzani 2000: 103–8; Bianchi 2012: 202–3).

Houses in Spain were constructed of the same mix of materials used in southern France and Italy. Dry-stone construction was a common form of building material before the tenth century, but subsequently pisé (known in Spain as *tâbiya or tapial*) set on stone footings became widespread. Studies of houses in Spain have tended to stress the complexity of the evolution of their plan, but there seems to be a general tendency for one-roomed houses to develop into clusters set around a central open space. The next stage is the formation of what has been termed a 'proto-courtyard', defined as an area incompletely enclosed by the surrounding buildings. The sequence of buildings at El Tolmo de Minateda (Albacete) demonstrated the gradual evolution of such proto-courtyards, with the kitchen, pantry and bedroom generally situated on the north side and facing in towards the central space (Lloret 2013: 252–4).

The houses of England have to be treated separately from those in the adjoining countries of Britain, and from those in Ireland. The form of houses in England owed little to those being erected in Wales or Scotland and were different in turn from those on the continent. They were constructed from numerous close-set timber posts and usually had opposed doorways set in the middle of the side wall. Aisled buildings do not occur until the middle of the tenth century and there is little evidence for byre-houses before the twelfth century, and then only in the west (discussed above) and north of England. We understand very little about the use of space in the early medieval houses, but there seems to have been a growing separation between the hall used for eating and sleeping for lesser member of the household, and the chamber used for business and for sleeping for the head of the house (Gardiner 2011).

In the north-west periphery of Europe, the prehistoric tradition of round houses continued well into the first millennium CE, only gradually changing into more elongated forms in the case of Scotland, or oval and rectilinear shapes in the case of Wales and Ireland. A D-shaped house at Carn Dubh in eastern Scotland dated to the period 600–800 CE was clearly influenced by two underlying round houses, and those at the contemporary settlement at nearby Pitcarmick were more elongated in form. These were byre-houses with the cattle stalled at one end of the building and humans living at the other, with a single entranceway serving both (Carver *et al*. 2012: 168–73, 188–91). The pre-Viking phase at Llanbedrgoch in north-west Wales had both a round house and contemporary large rectangular hall. Limited work elsewhere in Wales has uncovered oval-shaped post-and-wattle buildings, which have been compared to similar ones in Ireland, but such buildings have also been found in Durham, where structures with wattle sides have been recorded from the eleventh century (Carver 1979; Edwards 1997: 4; Redknap 2004: 148).

A greater number of sites have been excavated in Ireland and the publication of the waterlogged site of Deer Park Farms from the north of the island has particularly clarified their form. Irish round houses, which persisted from the prehistoric period, were replaced by rectangular forms between 800 and 1000. Comparison of the Deer Park Farms (Co. Antrim) with the similar waterlogged buildings in Viking-period Dublin suggest that the latter were a more rectilinear version of the former, but not fundamentally different. Both had walls formed of double bands of woven wattlework and sleeping benches set against the walls retained by low bands of wattle (Lynn 2011; Boyd 2015: 343–5).

This summary of early and high medieval house forms has enabled us to identify a series of broad types (Figure 3.2). In a large part of central and north-western Europe the hall was fundamental to the idea of the house from at least the Roman Iron Age onwards. In essence, this was a long building with a central hearth, generally with aisle posts and entered from a single door or often two opposed doors in the side walls. Variants of this plan are also found in France and

England from the early Middle Ages, but rarely did halls in those countries reach the size of such buildings in the Netherlands, Germany and Denmark. The investment in the larger halls seems to have been substantial and they were clearly intended to last for many years. We can contrast this with the wicker buildings on the north-west periphery which seem ephemeral by comparison and, on the evidence from Ireland, cannot have lasted longer than ten to twenty years (Lynn and McDowell 2011: 615). A third distinctive area are the pit houses, which have been found across eastern Europe. The practice of constructing sunken buildings (*Grubenhäuser*) occurred in most areas of Europe, but in the west these do not seem to have been used for occupation and served as outbuildings. The practical problems of insulation from the cold made sunken dwellings impractical in northern Russia and parts of Scandinavia where the tradition of log construction was established, although in many respects these were similar in general plan to the pit houses, but set above ground. Finally, we can group together the miscellaneous forms of mud, dry-stone, and stone- and clay-walled buildings, often set around a courtyard, in countries bordering the Mediterranean.

THE LATE MIDDLE AGES (1150–1450)

The period from 1150 onwards is marked by the emergence of broader, less localized patterns of construction. Conceptions of space and domestic form also began to converge in this period, although considerable local variation remained.

It is convenient to begin, as before, in the eastern Mediterranean, where the courtyard and linear arrangements of Greek houses of the earlier period persisted. However, in a number of areas, particularly the islands of the Cyclades, and in Boeotia and Attica, settlement became consolidated in *kastra* or defended villages. The uncertain conditions in Greece following the division of the Byzantine territories after the Fourth Crusade (1204) encouraged the population to seek protected sites beneath a citadel. The houses within the *kastra* on the Greek islands were very tightly packed together on a terrace, which was formed by quarrying into the rock. They often stood in a row, sharing party walls. These rows formed an enclosure with gaps to provide gateways into the settlement. If the houses had two storeys, the lower might be used for keeping animals and for storage, while the upper was used for living. The houses at Pergamon in Turkey typically consisted of a living room, kitchen, pantry with ceramic containers for cereals, fruit, wine and oil, a storage space for household goods, and another for fuel and fodder. Work on standing buildings has shown that there were few openings, apart from doorways, which if possible faced south for the light and to avoid the north winds (Figure 3.3). If a fire was lit indoors, as much later travellers reported was common, it must have been set in the centre of the room (Rheidt 1990: 199; Sanders 1996; Gerstel and Munn 2003: 154–8; Kourelis 2003: 174–80; Sigalos 2003: 213–

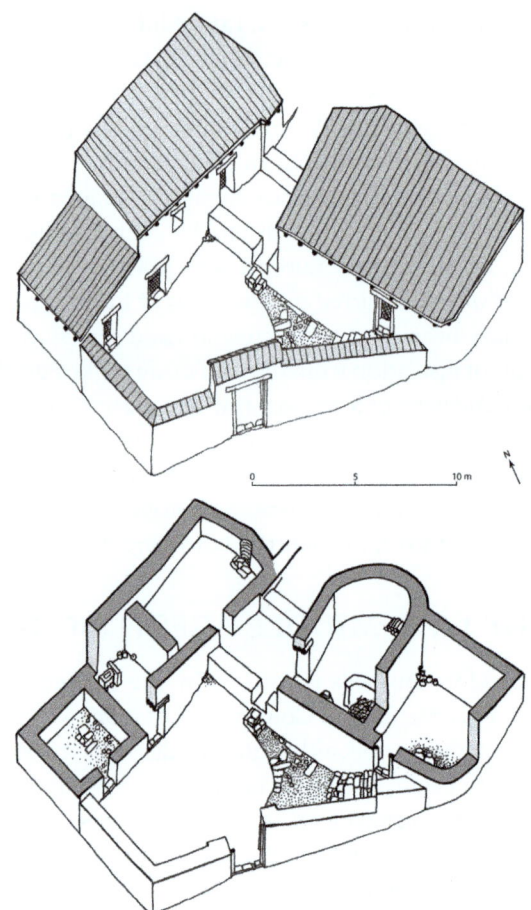

FIGURE 3.3: Reconstruction of complex 4 at Pergamon, Greece, dating to the end of the thirteenth century (after Rheidt, "Byzantinische Wohnhäuser"). © Mark Gardiner.

15). Similar defended sites can be found further north in Montenegro, where the towns, both those on the coast of the Adriatic and inland, were situated within fortified enclosures. While these clearly predate the use of artillery and are evidently medieval, the precise period of construction remains uncertain (Mijović and Kovačević 1975).

Although there was a superficial similarity between the courtyard houses in the eastern Mediterranean and those in the west, the basic principles of design were fundamentally different. The tendency towards the evolution of courtyards seen in the early and high medieval periods emerged in a fully developed form in Spain in the late Middle Ages. Excavations at Saltés (near Huelva) found a characteristic plan with the entrance from the street into the hallway or *zaguán*, which did not lead directly to the central patio, but ensured that the interior of the house was secluded from the street (Figure 3.4). The surrounding rooms were not interconnected, with the exception of the *alcobas* or bedrooms, and access was from the central courtyard. The grand courtyard houses of Granada were a variation on this basic plan, but were more elaborate in design and had an upper storey. Perhaps the most striking features of these urban houses were the pools in the courtyard and beds for plants, although the former might be seen as an elaboration of the wells in the courtyards of rural houses (Bazzana and Trauth 1997; Orihuela 2007: 174–5).

The houses of Sicily can be treated as representative of the central part of the Mediterranean as a whole. Most peasant houses outside the towns were single-storey buildings; only those in urban centres, and not all of those, were taller. Villages houses adjoined each other along the roads and even their back wall

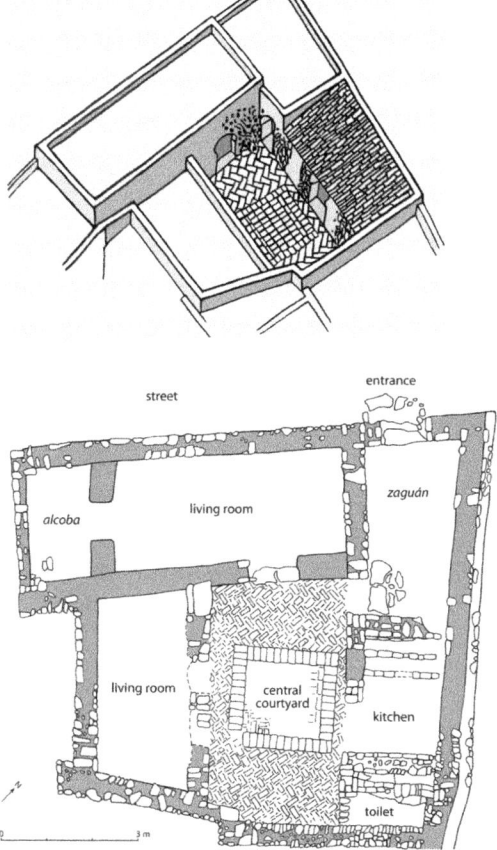

FIGURE 3.4: Plan and reconstruction of the mid-thirteenth-century House 1B at Saltés (Huelva), Spain (after Bazzana, "Espace Privé/Espace Public"; Bazzana and Trauth, "L'île de Saltés"). © Mark Gardiner.

was contiguous with a house behind, and in this respect they resembled the closely set houses of the Greek *kastra*. The houses were rectangular in form and made from rough stone bonded with clay. The space was formally organized with a hearth in the front room for cooking and an adjoining area for a table for eating. A second room behind the first was used for sleeping and storage. Ethnographic evidence suggests that there may have been a raised floor over the back room used for storage of agricultural tools and to serve as a bedroom for children. A platform in front of the house adjoining the street was used for washing and drying clothes, and had a bench to sit outside (Pesez 1984: 686–91; 715–26; 737–45).

Sunken buildings, which had been so common across eastern central Europe, were gradually superseded by ground-level houses, although the two forms existed alongside each other until the thirteenth century, when surface-built structures became predominant. The new ground-level houses constructed in the late Middle Ages were considerably larger than the pit buildings, typically having three rooms (Figure 3.5). The entrance was to the central room, which served as a kitchen and was equipped with an oven. Beyond this on the right-hand side of the entrance was a living room with a stove and on the left-hand side was the storeroom or bedroom, which was unheated. In some buildings a fourth room beyond may have served as a further storage space, often for grain. A variety of different building materials were used: stone bonded with clay, as at Svidna in Bohemia; or close-set timbers and daub, as at Szentkirály in the Hungarian Great Plain; or log construction, as at Sarvaly in Hungary; or a combination of stone for the body of the building and timber set on a low wall, as at Pfaffenschlag in Moravia (Figure 3.5) (Nekoda 2012).

Houses constructed entirely of logs have been found at Gdańsk and Pułtusk (Poland); the form at the latter was an interesting compromise between the three- or four-roomed houses found further south and the single-room buildings known from Russia to the east. Although these square buildings had only one room, separate structures might be joined together after construction to form a larger building. A typical farmstead included a house and buildings for storage and for keeping animals (Golembnik 1987: 173–8; Paner 2000: 491–4). Such houses tended to be smaller, and therefore easier to heat in the cold conditions found in Russia and Poland. In Hungary, where the winter conditions were less extreme, horizontal logs were jointed to vertical uprights to produce both longer single rooms and longer buildings than was possible with single lengths of timber, which rarely exceeded 4.5 m or 5 m long (Pálóczi-Horváth 2002).

A common style of house emerged across Fenno-Scandinavia. The style of log buildings known from Russia in the early Middle Ages was adopted more widely over the northern lands of Scandinavia and Finland in the eleventh century onwards, largely replacing the earlier three-aisled halls (Hauglid 1980: 309). The principal archaeological remains of log houses are often the stone

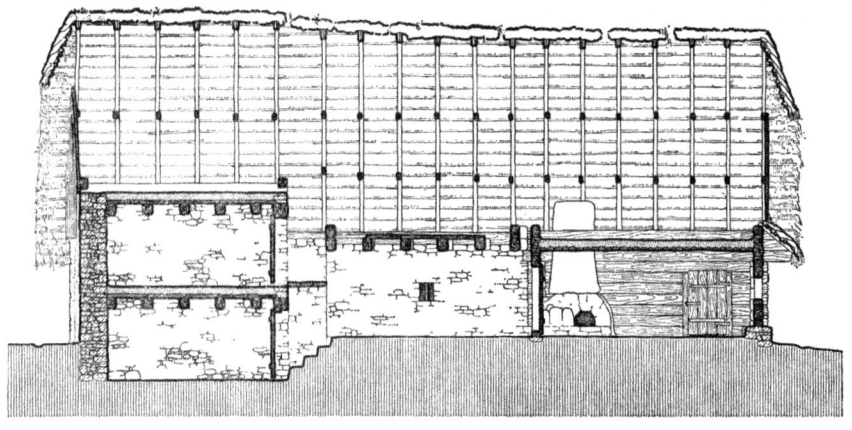

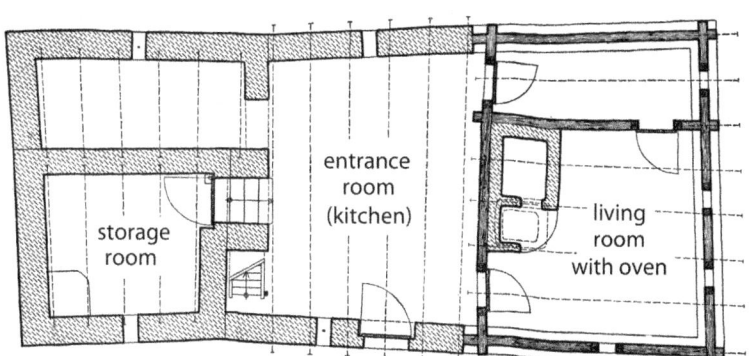

FIGURE 3.5: Section, elevation and plan of the later thirteenth- or fourteenth-century House I/60 at Pfaffenschlag, Czech Republic (from Nekoda, Pfaffenschlag, fig. 71a, b). © Mark Gardiner.

footings on which the timbers were placed. A small number of buildings of this type excavated in the countryside suggest that buildings with separate functions replaced the larger long-houses with living quarters and animal byres under the same roof. Excavations in towns suggest that log construction was established in Trondheim (Norway) from 1000 and in Sigtuna (Sweden) from the end of the eleventh century (Christophersen 1990: 107–8; Tesch 2001: 727–9). The most economical method of construction with logs was to build a square box with horizontal logs, the lengths of the sides being dictated by the timbers that might be obtained. The logs overlapped at the corners to ensure tight joints. This basic form meant that the smaller houses in Oslo were effectively the same as those in Novgorod and there was little development in plan throughout the late medieval period (Molaug 2001: 773–4). Both the Scandinavian and Russian houses were heated by stoves, which were placed in one corner of the room.

Construction with horizontal logs was not, however, the only building type in Scandinavia in the late Middle Ages. Two other types are also attested, but these required a higher level of carpentry. The first carried the weight of the room on a smaller number of principal posts with the body of the wall formed from horizontal planks, which were slotted into the sides of these main timbers. This form of building was known as *sleppvegg* construction and meant that the house size was not constrained by the length of the timbers. The other form of construction was similar, since it used principal posts to take the weight of the roof, but the infilling of the walls was with vertically set timbers slotted into a ground sill at the base and a wall plate at the top. This type of construction was used in stave churches known particularly from Norway, but also employed in houses, as the finds from Bergen have demonstrated (Reimers 1982; Skre 1996: 63–8; Viitnen 2001: 96–9).

Building practices in Finnmark in the north of Norway and in the North Atlantic islands (Faroes, Iceland and Greenland) were notably different. Turf-walled buildings, usually with an outer face of stone and sometime with three aisles, continued to be constructed because little timber was available and that only from driftwood. There is some evidence that in Iceland there was a separation of the animal byre from the dwelling over time. Houses with clusters of rooms up to eighteen in number, connected by a single corridor, have been found dating from about 1300 onwards in Finnmark, as well as Iceland and Greenland. The function of the rooms and the groups inhabiting such buildings remain poorly understood (Thorsteinsson 1982; Urbańczyk 1999; Amundsen *et al.* 2003: 81–3).

The high medieval log houses in Novgorod in Russia have already been described, and similar practices of building continued into the late medieval period. The houses may not have been only one-storey structures, although perhaps these were the most common type. Two-storey log houses with accommodation on the first floor have been suggested in Novgorod from the nature of the foundations, although, of course, the upper parts of these larger houses do not survive but have been reconstructed from representations in chronicles and icons, and from a wooden model of a house found in excavations. By the fifteenth century stone buildings were also being constructed and these too had a number of storeys. However, such buildings were only found on properties owned by rich citizens and in the quarter where foreign merchants stayed.

Log construction was used where there were abundant straight conifers – that is, in Scandinavia, and also eastern Europe and the mountains of the Alps and Carpathians. In the northern parts of continental Europe, Britain and Ireland, where deciduous trees were more common, timber-framing was widely employed. Timber-framing allowed a smaller number of trees to be used and enabled the posts to be raised above the ground on a stone sill. As a result, buildings, if maintained, could last almost indefinitely. While archaeologists have stressed the importance of this innovation, which allowed investment in buildings now able to last for centuries, the implications of the change were not apparently evident to contemporaries, who for many decades continued to set the timbers on the ground surface and not on stone sill walls. Buildings were therefore still prone to damp from the soil and liable to wet-rot (Gardiner 2014: 18–20).

There was immense variation in the types of timber-framing used, both within countries and between them. The fundamental ideas of assembling a timber building – what Harris has called the grammar of carpentry – varied fundamentally across Europe. Harris (1989: 4) has contrasted the English method of timber construction, which gathered the loads from the rafters and passed them to a small number of main posts, with the German approach, which had a larger number of main posts, each supporting a rafter and beam. Nor was this just a matter of carpentry technique; such differences had an effect on the interior organization of the building. The spaces between the main posts, or 'bays', also served to define the size of rooms. In England this could be done by varying the bay width; in Germany the smaller bays were kept a constant size and rooms were formed of different numbers of bays.

URBAN BUILDINGS IN LATE MEDIEVAL EUROPE

During the late Middle Ages, buildings in towns developed a character that sharply separated them from those in the surrounding countryside. Indeed, it has been suggested that the houses of merchants in Prague must have appeared entirely foreign in comparison with the surrounding area (Klápště 2006: 209). The most intense area of urban development in Europe occurred in a band running from north-east France and Flanders southwards to northern Italy. Two- or more storey stone houses appeared during the course of the twelfth century in this area, reflecting the pressure on space, the wealth of merchants who occupied them, and the particular requirements for rooms for retail. The general pattern of usage of these houses can generally be guessed, but the details remain obscure. Undercrofts (or cellars) were widely found in north-eastern France, where they were used for displaying and selling goods. Ground-floor rooms on the street frontage, often with large openings, served both for retailing and as workshops and, therefore, the upper rooms must have had a residential function. Whether they acted as halls or chambers and the position of the kitchen are all unclear (Schofield 1994: 30–4; Grandchamp 1999: 10).

Towns played a pioneering role in the use of new building materials, particularly inorganic substances such as stone, brick and tile. The crowded buildings in towns were particularly vulnerable to fire and the goods held there were often of high value. Brick and tile were expensive, but the urban elite were sufficiently wealthy that they could invest in ceramic building materials. The production of roof tile preceded the manufacture of brick and it was adopted over a wider area. It was used first for the houses of the aristocracy in Rome in the tenth and eleventh centuries, and in the twelfth century more widely replacing thatch and wooden shingles. The chronology in Flanders seems to have been similar, with a restricted use of roof tile from the tenth century, becoming more common in the later twelfth and certainly in the early thirteenth century. An alternative to ceramic roof tile was provided by slate, which was first used in England in the later twelfth century (Hubert 1990: 220–2; Debonne 2014: 11–12).

Brick appeared first in the Baltic area around the middle of the twelfth century and was initially used in church and monastic buildings as an alternative to stone. By the early decades of the thirteenth century it had been adopted for use in merchants' houses in Lübeck and later that century had spread as far north as southern Sweden, east to Novgorod, south to Vienna and west to the east coast of England, although it was not widely adopted for building in these peripheral areas. Even by the fifteenth century, brick was only used in isolated, prestigious buildings on the east coast of England, which contrasts with its widespread adoption along the southern coast of the North Sea and Baltic coasts of continental Europe (Mitchell 2013; Antipov and Yakovlev 2015).

Gradually, the use of these materials extended beyond the elite. Stone buildings had first appeared in the town of Deventer (Netherlands) in the later eleventh century, but from 1200 the local stone, tuff, was superseded by brick (Bouwmeester 2014: 248). The town council at Deventer agreed in 1334 to subsidize the cost of tiles in order to encourage their use after a fire had devastated the town, and in 1360 the subsidy was extended to brick for walls. These materials were so widely adopted in the succeeding decades that by 1425 the subsidy was withdrawn, as there was no longer a need to promote alternatives to thatch and wood (Spitzers 2001).

Neither the concentration of towns, nor the distribution of clay or loess deposits, nor even the shortage of alternative construction materials provide a sufficient explanation for why brick was adopted particularly on the northern coastal edge of continental Europe. The ever-present risk of fire certainly accounts for the use of brick, tile and slate, but it is not clear why these did not become universal building materials in all towns. For example, most houses in London in the fifteenth century were still timber-framed, including some of the most prestigious in the city, so it was not simply a question of expense. To a large degree, the choice of building materials represented a conscious cultural decision. Not only the form of buildings but also their materials carried a message. In coastal Europe, brick was quite clearly associated with commerce and it became a mark of 'Hanseatic culture' (Schofield 1994: 141–50; Mührenberg 2001: 851).

The wider context for the adoption of tile and brick was a shift from the near-universal use of organic materials, which were inevitably subject to processes of decay, to buildings that both inside and out were formed largely of inorganic materials and required less maintenance. Houses of stone became more common as commercial quarries developed, although outside towns they remained a minority in most of Europe north of the Mediterranean. In the interior of some houses, earthen or wooden floors were replaced by ceramic tiles, often decorated with heraldic shields, which became common in the thirteenth century. Stoves, which had played such an important part in heating houses in central eastern Europe from the early Middle Ages, were adopted more widely, appearing as far west as the Île de France. Nevertheless, the advantages of using a stove commonly fuelled from adjoining rooms or from the exterior of the building were not apparent to those living in north-west Europe, even though they removed smoke and fumes from the interior. Even within Denmark there was a contrast between the stove-using areas of the east and north and the open fires in the west (Roesdahl 2009: 281). In England, the open hearth in the centre of the hall, which required the room to be open to the roof, was almost ubiquitous until the mid-sixteenth century (Figure 3.6).

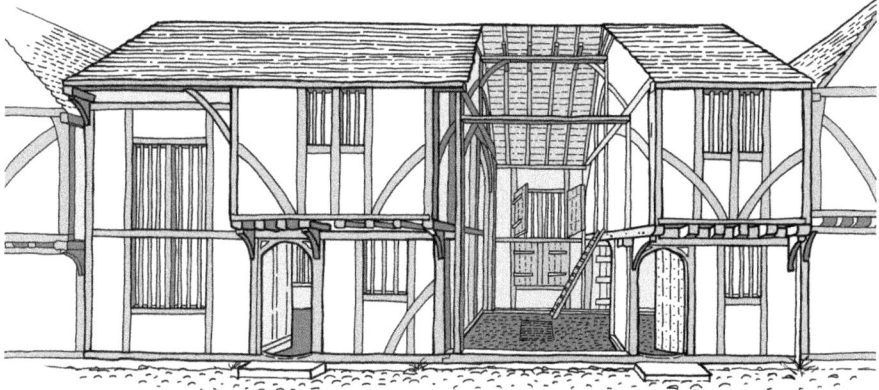

FIGURE 3.6: Reconstruction of the original form of fifteenth-century urban buildings in Sandwich (Kent), England (after Clarke et al., Sandwich). © Mark Gardiner.

By the mid-fifteenth century the transformation in building materials had affected or was having an influence on virtually all parts of Europe. New standards of living were being defined and there were new expectations of accommodation. The criterion for a beautiful town in central Europe was the presence of masonry buildings, tiled roofs and glazed windows. Paolo Santonino, secretary of the bishop of Caorle, recorded in his travel diary for 1485–7 the number of masonry buildings in the towns he visited: 130 at Celje, 400 in Kranj, 50 houses out of 200 at nearby Škofja Loka (all Slovenia) (Jaritz 2006: 252). Yet the same test could hardly have been applied in Scandinavia or Britain, where timber remained the predominant material, although tile and glass were commonly used.

CONCLUSION

The variety of house types in medieval Europe can be ascribed to the interplay of three factors: culture, materials and climate. Each of these has been mentioned in the regional survey of Europe. Stepping back further from the details of the building types, broader patterns begin to emerge. In northern and western Europe the core of the medieval house was the hall – a large, multifunctional space, which formed the largest room. The hall had a symbolic as well as practical purpose. It was a statement of status and might serve as a mark of lordship, and so persisted, most notably in Britain, throughout the period considered here (Gardiner 2015). Even those buildings that were adapted to fit into the constrained spaces of towns still retained a hall (Figure 3.6). Elsewhere, the hall ceased to have such a role. In Norway, for example, with the abandonment of three-aisled buildings, the hall ceased to be so important. In the Mediterranean, the courtyard plans had particular significance and were used in houses of higher status, providing an arrangement that allowed seclusion from the street, shade, and access to the open air. This was not just a response to the climate, but a reflection of the sharp separation of domestic and public life. If the hall and the courtyard houses represent continuity, perhaps the most dramatic change was in central Europe, where the small sunken buildings disappeared, to be replaced by forms which were similar to those further west.

How far can we consider the convergence of building forms to be an aspect of Europeanization? The concept of Europeanization has been applied to the emergence of common ideas of religion and society across Europe, but rarely to the development of common lifeways (Bartlett 1993; Svensson 2014). It is clear that there was still immense variations in style of building across Europe in 1450, and indeed there remains so in the present day, but the greater differences were gradually disappearing – at least in the central part of Europe. On the peripheries the situation was rather different. It would be some centuries before the accommodation of cattle and humans under the same roof finally vanished in parts of England and Wales, and in the *Hallenhause* of northern Germany, although there was a growing sense that humans and livestock should not live in such proximity. Generally, spaces within the house were becoming subdivided and separate functions were to be performed in different rooms, if the size of the building allowed. Cooking, for example, was not to be undertaken in the same place as sleeping and even eating was separated from cooking. It has already been noted that across Europe there was a gradual drift towards the use of inorganic materials in the home, and if organic materials were to be used, then these were to be processed or worked to remove them from their 'raw' origins. Worked and squared timber was preferred to wood with bark, limewashed walls to those with clay daub, and tile, planked or stone flagged floors to earthen ones.

The distinction between the domestic space and the natural world applied not only in the materials used for the former, but also in the creation of an interior environment, which was increasingly differentiated from that outside. Interior spaces were more effectively heated using stoves and lit using lamps and glazed windows. Draughts were removed from houses by the use of tightly fitting doors, by smaller rooms, and ceilings. Chimneys ensured that smoke no longer filled rooms. Furthermore, the spread of storeyed buildings, particularly but not only in towns, raised people above the cold and wet surface of the ground. By the end of the period considered here, buildings provided a warm and dry domestic environment suitable for the finely made furniture and fabrics that were increasingly found within houses.

ACKNOWLEDGEMENTS

I am grateful to Eva Svensson for the help she provided, to Edith Peytremann (France), Jan Klápště (Czech Republic) and Rumjana Koleva (Bulgaria) for providing information on buildings in their countries, and to Libby Mulqueeny for preparing the illustrations.

CHAPTER FOUR

Furniture and Furnishings in the Medieval House[1]

KATHERINE L. FRENCH

INTRODUCTION

Household furnishings serve the human needs of eating and sleeping, but they also enable storage, entertainment, work, relationships and status (Eames 1977: xviii; Carver and Klápště 2011: 204). Medieval furnishings consisted of a limited quantity of furniture; an abundance of soft furnishings, such as table and bed linens, wall hangings and cushions; and eating, drinking and cooking ware. Given modern furniture's role in design, its scarcity in medieval homes has interested scholars, who have tried to explain its dearth, pinpoint when people began acquiring specialized pieces, and when it began to accumulate in homes. Medieval furniture drew most of its inspiration and style from architecture, sharing the tracery and arcading that organized or framed space in meaningful ways. Coupled with textiles and plate, medieval furnishings transformed the daily habits of eating and sleeping into manifestations of estate (Eames 1977: xxii).

Studying medieval furnishing is hampered by its poor survival. Textiles and wood rarely survive in archaeological contexts, and even when intentionally saved, they are prone to decay. Metal survives better, and was saved more assiduously because it could be recycled and had fiduciary value, but everyday use is often difficult to understand. Ceramics survive in abundance but often as sherds and again with contexts that are sometimes difficult to interpret. Surviving furniture generally dates to after the twelfth century, and even that is rare and largely from very elite secular or ecclesiastical contexts (Mercer 1969:

17; Eames 1977: xi). However, the shared aristocratic social class of abbots and bishops and the common habit of adorning furniture with armorial devices means there is little reason to distinguish between lay and ecclesiastical furniture in terms of form, style, or use (Eames 1977: xxiv).

Lacking surviving examples, scholars studying medieval furnishings rely on contemporary texts and illustrations, whether from manuscripts or carved in ivory and stone. Illustrations help answer questions of style and form, but they are also useful for showing what existed in the material world (Carver and Klápště 2011: 202). While manuscript illustrations depicting textiles show how they interacted with furniture, we often have no way of knowing how common or idealized depicted arrangements were. After the twelfth century, not only does furniture increasingly survive, but so do inventories and wills, which provide lists of household furnishings. Legal conventions guide the composition of these documents, so like images they offer challenges. Their sparse descriptions make it difficult to know details and inventories do not provide a social or behavioural context, nor do they necessarily include everything that a room contained or a householder owned. Yet since they often list furnishings in the rooms where appraisers found them, we can compare them to illustrations to see possible room arrangements and theorize about how owners used items (Deets 1996: 116). The increased survival of wills and inventories over the course of the later Middle Ages allows glimpses into the homes of not only the very elite, but the middling and the poor as well.

A hallmark of medieval furnishings is that they are minimal, mobile and adaptable (Mercer 1969: 19; Eames 1977: xix; Barthémy and Contamine 1988: 414; Woolgar 1999: 50). This is a consequence of both housing and household structure. As Mark Gardiner in this volume demonstrates, medieval houses across the social spectrum had few rooms, which served multiple functions. William the Conqueror, for example, variously used both his hall and chapel in Caen Castle as the exchequer (Eames 1971: 53). As we have also seen in this collection, the aristocracy predominantly lived in castles, fortified residences whose balance between household and military functions swung back and forth with the fortunes of the territory. These households were open to an ever-fluctuating number of men according to need and season. The members of these households spent much of their time in the hall, making it crowded and, therefore, difficult to furnish. Lastly, the households of the medieval elite were also peripatetic, meaning they routinely moved about. England's King John (r. 1199–1216) moved on average twelve times a month; his son Henry III (r. 1216–72) moved less often, only about six times a month (Woolgar 1999: 46). These moves were among numerous holdings. Early in his reign Edward III (r. 1307–77) had upwards of twenty-five residences. By the later Middle Ages, this number declined, and Edward IV (r. 1461–83) had only about ten. With such a lifestyle, furnishings either needed to be transportable so as to accompany the household when it moved, or households needed to furnish all their dwellings, an expensive undertaking. If householders furnished all their dwellings, they then needed to be able to guarantee their furnishings' security in their absence. Security required protecting the castle from both outsiders and transitory and opportunistic insiders – household members left to guard the castle in the absence of the owner. According to the protocols of Edward IV of England, his bedding was to be returned to the Wardrobe of Beds each morning, so that 'no stranger shall touche hit' (Eames 1977: 288 n.565).

With limited furniture, the furnishings that take central stage in a medieval house were plate and textiles. They appear more frequently than furniture in both literature and legal records. They were easy to store and move and their value and beauty promoted any number of messages about status and estate (Mercer 1969: 21; Eames 1977: xx). Plate and textiles had utilitarian, symbolic and fiduciary roles: goblets could be used to quench thirst, ransom captives and celebrate mass. Table and bed linens, wall hangings and cushions helped insulate space, comforting its residents. They transformed a castle or manor house hall from a dark and often cold space by bringing colour, luxury and refinement to the hard, minimal furnishings that stayed put. Soft furnishings, like clothing, displayed status and projected luxury (Eames 1977: xx). Plate, in the form of dish and drinking ware, also offered luxury and display opportunities. At banquets, richly adorned tables and costly tableware enhanced the host's reputation. When the banquet was over, the plate could be secured. Often classified with jewellery in inventories, plate, like jewellery, had worth that could be realized in times of financial exigencies.

Technology and trade also influenced the kinds of furnishings a house contained, whether furniture, textiles, or plate. The demands of Germanic elites had kept Roman metal crafts alive, or promoted its rediscovery (Giannichedda 2008; Fleming 2010: 61–88). Gold- and silversmithing enabled the production of cups, plates and silverware (knives and spoons). Textiles, particularly silk, was also highly sought after, and while Europe did not produce silk, trade routes between Byzantium and the Middle East and Europe kept Europe well supplied with this highly desired textile. Even in the tenth century, middling women in Dublin had access to silk (Fleming 2007). Woodworking technology must also have played a role in furniture's design. Although the Romans had sawmills, they were rare in medieval Europe until the fourteenth century. The earliest documented sawmill in France was *c.* 1300, and later for England, Germany and Italy. Spain certainly had industrial mills as early as the seventh century, but current research suggests these were more likely to be paper or oil mills (Lucas 2005: 11, 15, 21). Lacking mills, carpenters fashioned planks by either splitting a log with an axe or using a two-man pit saw. Both methods required tremendous effort and skill (Eames 1977: 228). Yet evidence from shipbuilding and door and roof construction, which relied primarily on wood, shows that jointing techniques could be quite sophisticated and decorative (Geddes 1982). Thus the manufacturing of elaborate wooden furniture was not necessarily outside the bounds of early medieval technology, but it was impractical or unnecessary given the priorities and needs for mobility and security. Moreover it is likely that interest in textiles drove the simplicity of furniture styles. If furniture was to be covered up, this was another reason for not making it elaborate and costly. Even though luxury and display were an important goal for elite dwellings, not all their furnishings were luxurious. At Castle Acre in Normandy, archaeologists have recovered a great deal of local pottery, showing that the castle residents were using local wares probably on occasions that did not call for excessive display (Mellor 2004: 129).

Daniel Lord Smail has recently argued that as credit began to play an increasingly important role in the twelfth and thirteenth centuries, plate and textiles, which could be converted to cash, represented a better investment than furniture. He writes: 'The volume of available credit was not wholly dependent on the volume of coinage. It depended on the volume of available capital, which could take the form of goods' (Smail 2016: 27). For those who routinely used credit to survive during difficult times or to conduct routine business, it was easier to liquidate plate and textiles; when faced with creditors at the door, they were also easier to hide (Smail 2016: 28). While the development of legal structures to secure and recover credit may have played some role in the ways medieval people furnished their houses, the household-furnishing patterns Smail has identified predate the economic transformation of the twelfth and thirteenth centuries. Even as elite households grew less peripatetic, households in general were already used to mobile or minimal furnishings adorned with textiles and plate if they could afford them. The ability to seize goods to recover debt may have favoured soft furnishings, but it did not create a desire for them in the first place. As Penelope Eames (1977: 229), the foremost scholar of medieval furniture, argues, for elite and non-elite households alike, it seems likely the habit of household furnishings was entrenched as they were 'recognized as the means by which social realities were expressed'.

EARLY MEDIEVAL FURNISHINGS

In the early English epic poem, *Beowulf*, written down around the year 1000, the eponymous hero comes to the aid of King Hrothgar, whose lands are being ravaged by the monster Grendel. When Beowulf and his men arrive, Hrothgar entertains them in his hall Heorot with drink, food and story-telling. Afterwards, they are invited to sleep. Hrothgar's hospitality is enabled by a few furnishings, most notably benches (*benc*), a multipurpose item used for resting, feasting and storage. Control and provision of benches for one's men was political power. How visitors used these furnishings supported or undermined social order.

When Beowulf and his men first arrive, 'sea-weary . . . they sat on benches'. When the feast was set up, 'then a bench was cleared in the beerhall for the men of the Geats all together' (Liuzza 2000: 63 l.325–7, 68 l.491–4). Seating arrangements were not random. The king sits apart from the men on his own seat. Later in the poem, when Beowulf becomes king, this separate seat is described as a throne or more literally the prince's stool (*brego-stōl*) (Liuzza 2000: 126 l.2389).[2] Grendel's damage includes leaving 'the benches gory', and when Beowulf fights with Grendel inside Heorot 'from the floor there flew many a mead-bench . . . gold adorned (Liuzza 2000: 68 l.486, l.776). At bedtime, 'they cleared away bench-planks, spread cushions and bedding on the floor . . . there on the bench was easily seen over the noblemen the high battle-helmet, the ringed byrnie, the mighty wooden spear' (Liuzza 2000: 91 l.1239–48). Meanwhile Hrothgar and his queen, Wealhtheow, leave Heorot to sleep elsewhere. Once Beowulf has slain Grendel, he too is permitted to sleep elsewhere (Liuzza 2000: 73 l.663-5, 93 l.1310). Other furnishings include war trophies, in particular Grendel's arm, which Beowulf has hung on the wall (Liuzza 2000: 83 l.983). Later in the story, when Wiglaf enters the dragon's lair to avenge Beowulf's death, we learn it was festooned with wall hangings, possibly the kind that would have also adorned Hrothgar and Wealhtheow's bedroom (Liuzza 2000: 137–8 l.2767–78). The furnishings displayed Hrothgar's wealth and power and their destruction manifests the social disorder that came when a king was unable to defend his people.

Beowulf describes an ideal hall; archaeology grounds this imaginary in practice. Excavations at Yaevering in northern England have uncovered four sequential royal halls, the largest of which was about eighty feet long and forty feet wide (24.5 x 12.2 m). Recent work at Rendelsham, the likely hall associated with Sutton Hoo, revealed a hall of a similar scale and complexity (Hope-Taylor 1977: 124–49; Skull *et al.* 2016). Both excavations show a great deal of investment in such spaces, commensurate with the ideal described in *Beowulf*.

Although not specifically mentioned in *Beowulf*, the competing needs of mobility and luxury made chests one of the most common forms of medieval furnishings. Numerous examples still survive. They served as both furniture and luggage, coming in many sizes and shapes. Their basic variations were either flat or domed lids and either feet or flat bottoms. Feet kept the contents off damp floors and made it more difficult for vermin to climb aboard, but they were a hazard during travel. Flat lids could turn a chest into a seat or a table, but domed lids threw off rain and snow during travel (Eames 1977: 108–9). Among the grave goods found in the ninth-century ship burial at Oseberg, Norway were three chests. A burial for an elite woman, the grave contained the trappings of a well-appointed hall. The best-preserved chest is made of six oak planks, with the end planks forming legs (Figure 4.1). The cover was a portion of a carved-out log, giving it a slightly domed appearance. Iron bands and nails

FIGURE 4.1: Oseburg Chest, ninth century, Oslo, Kulturhistorisk Museum, photo by Ove Holst. © Museum of Cultural History, University of Oslo, Norway, ViO/CC BY-SA 4.0.

both decorated and strengthened it. Hollowing out logs for a chest or its cover was a common practice (Wyley 2005). In 1206, when he was collecting money for a crusade, Pope Innocent III ordered all parishes to be provided with trunks made from hollowed logs with two locks (Mercer 1969: 29). Small chests, more often termed coffers or caskets, carried jewellery and other precious items belonging to the householder. Coffers themselves enjoyed prestige, and surviving examples such as the Franks casket at the British Museum, carved of whalebone and dating from the eighth century, were precious objects in their own right (Mercer 1969: 35–6). Whether because they were small and portable, or because they held valuable items, coffers varied in style and design more than their larger counterparts. The gold, jewels and carvings that often adorned coffers suggests they were display items, and would themselves have been stored in large wooden chests when the household moved.

Another solution to the conundrum of mobility and security was for some furniture to be built into the walls of castles and manor houses. Building in cupboards and seats required architectural planning, and rearrangements required renovations, so this practice was not always practical. Few examples of built-in furniture survive for medieval secular buildings, as they generally have undergone more renovation or destruction, but several examples survive in monasteries and cathedrals. For example, at the abbey of Saint-Étienne in Obazine, France, there is a stone cupboard with wooden doors, dating to the late twelfth century (Eames 1977: 1). Like the doors of the abbey itself, the cupboard and its doors are Romanesque arches, showing a relationship between architecture and furnishings that was to endure throughout the Middle Ages. Seats underneath windows or around pillars were another form of built-in furnishings (Eames 1977: 203). Built-in furnishings were also common in the homes of lower-status people, such as the settlers living in long-houses in Iceland and Greenland (Roesdahl 2009: 276–7).

Because technology was not the determining factor in medieval furnishing's form, scholarly analysis focuses on the underlying principles of estate and how users incorporated it into form (Eames 1977: 181). Perhaps nowhere are the concerns of estate more evident than in the furniture upon which people sat. As we saw in *Beowulf*, Beowulf and his men sat on benches and Hrothgar sat apart. The most obvious example of seats promoting status is the throne – the seat of a king, bishop, or judge. Thrones have a long history as a symbol of sovereignty. While most household would not have had a throne, the grandest seat in the household usually went to the householder or his or her lord if he were present (Deets 1996: 166–7; Eames 1977: 181).

Solomon's throne, as described in 1 Kings in the Old Testament, served as an important inspiration for medieval European thrones. It was purportedly made of ivory and overlaid with gold. Six steps flanked by lions lead up to the throne. The throne had two arms, which were also flanked by lions. Another important model for medieval thrones was the curule or X-chair or stool, which also had ancient origins. Romans consuls, generals and other authorities specifically used this style of chair (Croom 2007: 97). These two models made elevation, lions and the curule form frequent elements in early medieval throne design. For example, the bronze chair of Merovingian king Dagobert (r. 629–639) was originally a curule chair that Abbot Suger (l. 1081–1151) allegedly modified by adding arms and a back. The 1082 seal of Philip I of France (r. 1060–1108) shows a curule seat, while in an early panel of the Bayeux Tapestry, which dates to about the same time, King Edward (r. 1042–66) sits on a stool adorned with lions. Late-twelfth- or early-thirteenth-century examples of curule stools, such as the one from Admont Abbey in Austria used by its abbots, folded for additional ease of packing (Eames 1977: 184). The stool at Admont Abbey is made of pear wood and has lions' heads on the top of the Xs (MAK, Austria H1705/1935).

Not every important chair was curule in shape. The kings depicted in the Bayeux Tapestry also sit on a variety of other chairs or benches. Another form of early medieval chair is one assembled from boards and/or posts. The so-called Suntak chair, now at the Västergötlands Museum in Sweden, is basically a box with arms and a back, held together with nails. Portions of this chair date to the early twelfth century, with modifications made from recycled oak in the thirteenth. Intentionally, its arms do not match, with the left arm bearing the head of a beast, identified by some as a wolf or dog, but perhaps a lion, carved by someone who had never actually seen one. At one point the chair was painted in red, yellow and black. The chair comes from the parish of Suntak in Västergötland, and as an artefact of the early stage in Sweden's Christianity, it was likely the chair of the bishop or local patron (Löfgren and Isaksson 2012). Another Nordic ecclesiastical chair, the so-called Blakar chair now at the Kulturhistorisk Museum in Olso, Norway, is made of pine, and is also a box with arms and a back, and was also painted. The Blakar chair has much more elaborate carvings on the front and sides and through-mortice and tenon joints connecting the back and front (Löfgren and Isaksson 2012: 1672; Roe 1907: 12). Given the ecclesiastical context and the elaborate carvings of both of these chairs, it is difficult to know how typical they were, but these various styles might have had domestic analogues. The Blakar chair shares elements of the elaborately carved chairs used by the kings, queens and bishops of the Lewis chess set.

Another way chairs and stools were invested with authority was by being placed under canopies. Whether a chair or a bed under a canopy, or a cup with a cover, covering signalled the user's status and import (Eames 1977: 198, 202). For example, Holy Roman Emperor Otto III (r. 996–1002) is depicted in his gospels sitting on a box chair with lion arms, covered by a stylized building supported by columns and adorned with a canopy of draping cloth (Bayerische Staatsbibliotheck: Clm 4435).

If there were seats of prestige and power, there had to be more humble ones. Beowulf and his men all sat together on benches, showing that some seats accommodated more than one person. Some would have had backs, but many would not. Called forms, they were likely the most common type of seat throughout the Middle Ages (Eames 1977: 181). They could be adorned with costly metal fittings, as those Beowulf and his men sat on, or be quite rudimentary. Illustrations show that stylistically forms and benches could be dressed up with carvings around the legs that mimicked the arcading in buildings. A mid-fifteenth-century Flemish drawing depicts a jumble of different styles of chair as a metaphor for social chaos. The chairs, which workmen sweep together, are curule chairs, humble three-legged stools, and chairs with backs. In a well-ordered world, this variety of seats would not be so intermingled (Figure 4.2).

We know far less about medieval tables, because so few survive and they were not as important as chairs. Most tables mentioned in documents are described as trestle tables, which would have made them easy to remove once the meal was finished to make way for entertainment or sleeping. Their mobility speaks to the varied uses of the hall. They were probably not elaborately carved, and were instead routinely covered with tablecloths.

Beds, like chairs, helped create social status and display estate. Only a few medieval beds still survive, and most that do are from the later Middle Ages, so it is difficult to know what early medieval beds looked like. For the warriors sleeping in the hall, one suspects their beds were not more than pallets, which, like the tables, could easily be moved when not in use. Archaeologists have recovered several bed frames from Viking ship burials, including five from the

FIGURE 4.2: 'Shoveling Chairs' fifteenth century, Flemish, Circle of Rogier van Weyden, NY. © Metropolitan Museum of Art, NY Lehman Collection.

Oseberg ship burial (Museum of Cultural History, Oseberg). Of the five, one has headposts carved with fantastical animal heads (Figure 4.3). Analysis of surviving Nordic beds suggests the large carved posts were a regional design (Roesdahl 2009: 274). Like the Blakar chair, this Oseberg bed has mortice and tenon joints that connect the slats to the sides and the sides to the head and foot (Hoffman 1983: 353–6). The carvings on the prominent headposts of the Oseburg bed also suggest it was meant to be seen, and indeed this style continued in the Nordic regions throughout the Middle Ages, representing a different bed tradition than in the rest of Western Europe, where textiles covered frames. Regional conservatism, suggests E. Roesdahl (2009: 274), might be related to the bed's strong connection to family and lineage. Also among the Oseberg finds are a variety of textiles, including silk tapestries, coarse woollen cloth, rugs and embroideries. Some of these may have been bed linens. A description from *Eyrbyggjasaga* describes a bed with a valance and bed curtains and 'English' coverlets, suggesting not only a textile trade, but cultural adaptations (Hoffman 1983: 365). We get a glimpse of the importance of textiles to beds in other parts of Europe in around 1100, when Abbot Baldric of Dol describes, in his praise poem of Adela of Normandy, the hangings that adorn her chamber and bed. The hangings have scenes from the Old Testament, Greek mythology and Roman history. The hangings around her bed include a scenic depiction of her

FIGURE 4.3: Reconstruction of an Oseburg Bed, original ninth century, Oslo, Kulturhistorisk Museum, photo by Kojan & Krogvold. © Museum of Cultural History, University of Oslo, Norway, ViO/CC BY-SA 4.0.

father, William's invasion of England (Woolgar 1999: 73). An eleventh-century inventory from a Catalan magnate, Arnal Mir, shows his bedchamber also well fitted with textiles: tapestries, rugs, feather cushions and bed linens (Duby, Barthélemy and de la Roncière 1998: 60). In both instances, it is the textiles rather than the bed frame that attracts attention.

Medieval textiles, such as the Bayeux Tapestry or the fragments from the Oseberg ship burial, are exceedingly rare. Despite their paucity now, they were central to early medieval furnishings. We know they hung on walls, adorned beds and tables and covered floors. To prepare for his coronation, Roger II (r. 1130–54), the first Norman king of Sicily, draped his castle walls in scarlet and purple hangings, likely from Byzantium. Their splendour impressed the abbot recording the ceremony (Mellor 2004: 131). The pieces of textiles that survived in the Oseberg burial show not only a variety of weaving patterns, but also intricate embroidery of silk, in a style similar to the Bayeux Tapestry (Ingsta 1995: 140–4). These and the surviving examples of early medieval clothing, such as Roger II's coronation mantle, provide a glimpse of the vibrant and abundant hangings and coverings that we have lost.

The mobility of early medieval elite households drove furnishing decisions towards movable goods such as plate and textiles, which had practical, fiduciary and symbolic value. The early medieval culture of gift giving also contributed to the emphasis on plate and textiles. Still, the surviving examples of furniture show that despite the lack of sawmills, woodworkers were capable of skilled work, and their designs, which often imitated architecture – or, in the case of the Norse, ships – tied furniture to the rest of the built environment.

LATE MEDIEVAL FURNISHINGS

Sometime around 1225, John de Garlande (1981) an English-born teacher in Paris, composed a *Dictionarius* to help his students learn their Latin vocabulary. In doing so, he takes his students on a tour of Paris, with its streets and artisans, through fields with their animals, his own garden, and a trip he went on that included a shipwreck. Among his descriptions is what a well-off man would have in his house:

> In the lodging of a worthy man there ought to be these: a proper table, a white table-cloth, a hemmed towel, high three-legged stools, strong trestles for a table, firebrands, a crane for suspending pots over the fire, a hearth, candlesticks, logs, bars [a kind of game], stools, benches, an armchair, a bedstead and folding-chairs made of polished wood, a quilt, a bolster, and cushions, a sieve, a bucket, a flour-sieve, a milk pail, a cheese vat, and mousetraps.
>
> —de Garlande 1981: 57

Whether or not de Garlande is describing the furnishings of more than one room, he expects a variety of seats: two kinds of stool (*tripodes alti* and *sedilia*), benches (*scanna*) and two kinds of chair: an armchair (*cathedra*) and a folding chair (*fercula*). There is a bed and the fireplace is well provisioned for warmth and cooking. Notably, there are no chests, which would continue to be common in late medieval houses. In the next paragraph he tells us what items would be needed by a cook: 'caldrons, and pitchers, plates, and frying pans, basins, water-jugs, pots, mortars, saucers, and trenchers, vinegar bottles, spoons and bowls, gridirons, and graters, meat-hooks; moreover they have ovens, chafing-dishes, [and] furnaces' (de Garlande 1981: 59). Such a well-appointed kitchen could roast meat, simmer stews, make sauces and warm drinks. Textiles are prominent, but unusually, the furniture and kitchenware take pride of place. While we have no equivalent sources for the ninth century, read against what does survive, both textually and archaeologically, de Garlande's text suggests that something has changed by the thirteenth century. He describes what we might call a 'cosy' dwelling, with a concern for comfort, and an increased specialization of furnishings; as the reference to a folding chair of polished wood implies, there was also a concern for aesthetics that had only been directed to armour and weapons in *Beowulf*.[3]

De Garlande's description of a 'worthy home' finds echoes in the late-fourteenth-century *Ménagier*'s household book, another French production (Greco and Rose 2009). Written ostensibly by an elderly man for his new and young wife, the author is similarly concerned with comfort, and the ways in which furnishings both enabled and promoted his prosperous identity. While the handbook does not contain a detailed description of the furnishings, we do get a sense of how furnishings organized the household and its activities. The couple sleep in a bedroom, and there are detailed instructions for how to care for the bed to keep it free of flies, fleas and other filth. The spare linens are to be stored in chests to keep them clean. The *Ménagier* also assumes that there will be tables, benches, sideboards and other furniture (Greco and Rose 2009: 139–40). In directing his young wife on how to manage servants, he mentions that his house has a kitchen, an attic and multiple chambers, many of which have fireplaces; altogether there are at least three storeys. The servants have their own space to eat, but once they are finished, the table is to be removed and the space turned over to other purposes (Greco and Rose 2009: 222–3). While the details on the actual furnishings are thin, there is no doubt that the *Ménagier* values comfort and takes pride in his home. His pride also has a moral quality to it; keeping a house according to his dictates included behaving in a certain way, which would keep the young wife away from sin. Indeed, his concern for mice, flies and fleas could be understood as a spiritual allegory (Calkins 1995: 200) (Figure 4.4).

This change in attitude towards household furnishings coincides with a number of other changes starting in the twelfth century. These included the economic expansion of the twelfth century and the rise in consumption after the plague. Overall, houses were furnished with more items and with items from further away. Other changes included a more sedentary life for elite households (Gilchrist 1999: 118). Under these conditions, the nobility spent more energy and resources on furnishing their castle for comfort, luxury and aggressive self-promotion. Wealthy merchants, who manufactured or imported the luxury items now adorning court rooms and private chambers, also improved their standards of living, sometimes imitating, sometimes adapting what was in aristocratic homes. The rediscovery of sawmills made the production of wooden planks easier and cheaper and wooden furniture became more common and more specialized. There is a similar trend in ceramic ware, the material most commonly used for eating and drinking vessels. By the twelfth century, European pottery manufacturing was specialized, with local and regional traditions interacting with broader trends (Carver and Klápště 2011: 190). Ceramics also became more colourful; majolicas came from the Mediterranean and decorated and highly glazed stoneware came from the North Sea. These ceramics were traded across Europe, with majolicas being found as far north as Norway, and the glazed pottery of the North Sea becoming

FIGURE 4.4: 'Blind Tobit,' 1470-79, French, *Bible Historiale*, London, British Library, Royal Mss 15 D I fol. 18r. © The British Library Board.

ubiquitous in England, northern France, Denmark and the Low Countries (Carver and Klápště 2011: 191–2). Both of these ceramic traditions made colourful table settings affordable for many people, not just elites. In central and eastern Europe, colourful embossed ceramic tiles adorned the panel stoves that heated houses and eliminated the smoke of an open hearth. These elaborate stoves started out in elite contexts but by the fifteenth century were in modest homes as well (Klápště 2016: 151). Finally, the later Middle Ages are also better documented; we just know more about household furnishings altogether. De Garlande and the *Ménagier* discussed household furnishings as a manifestation of identity, but furnishings also embodied the virtues of comfort, 'cosiness' and morality. These are new attitudes projected onto the house and were connected to the growing economy and the values of the expanding merchant class.

Late medieval increased consumption did not impact every group in the same way. Peasants and townspeople had very different patterns of consumption. Investment in household wares, many of which could be turned into cash if necessary, was more of an urban practice, while the peasantry used the majority of their resources for land, livestock and food (Oyer 1989; Goldberg 2008; Smail 2016: 61–4). The inventory from Robert Oldman of Cuxham, Oxfordshire from 1349 shows him having minimal furnishings, most of which were textiles: a canvas cloth, two rugs, probably used as beds, some linens and tablecloths. His only furniture was a bench and two stools. Oldman was a well-off peasant, with land and animals worth four times his meagre furnishings (Dyer 1989: 170–1). The inventory from one Jacme Sptalier, a poor man from Marseille, from 1350 shows only a marginally better-furnished house. For furniture he had a table with its trestles and two benches. In addition to his tablecloths, bed linens, coverings and pillows he had an iron bucket, a small shield, three jars and three saddle pads (Smail 2010: 68). Neither man seems to have had a bed, but they probably covered a straw pallet with their linens. For those below the merchants and well-off artisans, furnishings of all kind were more limited.

At the other end of the social spectrum was the aristocracy. They adapted their furnishings, as military defence became less immediate, but status and power remained essential. Writing about the Burgundian court in the fifteenth century, Georges Chastellain said: 'After the deed and exploits of war, which are claims to glory, the household is the first thing that strikes the eye and which it is therefore, most necessary to conduct and arrange well' (Huizinga 1924: 31). Chastellain's observation was by no means the first evidence of aristocratic concern for the state of their households. Eleanor of Provence (r. 1236–72), wife to the English King Henry III (r. 1216–72), introduced a number of new furnishing ideas during her reign. Her private rooms at Clarendon Palace, an undefended hunting lodge, were warmed by a fireplace rather than an open hearth, the walls painted with vivid imagery, and the coloured floor tiles had images of 'knights in combat' (Gilchrist 1999: 131; Mellor 2004: 126). Her windows looked out on her private gardens. Luxury marked her space, as it did the other female spaces of elite homes (Gilchrist 1999: 125). Her husband, apparently inspired by his wife's French ideas of interior decorating, had his bed and canopy at Westminster Palace painted green with gold stars (Eames 1997: 74–5).

New forms of furniture furthered the culture of self-promotion in elite households. The buffet or sideboard developed in the late fourteenth or early fifteenth century as a piece to display plate and from which to serve wine. There are no surviving examples, but descriptions – particularly from Alienor of Poitiers' book of court etiquette, *Les Honneurs de la Cour* – suggest they are large stepped pieces, much like a staircase, with a series of open shelves. Alienor's text, also written about the Burgundian court, explains that the number of shelves reflected the status of the owner. The queen of France could have five stages, countesses had three, while lesser nobles could only have one (Eames 1977: 57). The buffet would have been draped with rich textiles, which were also subject to regulation. Only the queen could have crimson cloth of gold, a countess had velvet (Mercer 1969: 83).

Furnishing styles also varied by region and culture. In Spain, inventories from elite and urban houses identified numerous items, from textiles to glass and metal ware, as Moorish, Alexandrian, or 'in the Damascene style'. For example, Bernat de Sarrià's inventory includes 'red leather Saracens [sic] mattresses'. Another inventory lists 'an almería silk *alquella* or bed canopy' decorated with leaves and the king of Sicily's coat of arms (Amenós 2015: 32). While we do not always know what this means stylistically, we can guess from surviving examples. Moorish ceramics, for example, were often glazed in greens and violets with repeating motifs. Whatever their design, Arab objects were typically marked as luxury items.

The chest also underwent some changes in the late Middle Ages. By the fifteenth century, workaday chests made of boards with lids fashioned from hollowed-out tree trunks were common (Pickvance 2012: 105–8). Panel chests with flat tops that doubled as serving pieces or seats were also increasingly common. These panel fronts became a surface for design. A fourteenth-century French chest at the Victoria and Albert Museum in London has carvings of two knights jousting (Mercer 1969, Fig. 91). In Spain, chests manufactured by Christian artisans had painted fronts, while Arab-influenced ones were apparently plain (Amenós 2015: 30). In northern Europe, chest panels also came to sport a new motif, the linen fold – a design that became common on furniture and wainscoting (Figure 4.5). The linen fold is important because it had no precedent in architecture. Its appearance was another manifestation of the growing importance of wooden furnishings. Probably originating in the Low Countries, it would remain a popular

FIGURE 4.5: Fifteenth-century French or south Netherlandish chest with linen fold panels, NY. © Metropolitan Museum of Art, NY Lehman Collection.

motif in northern Europe into the seventeenth century (Mercer 1969: 88–90; Eames 1977: 275–6). Surviving household inventories suggest the ubiquity of chests, without necessarily explaining what they looked like. In 1380, the forty-two chambers in the Château Cornillion complex contained seventy-four chests. On a more humble level, in 1425, John Andrew of London kept a chest at the foot of his bed, which held all his clothes (LMA: DL/C/B/004/Ms9171/3 f. 154). By the later Middle Ages, much chest manufacturing was centred in the Baltic, connected in part to the timber industry that supplied timber to much of medieval Western Europe (Pickvance 2012: 125–8, 131–2).

In Italy, particularly Florence, the elaborately painted and/or carved marriage chest, *cassoni* or *forzieri*, became a celebrated piece of furniture, subject to competition among leading households. It had pride of place in the procession that ushered the bride from her parents' house to her new husband's house. While ostensibly used to carry the bride's trousseau, its images, usually from non-biblical sources, were also frequently important for promoting an ideal of marriage or the family's lineage (Mercer 1969: 93–9; Musacchio 1999: 159–89; Lindlow 2005). By the beginning of the fifteenth century, the elaborate carvings and paintings on the *cassoni* began to assume what we think of as Renaissance styling and imagery, making them quite different in appearance from the chests in northern Europe, many of which still depended stylistically on gothic architectural forms.

Perhaps the most obvious piece of furniture to promote morality and identity was the bed, because of its association with birth, marriage and death (French, Smith and Stanbury 2016). It is also one of the few pieces of furniture with gendered associations. As the place where marriages were consummated, it was a space of male potency and dynasty, but when associated with childbirth it became a female space. The symbolic import of beds was not lost on medieval owners. We know that some beds had elaborately carved posts and headboards that addressed these themes. For example, when the peasants stormed John of Gaunt's Savoy palace, outside of London, during the Rising of 1381, one of the chronicles explains that 'they took all the torches they could find, and lighted them, and burnt all the cloths, coverlets and beds, as well as the very valuable head-boards (of which one, decorated with heraldic shields, was said to be worth a thousand marks)' (Dobson 1983: 157). In general, however, textiles still remained the major visual focus for beds. Most bed frames were probably quite modest, with the canopy attached to the ceiling by a frame, rather than to the bed. The essential parts of the canopy were the celour (the canopy), the testor (a curtain or board at the head of the bed) and three bed curtains, usually on rings so they could be pushed aside. The whole ensemble might be finished off with a valance (Eames 1997). The type of cloth, its colour and decoration was open to personal choice, or in royal households determined by rank. The size of the celour was also rank determined. A full celour was more prestigious than a half or demi-celour.

Childbirth garnered special preparation for the bed. Royal beds were the birthplaces not only of future monarchs but of dynasties. When Elizabeth of York gave birth to Margaret Tudor in 1489, a chronicler noted that the wall hangings were of 'rich cloth of blue Arras, with fleur-de-lis of gold' and her 'bed [was] made up of a wool-stuffed mattress, a featherbed, a down-filled bolster and four down pillows, the finest linen sheets and pillow cases, a linen quilt, and a coverlet or ermine and cloth of gold' (L'Estranbe 2008: 85–6). Adorning childbirth spaces was not only for the royals; across Europe, women of means, including the wives of merchants and artisans, had special furnishings for the birthing chamber, such as special linens for the bed (Musachio 2016: 131) (Figure 4.6).

FIGURE 4.6: 'Lying in of Siware at the Birth of her son Edmund,' 1434-39, probably English, Bury St. Edmunds, Presentation Copy of John Lydgate's *Lives of SS Edmund and Fremund*, London, British Library, Harley Ms 2278 fol. 13v. © The British Library Board.

Bedding was decorated even for regular use. In the 1397 inventory of the goods of Thomas of Woodstock, first duke of Gloucester, there was 'a large bed of cloth of gold, comprising coverlet, tester and whole celour of fine blue satin worked with gold garters, and 3 curtains of tartarin "beaten" to match, with 2 long cushions and 4 square cushions matching the bed'; it was valued at £182 3s (Eames 1971: 43; French, Smith and Stanbury 2016: 66). According to inventories, saints were a popular image for bed curtains and coverlets. They would have provided spiritual protection and asserted Christian decorum for the occupants. Thomasyne Percyvale, widow of the lord mayor of London, had matching coverlets with St George on them (LMA: PROB11/17/332). The bed of London ironmonger Richard Fawkener had a 'celor and curteyns stayned with fawcons [falcons]', a play on his name, but also an invocation to family, lineage, and identity (French, Smith and Stanbury 2016: 66).

Not only was the bed a potentially colourful and expensive display, sleeping arrangements remained predicated on rank. Whether castle or peasant cottage, the householder slept in the grandest bed with the best linens and curtains, and children and servants slept in more modest, temporary beds (French, Smith and Stanbury 2016: 63–4). According to the 1488 probate inventory of London stockfishmonger Thomas Cowper, his bedroom had a variety of beds: a 'standing bed' with a 'running bed' or trundle bed underneath it, and a cradle (French, Smith and Stanbury 2016: 64).

Another focus of household order and morality was eating. Christian Eucharistic theology embedded the themes of sacrifice, redemption, largesse and social harmony in meals. Sharing a drink symbolized peace and prosperity. As a result, eating and drinking together did more than symbolize household order, it *was* household order (Bynum 1987; Wright 2008: 249; French 2014). These messages were emphasized by the religious images that adorned much dining and drinking ware. Whether incised, like much of the ceramics from Germany, or glazed, like the majolica from Spain and Italy, or engraved in gold, silver or pewter, the saints, the holy family, or pious phrases were common decorations in eating and drinking ware (Figure 4.7).

The centrality of eating together was also fundamental to canon law's concept of marriage and divorce. The canonist Gratian admonished separated couples: 'you shall not eat with her, drink with her at the same table, or stay with her under one roof' (Butler 2013: 134). Advice on choosing a wife from a late-fifteenth-century English poem recommends that prospective grooms value meekness over wealth, explains that a courteous and good wife who 'serves you well and pleasantly . . . with rest and peace a nice meal of homey fare . . . is better than to have a hundred dishes with grumbling and with much care' (Furnival 1868: 50–1).[4] Eating habits not only defined marriage, they embodied notions of status and identity. In great houses the lord ate on the dais with his household spread out before him (Grenville 1997: 66–9; Girouard

FIGURE 4.7: 'Feast of Herod and the Beheading of John the Baptist,' c. 1330, Giovanni Baronzio, NY. © Metropolitan Museum of Art, NY Lehman Collection.

1978: 25–31). In the late Middle Ages, the elite's gradual retreat to parlours or private chambers for meals garnered criticisms from moralists (Morgan 2017: 111–12). The English poet John Lydgate wrote a hugely popular poem called 'Dietary' in the first half of the fifteenth century that juxtaposed the banquet behaviour of aristocrats, which embodied the values of largesse, opulence and abundance, with the bourgeois eating habits, which were restrained, moderate and focused on self-mastery (Sponsler 2001; French 2014). While wealth and estate demanded new layers of deportment and behaviour, and more luxurious dining ware, the morality of the home and hierarchy, whether between a husband and a wife or the lord and his retinue, remained.

CONCLUSION

Household furnishings were more than a means to accommodate sleep, provide warmth, and deliver food. They organized space, created and supported identities, and promoted moral behaviour. The lack of emphasis on furniture and the importance of textiles and plate had less to do with technology or legal structures, and more to do with lifestyle. Furniture's indebtedness to architecture suggests that it was understood as an extension of the building and it was a complement and extension to how a building delineated space. Even when households moved less often, these concerns would remain, even as new values of comfort and 'cosiness' became important.

CHAPTER FIVE

Work and the Home

TANYA STABLER MILLER

INTRODUCTION

The relationship between work and the home is a rich perspective from which to examine gender, socio-economic status and historical change. While twenty-first-century information and communication technology has increasingly brought certain types of work into the home, effectively blurring the line between 'working time' and 'leisure time', the association of work and home, specifically the home as a site of work, was a marker of the pre-industrial age. The rise of industrial capitalism, historians have argued, effectively separated waged labour from the home, thus redefining the meaning of work in ways that still shape modern assumptions about productive labour. Yet, the image of the medieval home workshop governed by a master artisan or craftsman, an image informed by nineteenth-century discourses, has obscured the diversity of medieval work and the varied ways in which women and men contributed to the household economy. In the early twentieth century, feminist historians interested in the history of women's work identified industrialization and capitalism as the chief culprits in the denigration of women's work (Clark 1982). Before the industrial revolution, the argument goes, work took place in the home, with both husband and wife performing complementary tasks in the interest of the family-based economy. By separating work from the home, industrialization introduced individual wages, factory hours and specific labour requirements. Expected to remain in the domestic sphere, most women could not compete in this new system (Clark 1982: 290–338). Although recent work by medieval and modern feminist historians has done much to challenge and correct these arguments, examining the relationship between work and the home still provides historians with fruitful ways to approach the history of women's work and complicate what we mean by complementary tasks (Hanawalt 1999). Clearly, moreover, understandings of this relationship frequently reflect modern priorities and assumptions about work and gender.

An analysis of work and the home also brings to light the ways in which the rise of medieval cities, with their guilds, work regulations and wages, shaped and reshaped the meaning of work by privileging waged labour and profit-oriented ventures over domestic work. Although all members of the household – parents, children, and household servants or apprentices – contributed to its sustenance, medieval officials tended to identify only the names and official occupations of the head of the household – usually male – thereby occluding the productive labour of wives, apprentices and dependent children (Beattie 2000). Tax and guild records, moreover, fail to account for the diversity of household labour, identifying only certain types of labour and ignoring work that fell outside the guild structure. Although family members, particularly women, laboured in the home – cooking, cleaning, spinning wool, brewing ale and caring for family members – unwaged work, then as today, frequently escaped the attention of observers. Documentary sources also tend to record the work identities of people at the higher end of the socio-economic scale, further privileging certain occupations over others. The relationship between work and home was far different for a poor-wage worker, a woman doing piecework for little pay, or a merchant managing the work of others while selling finished goods from his home or in the marketplace.

The relationship between work and the home also varied across regions, between urban and rural settings, and over the course of the development cycle. As Tovah Bender in this volume discusses, scholars have generally characterized north-western European households as composed of partners who married late (about the mid- to late-twenties), were of similar age, and had few children. By contrast, the 'Mediterranean' or 'southern European' family was typically composed of older men married to younger women (Hajnal 1965). Although recent research has complicated this picture, these models point to differing household composition and labour relations. In north-western European families, for instance, women from propertied families tended to have access to training opportunities and capital, allowing them to participate in the urban economies of northern cities (De Moor and Van Zanden 2010). Scholars working on Italian cities, by contrast, have generally found that few women participated in the labour market. However, these studies have tended to focus on elite Italian families, thereby overlooking the preponderance of non-elite women performing low-paid, semi-skilled work (Chojnacka 2001).

Life cycle, too, shaped the sort of labour that was done within and in support of the home. The work experiences of young, unmarried people differed significantly from older, married people. Families with young children organized household labour differently from elderly couples, single mothers and widows. For women in particular, life cycle determined access to certain types of labour, with singlewomen generally having fewer opportunities to engage in high-status labour than the widows of propertied artisans and merchants (Howell 1986; Bennett 1996).

Clearly, the relationship between work and the home varied significantly across time and space, making broad generalizations impossible. Yet, how work within the home was characterized, valued and documented reflects assumptions about gender and socio-economic status as well as the realities of occupational structure and the economy.

WORK AND THE RURAL HOME

In the pre-modern world, the family was generally the basic unit of production, although as we will see, cities attracted a large number of single people, leading in some cases, as Bender explains in this volume, to households composed of non-relatives. In the early medieval period, however, the cities of Latin Europe, particularly in the north, had shrunk or disappeared. 'Those who work' were the serfs or free peasants who laboured on rural estates and monastic lands. Some estates had women's workshops, or *gynaecea*, in which women engaged in cloth production (Herlihy 1990: 77–90).

Agriculture supported most medieval households. All family members, male and female, young and old, contributed to the household's survival by participating in agricultural labour outside and around the home, as well as domestic tasks within, particularly in the realms of food and clothing production. Peasant families provided for their own needs by brewing ale, spinning wool and weaving textiles for home use. Such labour could supplement the family income, too. In thousands of peasant homes, for example, women brewed ale for domestic consumption as well as for sale. In medieval England, almost half of rural households brewed ale for profit, with many women selling ale to their neighbours for a profit on a regular basis (Bennett 1996: 14–36). Some rural households had the opportunity to specialize in crafts that could be accommodated in the home, particularly spinning, fulling, dyeing and weaving textiles. Thus, peasant households did not necessarily bake their own bread or make their own clothes, but rather bought them from locals who specialized in these crafts (Hanawalt 1986: 113). Rural villagers could also practise crafts such as smithing or carpentry in addition to working their lands, or seek waged labour on others' estates to supplement the family income. This bucolic image of peasant families working in and around their own homes, however, ignores the fact that for many families, the home was mainly a place to eat and sleep. Members of poor rural families – both male and female – by necessity found work wherever they could as wage labourers outside their home (Goldberg 2001: 215).

The relationship between work and the rural home reveals ways in which space was gendered. While historians have debated the extent to which medieval people organized space into public and private sectors, with its concomitant assumptions about male and female domains, such divisions have guided thinking about work and spaces within the home, as Eva Svensson shows us in this volume. In rural contexts, while women tended to work at tasks associated with the household, such as cleaning, cooking, brewing, spinning and carding wool, they also worked in the fields, weeding, reaping and threshing. Male family members tended to work primarily outdoors, suggesting that some types of labour – particularly ploughing – were gendered. Women might work as retailers in the home but they could also be found in the marketplaces. Women could also supplement the family economy in a quintessentially domestic manner by taking in lodgers (McIntosh 2005; Whittle 2013) (Figure 5.1).

FIGURE 5.1: Winter Work from *The Golf Book* (Bruges, c. 1540). London, British Library, Add. Ms. 24098, fol. 18v. © The British Library Board

The medieval English 'Ballad of the Tyrannical Husband', a fifteenth-century text about peasant life, portrays the gendered division of labour thought to be typical of rural households. In the ballad, the husband, exhausted from working the fields all day, comes home to find that his wife has yet to prepare dinner.

> Then he began to chide and said, 'You're an evil shit!
> You should go all day to plough with me,
> To walk in the clods that are wet and muddy,
> Then you will know what it is to be a ploughman.'
> The goodwife then swore, and thus did she say,
> 'I have more to do than I may do;
> And if you were to follow me for one day,
> By my head, you would be weary of your work.'

The wife goes on to describe her daily duties, which she executes while sleep-deprived from caring for the children throughout the night.

> After I lie awake all night with our child,
> I get up in the morning and find our house a mess.
> Then I milk our cows and turn them out in the field,
> While you are still sound asleep, Christ protect me!
> Then I make the butter later in the day;
> After that I make cheese – which is not as easy as you think.
> Then while our children are crying and must be got up,
> Yet you will blame me if any of our goods are missing.
> When I have done all this, yet there is even more still to do:
> I feed our chickens otherwise or else they will be scrawny;
> Our hens, our capons and our ducks are all together,
> Yet I tend to our goslings that go to the green.
> I bake, I brew, or else it will not be well;
> I beat and swingle the flax, as I have always done,
> As I trample it, I warm up and cool down,
> I tease wool and card it and spin it on the wheel.
>
> —Wright and Haliwell 1841–3[1]

As the 'Ballad' suggests, gender influenced the division of labour, with women taking responsibility for most domestic tasks. Nevertheless, in reality the survival of the household unit was paramount, making a strict separation of spheres impossible to maintain. Women sheared sheep, herded cattle, took grain to the mill, and sold produce in the marketplaces (Figure 5.2). Men in peasant households, for their part, engaged in domestic tasks during the winter months alongside their wives. Childcare responsibilities, likewise, did not

FIGURE 5.2: Pig Slaughtering from *The Golf Book* (Bruges, c. 1540). London, British Library, Add. Ms. 24098, fol. 29. © Art Media / Print Collector / Getty Images.

necessarily keep women exclusively in and around the home. Older children took care of younger siblings, freeing their mothers for all sorts of labour, including waged labour on other people's lands.

Children also worked in and around the rural home, taking part in weeding, gathering and herding. Children learned agricultural and domestic work from their parents, identifying with their father's or mother's labour. Teenagers tended to live at home with their parents but may have occasionally helped out on the lands of their neighbours if their own household had more help than it needed (Hanawalt 1986: 167). Following the urban revival of the eleventh century, labourers from the countryside frequently migrated to the cities in search of work and opportunity, helping to offset the high mortality rates associated with urban life. In the years of labour shortages after the Black

Death, teenagers and young people worked as servants and labourers in and around the homes of others, engaging in what scholars have termed 'life-cycle service' (Goldberg 1992).

WORK AND THE URBAN HOME

The turn of the millennium brought significant changes to western Europe. A decline in warfare, increased agricultural production, a demographic boom, and the revival of trade and commerce fuelled an urban revival, particularly in northern Europe (Nicholas 2003). Urban growth was sustained largely by migration, as men and women migrated to towns in search of work opportunities. Well trained in various domestic skills, such as brewing, baking and weaving, migrants set up households in the developing towns and supported the growing markets and fairs as contributors and consumers for new industries in food production, textiles and, eventually, luxury commodities. The invention of the treadle-operated horizontal loom significantly expanded the production of heavy woollen cloth, transporting the textile industry from the countryside into the developing cities. Cities made it possible for spinners, warpers, weavers and dyers to work and reside in close proximity, while providing cloth merchants access to markets (Munro 1988; Hunt and Murray 1999) (Figure 5.3).

As in rural contexts, the family remained the basic unit of production in the cities of western Europe. Many urban households engaged in a range of formal and informal occupations, with family members of both sexes and all ages expected to contribute to the subsistence of the household. Much of the work that took place in urban homes was informal and unorganized, arising out the need to meet the household's basic needs (food and clothing). Urban families with enough real estate grew some of their own food and kept animals, much like their rural counterparts, selling whatever surpluses they had in the markets or out of the home. Thus, one of the most common areas of labour, but hard to identify and classify, was victualling. Urban households, particularly its female members, sold surplus food and drink on a casual, ad hoc basis. Clearly related to their domestic duties, women sold fish, produce and ale (Swanson 1989).

Urban growth expanded the work opportunities available to city dwellers; specialized tasks, moreover, reshaped the home physically. As cities became increasingly crowded and urban markets more consistently supplied, families relied on professional bakers and butchers, as well as produce imported into the city marketplaces. Food production on a more formal basis, for example baking and butchering, required modifications to the home, and therefore a degree of capital investment. Bakers needed special ovens, separate from living spaces. Butchers, too, ideally lived near water or areas accommodated with ways to remove or dispose of offal. Fulling and inn-keeping required additional rooms

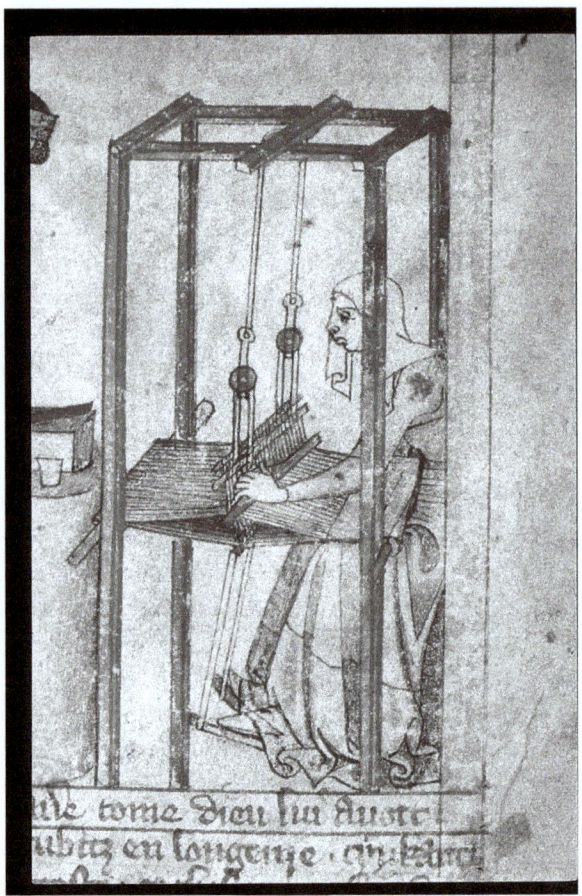

FIGURE 5.3: Woman Weaving on a Horizontal Loom from *The Egerton Genesis Picture Book* (English, third quarter of the fifteenth cent.) London, British Library, Egerton Ms. 1894, fol. 2v. © The British Library Board

or outbuildings. Tanners, who had to endure noxious conditions, often had outbuildings in which to work. Urban craftspeople who sold cloth, shoes or luxury commodities out of the home needed to ensure proper lighting for work and retail purposes. These needs shaped the design of urban homes, which were often set at right angles to the street, with the shop on the ground floor and living quarters above. Most workshops opened onto the streets for retail purposes. The statutes for the Parisian makers of leather buckles required masters to maintain their shops on the street 'by an open window or open entry door' (Roux 2009: 121). Work needs dictated the size of the windows (large to afford plenty of light as well as room to display inventory) and architectural features such as shutters and awnings. The home workshops of well-to-do craftspeople often featured shutters that hinged at the top and bottom. The lower shutter could serve as a counter, or sale window, by adding legs for support. The sale window was a convenient space from which to display goods and required additional features such as awnings to protect inventory and provide an inviting space for passers-by. The shutters could be closed at the end of the working day for security. Concerns over keeping inventory secure led to some home workshops being fitted with narrow doorways to control traffic in and out of the shop (Clarke 2000: 64). The confluence of work and domestic space is apparent in the fact that many urban residents used the workshop as a living space in the evenings (Figure 5.4).

The growth of cities and the expansion of trade led to increasing diversification of labour as well as efforts to organize and protect trades,

FIGURE 5.4: Silk Shop from *Tacuinum Sanitatis* (Italian, 1390–1400) Paris, Bibliothèque nationale de France Nouvelle acquisition latine 1673 fol. 95r. © Bibliothèque nationale de France.

occupations and workers through associations called guilds. Guilds were self-regulating social, religious and economic associations of merchants, artisans, or other professionals. Guilds set quality standards, work conditions and training requirements for their members, in many cases stipulating specific requirements for entry, including periods of apprenticeship training (Figure 5.5). More importantly, perhaps, guilds provided crucial support networks for urban men and women, allowing newly arrived migrants to forge alliances, build reputations and create relationships of mutual trust. Such relationships were crucial for securing credit, raw materials, tools and hired labour in the pre-modern city (Rosser 2015). While there existed considerable variations among the guilds – some being more economically important and thereby more exclusive and

FIGURE 5.5: Market Scene from *Livre du gouvernement des princes* by Gilles Romain (Barcelona, 1480-1500). Paris, Bibliothèque nationale de France, Arsenal 5062, fol. 149v. © World History Archive / Alamy Stock Photo

politically powerful than others – most developed hierarchies of apprentices, journeymen and masters. Apprentices were usually young boys (but sometimes girls) who learned the craft or trade in the home of a master (or mistress). Masters and mistresses taught their own children the family trade with the expectation of keeping the business in the family. Masters could also take in children from other families, who signed contracts and paid fees to place their children in another household to learn a trade. Guild regulations specified the number of apprentices a master could support in addition to their own children. Apprentices who completed their training often became journeymen – or labourers paid by the day (*journée*) – working in the homes of masters. Journeymen could sometimes save enough to become masters; however this was less feasible in some of the more exclusive guilds, which privileged the sons of current masters. As full members of the guild, masters set the rules for their own profession and enjoyed political power. As masters, they owned their own home workshop and dominated its members (both kin and non-kin), exemplifying the relationship between home and work in the Middle Ages (Epstein 1991).[2] Still, there could be considerable fluidity among and interaction between these groups, muddying the traditional image of a rigid, hierarchical guild structure (Rosser 2015: 166–83).

Guilds gradually took increasingly greater control over the rhythms of work in the medieval urban home. Guild statutes and the liturgical calendar regulated the hours and days of work. Workers could not labour after dark, or on holy days. These rules ostensibly protected quality, respected the liturgical feast days, and avoided unfair competition among masters. Bells signalled the start and end of the working day, following the liturgical hours of the day (Le Goff 1980). Some guilds specified how much labour workers could perform in the winter as compared with the summer when days were longer (Stabel 2014: 9–12). Although guilds generally required members to stop work on feast days, the needs of the industry sometimes compelled urban authorities to make exceptions. Members of more powerful guilds, moreover, could afford to bend the rules, thus having more control over the timing of work in their own homes. Workers who commenced before the bell tolled to signal the start of the working day received heavy fines, while masters could dock their journeymen's pay for showing up at their work stations after the bells had tolled (Stabel 2014: 15). Bells also dictated when journeymen started and ended their work days in their masters' homes.

Many of the most powerful medieval guilds were those related to the textile industries. As we have seen, wool working had long been practised in peasant households and, in more formal settings, on rural estates in 'women's workshops' or *gynaecea*. Technological advancements, such as the adoption of the treadle-operated horizontal loom, mentioned above (and later the broadloom, which, being twice as broad as the horizontal loom, increased production significantly) and the concomitant organization of the industry led to the rise of specialist weavers. The urban take-off of the twelfth century, in fact, was accelerated by the growth of the cloth industry, with Europe's most important urban centres in Italy and the Low Countries centred on the manufacture and trade of wool-based textiles. In many northern European cities, the wool industry employed over half of the population and weaving became, for many households, a full-time occupation in which all family members were engaged (Stabel 2015: 34) (Figure 5.6).

As the textile industry became increasingly lucrative and export-oriented, it came to be organized by weaver-draper entrepreneurs. The drapers (or *lanaivoli*,

FIGURE 5.6: Cloth Dyeing from *De proprietatibus rerum* translated into French by Jean Corbechon (French, 1482). London, British Library, Royal Ms. 15 e iii, fol. 269. © Universal History Archive / Getty Images.

as they were called in Italy) organized domestic labour in what is known as the 'putting out' system. In this system, the draper purchased the wool and then 'put out' material in the various production stages, all of which took place in homes. The draper might have the wool sorted and beaten initially in his or her own home workshop before putting out the wool to other specialist workers, such as spinners and warpers, whom the draper paid by the piece. These pieceworkers might be urban or rural labourers seeking to diversify and supplement their household income. In most cases, pieceworkers were poorly paid and female (Munro 1988). Their work, moreover, fell outside the guild structure. Nevertheless, mutual interests and a common economic setting led to considerable fluidity and cooperation among related crafts that cut across formal distinctions of work status, as well as the walls of individual home workshops (Rosser 2015: 164–5).

Although wool spinners and warpers were essential to the wool industry, their work goes largely unmentioned in the extant sources. In medieval Paris, for example, the city's estimated 450 wool weavers would have required at least 1,700 wool spinners to supply them with spun wool. Tax records from the late thirteenth and early fourteenth centuries, however, list an average of only seven wool spinners per year, all of whom were women. The small number of taxed wool spinners indicates that the vast majority of Paris's wool spinners were either married, making them invisible to the tax assessors, or simply too poor to pay the minimum tax. Drapers also took advantage of cheap rural labour, putting out wool to workers in the countryside (Belhoste 2000).

The draper usually employed other weavers – journeymen or apprentices – to work the looms in his shop. Other members of the household, particularly wives, worked in related tasks or in the retail side of the home workshop. Women's position as wives and partners in the home, however, meant that some women, particularly those from elite families, were able to work as drapers alongside, or in place of, their husbands. These women likely broke into this industry through their position in the family (Farmer 2010). One striking example from thirteenth-century Paris is Ysabel of Trembley, who came from a prominent alderman family and had been married to a wealthy draper, Jean Brichard. Her husband's draper business was notably successful; Jean supplied fine wool cloth to the Count of Artois. After Jean's death, Ysabel took over the family business. Her success is evident in royal account books from the early fourteenth century, which reveal that Ysabel supplied the French royal household with almost all of its luxury woollens (Farmer 2010: 94).

Drapers also utilized the labour of fullers. Fulling – the beating of woven wool cloth to soften it – required investment in vats and access to water-powered fulling mills. The necessity of capital investment and proximity to water certainly affected the household. Tax records suggest that fulling was a male-dominated task. Female fullers are not found in the tax registers for medieval Paris, although female family members were recognized as essential for the survival of the business. Guild regulations suggest that fullers could train their children and nephews in the craft and that widows could continue this training if necessary. One statute from the fullers' guild of Paris stated:

> If a master dies, his wife may practice the craft and keep the apprentices, freely, in the manner described above; and with the two apprentices she may teach the children of her husband and her brothers born of a legal marriage.
>
> If a widowed woman practicing the aforesaid craft of fullers marries a man who is not a member of the aforesaid crafts, she may not practice the craft; and if she marries a man who is a member of the craft, even if he is an apprentice or a worker, she may practice it freely.
>
> —Amt 2013: 196

WORK AND INHERITANCE

Clearly, the preservation of the family business was in the interest of all members of the household. While Italian families typically relied on training and working closely with members of the patrilineal line (brothers, sons and nephews), northwestern European families seem to have privileged the nuclear family centred on the conjugal pair. Guild regulations and property laws in northern European cities generally reflect this preference, allowing male and female children to inherit family property and providing widows with extensive rights over the family property, including the workshop. Among elite Italian families, however, women did not tend to manage family property after their husband's death (Herlihy and Klapisch-Zuber 1988).

Fiscal and guild records from thirteenth- and fourteenth-century Paris show that women often maintained control over their husband's workshop after their death, suggesting that the relationship between home and work made widows important in the continuation of the family business. Indeed, their work in the home meant that widows were generally perceived as competent to manage workshops in their own right, not as placeholders for their children. Tracking households across the tax rolls compiled during the reign of Philip the Fair (r. 1285–1314) shows remarkable stability of family businesses, even upon the death of male householders. Although most of the households listed in the tax registers are represented by the male head, in dozens of cases widows are listed as head of a household composed of dependent children who, in subsequent years, leave the household to start their own workshops. The tax rolls clearly show that widows continued to manage the original workshop in their own right. In 1297, for example, a woman named Marie of Dreues took over management of the home workshop after the death of her husband. While her son Guillot was listed alongside her between 1297 and 1300, by 1313 Marie was taxed alone, suggesting that her son had left the household to establish his own business elsewhere (Archer 1995: 167). Similarly, the tax rolls list Robert d'Anvers as the head of his family business in 1297; in 1298, his widow Richeut is listed along with a son. By 1300, Richeut is listed alone as the head of the family business. Guild regulations supported these transitions, demonstrating the ways in which the relationship between home and work privileged the conjugal pair.

Similar patterns of inheritance are evident in other northwestern European cities, such as Leiden and Cologne, where women frequently carried on the family business after their husband's death (Howell 1986). As in Paris, the desire to preserve the home workshop trumped gender. Widows maintained the masterships of their deceased husbands. Guild regulations implicitly encouraged widows to remain single or remarry within the guild. In theory, widows could maintain masterships in their own right if they remarried outside the guild, so long as they satisfied the guild requirements. Regulations for the linen weavers' guild in medieval Leiden, for example, state:

> [S]hould a master of the aforesaid trade die, his widow may maintain the mastership as long as she likes without paying new fees; however, should she remarry with a man who is not a master (in this trade), she is obligated to satisfy the requirements of the brotherhood and all else required of those setting up masterships anew.
>
> —Howell 1986: 74

WOMEN, WORK AND THE HOME

In spite of the household's function as an economic unit, documentary sources, such as fiscal or legal records, tend to identify only the male household heads, while ignoring other members of the household and obscuring the fact that many urban households were multi-occupational. For these reasons, it is difficult to know precisely how female members contributed to the household economy. The tax rolls of Philip the Fair, for instance, only record the names of female taxpayers in the absence of a male head. Thus, married women, even if occupied in a profession, remain invisible. Inventories reveal that the medieval home was the site of many different types of work, not just the official occupation by which the (typically) male head was identified. Descriptions of brewing equipment and cloth-making tools in households headed by men in different trades suggest that someone in the household, likely wives, brewed or engaged in cloth making (Goldberg 2001: 63). Then as now, the domestic labour in which most women engaged, because unpaid, is not acknowledged in the extant records.

Fiscal and guild records sometimes reveal that women were members of craft guilds that were different, albeit related to those of their husbands. Cologne was one of three medieval cities with guilds that were exclusively female. The most important of these guilds was the silk makers. Membership in the guild, however, seems to have been restricted to women married to men in a related trade, typically men who were silk merchants. The silk mistresses' position in the home, which was often the site of a family business in silk merchandising, was what gave them access to lucrative work (Howell 1986: 124–60). The silkwomen of London, although never organized into a formal guild, were also usually the wives of members of the city's mercantile class (Dale 1933).

Indeed, women's ability to maintain control over workshops was the result of the confluence of home and work that characterized medieval labour. Women's position in the household and their responsibility for domestic labour, particularly household management, gave them recognition as their husbands' partners and the key to the preservation of the family business. Indeed, many historians have argued that women's access to what is termed 'high status labour' is contingent upon their place in the home, drawing influential conclusions about the effects of capitalism on the household, the family, and women's productive labour. In her pioneering book *The Working Life of Women in the Seventeenth Century* (1919), Alice Clark connected the decline of the family economy with the rise of capitalism, which, she contended, separated work from the home. Women's responsibilities in the home – particularly caring for children, cooking meals and cleaning – shut them out of the world of compensated labour, a shift that dramatically affected women's access to most types of work. Women, or course, continued to work in the home well beyond the rise of industrial capitalism, labouring at a range of domestic tasks within the domestic sphere. Domestic work, however, came to be regarded as 'not work', a perception that lingers into the modern age.

Other historians have argued that capitalism and industrialization had little effect on the status of women's work (Bennett 1996). At every stage in history, women working both within and outside the home laboured in tasks that were considered low skill and thus poorly compensated. Judith Bennett's classic study on female brewsters in medieval England demonstrated that brewing had traditionally been the preserve of women, since it was easily accommodated in the home and carried out in the course of a woman's other daily domestic duties. As in the case of weaving, however, the introduction of new processes led to the commercialization of the industry. Ale soured quickly and thus was brewed in small batches (and thereby well suited to women's daily domestic routines). As brewers added hops, an import from Eastern Europe, they found the new brew, identified as beer, lasted longer. Over time, as brewing required capital investment and had profit potential, unattached women experienced greater difficult competing. Wives might still help their beer-brewing husbands as retailers and shop aids, but brewing was no longer 'women's work' once it became profitable (Bennett 1996: 145–57).

Clearly, the relationship of home and work was what allowed women to participate in certain types of productive labour. Although women can be found in just about every profession practised in medieval Paris, most of the professions to which Parisian women had access were only open through the family (Frappier-Bigras 1989). Singlewomen or widows unable to draw on the wealth of the conjugal household or continue their deceased husband's profession found these crafts closed to them. The wool weavers' guild, for example, admitted no women save for the widows of masters. The tax rolls show that most female wool workers were concentrated in the lowest-paid crafts in this industry, such as wool spinning, a task that required minimal tools, little technical knowledge, and was easily accommodated to domestic responsibilities. Regulations for other Parisian guilds were hostile to unmarried women. The statutes for the strap makers' guild, for example, state that wives could not learn the craft unless they themselves were the daughters of strap makers. Daughters, moreover, were not permitted to enter the guild independently and could practise the craft only if they married within the guild.

BEGUINE HOUSEHOLDS: THE WORK OF SINGLEWOMEN IN THE HOME

There were sectors of the medieval urban economy in which women could achieve high labour status apart from the family. As the seat of the French monarchy and part-time home to just about every important French noble and ecclesiastic, Paris had a robust luxury market. Thus, royal and aristocratic interests were best served by organizing and supervising the production of luxury goods. Consequently, the silk industry, which was just taking off in Paris in the latter half of the thirteenth century, came under guild organization as early as the 1260s. In fact, by the 1290s, there were seven guilds related to the production of luxury-silk commodities. Five of them were exclusively female in membership and the other two were dominated by women (Archer 1995: 111–17; Farmer 2002: 141–2).

Paris was also a city with a significant population of singlewomen. Historical demographers have argued that in northern cities where work opportunities were abundant, women tended to marry late or not at all, suggesting that in times and places where women had control over their own resources, they might *choose* to remain single (Schmidt, Devos and Blondé 2015; Stabel 2015). Indeed, the work opportunities, inheritance practices and cultural ideals of northern medieval cities allowed for at least the possibility of choice (Stabel 2015). These factors were important in supporting what is known as the beguine movement. Beguines were women who took personal, informal vows of chastity and pursued a life of contemplative prayer and active service in the world. In organizing their days around prayers, beguines lived like nuns, although they were never officially recognized as an official, papally approved religious order. They did not follow an approved rule, they did not live in convents, and they did not give up their personal property. In fact, beguines were free to abandon their religious vocation at any time since it was not enforced by any binding monastic vow. In medieval Paris, many beguines congregated together in households, supporting themselves by their own labour. Tax registers attest to the ubiquity of the beguine household. These records also show that almost all of these women worked in the silk industry.

A particularly specialized and lucrative textile industry, silk was also carried out in home workshops. Spinners, reelers, dyers, warpers and weavers worked out of their homes rather than in a central workshop. As in the wool industry, pieceworkers laboured using materials supplied by merchant entrepreneurs called mercers. Considering the high cost of raw silk, the mercers dealt with their workers directly and closely supervised all stages of the process. Mercers dispatched shop boys to deliver skeins of silk to the dyers and weft thread to the weavers (De Roover 1950: 2915).

Mercers came to dominate the silk industry by the late thirteenth century, organizing silk workers and marketing finished silk cloth and accessories at Les Halles or other venues. One of the four most influential and politically powerful corporations in medieval Paris, the mercers nevertheless permitted women to attain the status of mistress of the craft (Bove 2004). Many mercers rose to prominence supplying high-value luxury cloth to aristocratic households. Mercers with more modest clients also dealt with silk, albeit less prestigious items such as narrow ware and mercery goods.

The overlap between work identity and religious identity suggests that the silk industry was particularly accommodating to women who wished to live lives of chastity, prayer and active service, while remaining in their homes rather than moving into an official beguine community (or beguinage). Well-remunerated, socially valued and culturally associated with women, silk work facilitated the creation of female-centred household production units, which provided women with resources, support systems and a work identity independent of the conjugal household. Guild regulations suggest that silk technology passed among women, specifically female masters and apprentices, while fiscal and property records offer glimpses into home workshops composed of women who trained and worked with one another (Miller 2014: 59–80).

These households and networks were important sources of support. Coming together for the purposes of prayer, work and mutual support, Parisian beguines could support themselves and their households through earnings from silk work, an industry that facilitated the creation of strong ties among lay religious women of diverse socio-economic backgrounds and broadened their social networks. Indeed, silk work was such an important facilitator of beguine households that the vast majority (over 90%) of Parisian beguines for whom an occupation is known performed tasks related to the production and marketing of silk and luxury items made from silk (Miller 2014: 65–7).

The Parisian tax rolls reveal that several beguines worked as mercers, managing home silk workshops composed of other lay religious women. While much about these households is obscured by the nature of the sources, it is clear that silk served to bind these women together in supportive and stable households. The workshops of the beguine mercers Isabelle of Cambrai and Marguerite of Troyes, for example, located on the rue de Quicampoix, were at the centre of a cluster of beguine silk workers appearing in the tax assessments between 1296 and 1300. With the help of these beguine employees, Isabelle ran a modestly successful workshop that produced small silk goods, such as kerchiefs (Miller 2014: 172). The rolls indicate that she continued to run a home workshop with other beguines at least until 1300. Although it is impossible to know how these households were organized or even how many women came and went during the four years these households turn up in the records, it is clear that Isabelle and her companions trained and employed other beguines in their workshops, perhaps even helping to set up other women in the silk business (Figure 5.7). These workshops should change scholarly views on women, work, and the household production unit, which scholars – as we have seen – traditionally associate with the family. Rather than envision a household in which women contributed as wives, widows or daughters of masters, we might imagine a community organized and sustained by women who trained, worked and prayed together.

HOME, WORK AND MASCULINITY

Still, in most medieval cities and for most professions, marriage and the establishment of an independent home workshop went hand in hand. Indeed, some guilds dictated that only masters of the craft were allowed to marry and set up a workshop (Goldberg 2001: 62). Masters defined themselves against other men, locating their authority in their ownership of a workshop, membership in a guild, and ability to control their subordinates. Many of the craft statutes for medieval Paris required masters to have hearth and home to take care of their family members and apprentices (Roux 2009: 180).

The formalization of crafts into guilds articulated a hierarchy of labour – apprentices, journeymen and masters – that not only marginalized certain types of domestic labour (work generally associated with women) but defined masculinity by the possession of a workshop, economic success and civic authority (Riddy

FIGURE 5.7: Gaia, Caecilia, or Tanaquil Spinning, Combing, and Weaving from anonymous French translation of *Des cleres et nobles* (French, first quarter of the fifteenth cent.) London, British Library, Royal 20 CV fol. 75. © The British Library Board

2003: 213). To be a master was to possess a home, independence and authority, but over the course of the Middle Ages it became more and more difficult for men to become masters. The ideal progression from apprentice to journeyman to master was increasingly divorced from reality as master status became hereditary and expensive. Thus, some men spent their entire working lives as journeymen working in the homes of their employers (Karras 2003: 129–37). To work in one's own home, then, distinguished masters from men of journeyman status. Indeed, by the later Middle Ages, managing one's own home workshop came to be regarded as a marker of status. Day labourers, for their part, increasingly lived in rented rooms, sometimes above or near their masters, conveying through their living spaces their subservient labour status (Goldberg 1999).

Work rules also contributed to the separation of the worker from the household, at least conceptually. The craft associations of medieval Leiden, for example, required workers to serve longer apprenticeships and to work as free journeymen before they could be designated as masters (Howell 1986: 91). As labourers came to be subject to regular schedules and strict deadlines, moreover, hierarchies within the family production unit became increasingly pronounced (Stabel 2014: 39–40). Some craft associations began to interfere with the traditional divisions of labour within the medieval home workshop, forbidding wives to manage their husbands' accounts or perform even the most menial tasks within the workshop (Howell 1986: 91).

As heads of their own households, masters supervised and controlled the behaviour of residents, including apprentices and servants, as well as day labourers or journeymen. Many urban and rural homes employed live-in servants. In exchange for their labour, servants received room and board, as well as a small wage. In rural households, servants performed whatever labour needed to be done, whether agricultural or domestic. Urban households typically employed servants to help out in the shop or to perform domestic tasks. Elites employed servants to manage the day-to-day tasks – cooking, cleaning and laundry – of the household. Cognisant of the prevalence of servants, guilds usually tried to distinguish between the work and training of apprentices and servants and journeymen. Apprentice contracts, for example, routinely forbade masters from using their apprentices as servants.

In northwestern Europe, where men and women tended to marry relatively later than their southern European counterparts, young people often worked as servants before marriage (Smith 1992; Goldberg 1992). While many women and men engaged in 'life-cycle servitude' that ended when they married and set up their own independent households, many women at the bottom of the socio-economic ladder laboured in the homes of others for their entire lives (Farmer 2002: 27–30). In southern Europe, typically only poor women worked as servants before marriage; women from more prosperous families tended to marry young, moving straight from their father's home to their new husband's home (Herlihy and Klapisch-Zuber 1985: 202). Some of these women might later become domestic servants in their widowhood. Thus, while many people engaged in life-cycle servitude as young people, others worked in another's household as widows or older singlewomen. Despite the hierarchical and economic frame of these relationships, servants, as members of the household for long periods of time, sometimes developed close affective bonds with their employers (Farmer 1998: 362).

Domestic servants were expected to be under the control of the master and mistress of the household in which they laboured. Moralists warned elite householders that they were responsible for ensuring that their male and female servants avoided engaging in sexual activity outside of marriage (Farmer 2002:

48, 113). Although these same moralists viewed female servants as a greater threat to the household – characterizing female servants as especially wanton and lustful – in reality female servants were particularly vulnerable to sexual exploitation by their masters (Hanawalt 1993: 187–8).

Some wealthy families owned slaves, bringing unfree labour into their homes. Although some historians have argued that slavery had declined, and in some regions died out, after the collapse of the Roman Empire, western Christian traders continued to supply enslaved peoples to eastern markets.[3] In Sweden, for example, slaveholding persisted into the fourteenth century (Karras 1998). Although expansion of long-distance trade, as well as Frankish and Venetian conquests in the Byzantine Empire in the thirteenth century, indeed led to a revival of the slave trade in Latin Europe, the enslavement of women was remarkably consistent throughout the Middle Ages, calling into question arguments for decline (Stuard 1995; McKee 1998). Because maintaining enslaved people was so expensive, typically only wealthy families engaged in slave owning. There is abundant evidence, for example, of a demand for enslaved women in the households of wealthy Italian families. These women performed mainly domestic tasks, such as weaving, cooking, cleaning and caring for children. Many may have been kept at least in part to satisfy the sexual desires of their masters (McKee 1998: 319–20). In late medieval Iberia, particularly Valencia, the population of enslaved peoples was particularly diverse, with a sizable number of Muslims and black Africans enslaved in the course of the *Reconquista* and Portuguese exploration. In contrast to the Italian scene, both urban and rural households utilized slave labour, both within and outside the home. Enslaved men worked in the fields and women worked in silk workshops, picked fruit and sold it in the marketplaces (Blumenthal 2009: 80–4). Some households endeavoured to integrate their enslaved occupants through baptism and education, maintaining a paternal hold over enslaved men and women. Concerns about miscegenation and distrust of Muslims, however, meant that these groups experienced more difficulty integrating into Christian households as enslaved persons and into Valencian society as freed persons (Blumenthal 2009: 3–4).

The master of the home was expected to be the master of all of its members and the work they performed. Inevitable tensions resulted as wives resented the enslaved women who bore their husband's children and as apprentices or journeymen defied their master's authority by running away or bringing scandal on the household. A court case from medieval York suggests some of the ways these hierarchies played out in the home. The court records reveal that an apprentice, John Warrington, seduced one of his master's female servants. After making him swear never to commit such an offence again, the master caught John with another servant, a woman named Margaret, at which point the master tried to force him to marry Margaret. John did not wish to go through with the marriage unless the master gave him enough money to set up his own shop. Although John ultimately refused the marriage, the case illustrates some of the tensions that arose within the home workshop. Apprentices, even if they were fully grown men, could not take wives without possessing a workshop. The master, for his part, assumed responsibility for the household, including the sexual behaviour of those living within it (Goldberg 1999: 59–60).

SPACE AND DOMESTICITY IN THE LATE MIDDLE AGES

By the late Middle Ages, the growth of competition and increased organization of working life had a profound effect on the home and its occupants' relationship to labour. As artisan-merchants began to acquire greater civic authority and social status in medieval cities, they used their wealth and power to control not only the organization of work and the market, but also to forge for themselves an image of mercantile honour. This image was based on successful management of the workshop and the home, financial independence and civic authority, all of which they viewed as mutually reinforcing. Merchants and artisans were good businessmen and householders, therefore they were 'fit to govern others' (Howell 2013: 565).

As several historians have recently argued, the social, economic and political ascendance of the merchant capitalist brought with it a firmer demarcation between the domestic and commercial spaces, dramatically affecting ideas about home, work and 'domesticity'. New emphasis was placed on women's role in the domestic sphere, as women who necessarily ventured outside that sphere risked suspicion as 'common' women. Families at the upper reaches of the socio-economic scale conveyed their status by observing these distinctions. Virtuous women concerned themselves with household management, not with running a workshop or going to the markets. Thus, women who were obliged to labour outside the home, whether as laundresses or hucksters, might be regarded with distrust (Hanawalt 1998: 76, 84).

Advice literature emphasized the role women played in managing the household, suggesting a gendered division of labour and a clear distinction between domestic and common spaces. The Goodman of Paris's advice book for his young bride conveys this ideal, counselling his wife to rely on female domestic servants – in this case a beguine named Jeanne – to supervise household tasks:

> *Item*, concerning chambermaids and house varlets, who are sometimes called domestics, understand, my dear, that I leave you the power and authority to have them chosen by Dame Agnes the Beguine (or another woman you choose to have in your service), to hire, pay, retain, or dismiss from service as you wish, in order that they may obey you better and fear to anger you.

> Nevertheless, you should consult me privately about this and act according to my advice, because you are too young and could easily be deceived by even your own people.
>
> —Greco and Rose 2009: 216

Male servants, on the other hand, had responsibilities outside the home and should be overseen by a male steward. While the young wife ought to hire labourers seasonally, she needed the help of a male superintendent when dealing with these 'rough men' (Greco and Rose 2009: 215–16).

As for the work that the wife must do in the home, the Goodman described rooms that needed to be tidied and cleaned and linens to be aired. He also included remedies, recipes and cleaning advice for his bride, whose sphere of activity was strictly limited to the home:

> [Y]ou must be in charge of yourself, your children, and your belongings. But in each of these things you can certainly have assistance. You must see how best to apply yourself to the household tasks, what help and what people you will employ, and how you will occupy them. In these matters, you need take on only the command, the supervision, and the conscientiousness to have things done right, but have the work performed by others, at your husband's expense.
>
> —Greco and Rose 2009: 181

Yet, the needs of most working families necessarily pushed working women outside domestic spaces. For some tasks, such as retailing, women would have occupied intermediary spaces. Indeed, shops were an important liminal zone, with work and commerce taking place in and near domestic spaces (Rees Jones 2003).

Demographic and economic recovery during the post-Black Death period led to changes in working life and household space. Prosperous merchant families were able to acquire more space in the less-crowded conditions of late medieval cities, building larger homes with clearly demarcated spaces for entertaining, eating and sleeping. The urban houses of the wealthy could now have separate spheres for work space, retail space and domestic space, with work space increasingly regarded as 'male' and domestic life as 'female' (Rees Jones 2003).

In contrast to their poorer neighbours who lived in single rooms of simple cottages, prosperous urban householders had the rooms and space to establish a 'domestic geography' (Riddy 2008: 15). The masters supervised the work of the apprentices and servants and were able to separate these work spaces from domestic spaces. This domestic geography conveyed orderliness, control and industriousness. As masters and owners of the workspace, moreover, they controlled the timing and intensity of work. A well-furnished home was essential to merchants who wished to impress their peers, negotiate contracts with potential clients, and convey an air of prosperity, honesty and creditworthiness. Less prosperous craftspeople could hardly afford to compete. Some rented stalls to sell goods, or worked in the shops or out of the undercrofts of wealthier craftspeople.

In many ways, then, the question of labour in the home is one that relates to power, gender and status. Working in the home was to have some control over the process and intensity of one's own labour. Throughout the Middle Ages, work was inextricably tied to home life. It sustained it, reflecting its priorities, gender and social relations, as well as how these factors changed over time.

CHAPTER SIX

Gender and the Home: Archaeological Perspectives

EVA SVENSSON

'When Adam dalf (dug) and Eve span (spun) . . .'
—Thomas of Walsingham 1874: 321

'I write of the good behavior and deeds of ladies and gentle women, who because their goodness, were worshipped, honored, praised, and revered in time passed and will be forever because of their deeds and goodness, in the hope that my daughters should learn from their good example.'
—de La Tour Landry 1868: 3

GENDER AS A STRUCTURING PRINCIPLE IN DAILY LIFE

To medieval people, gender, and gendered actions, were both given by God in an original order and learned in relation to one's status in society, as expressed in the two introductory quotations by John Ball and Geoffrey de La Tour Landry, both from the late fourteenth century. Being born a (biological) man or woman was decisive for an individual's life course, even if there sometimes were also blurred borders and examples of transgressions, such as Jeanne d'Arc. But there were many different ways of constructing masculine and feminine identities, and urgent needs could interfere with ruling gender constructions and produce non-traditional behaviours.

Gender theories centre around the relationship between biology and social contexts for shaping people and societies, and there are different positionings along the scale from biological determinism to social constructivism. There is also a close connection between today's political agendas, activism and the use of gender theories in research, especially with respect to the idea that gender is socially constructed (Gero and Conkey 1991; Butler 1993; Gilchrist 1999: 26–30). For studies of gender in historical periods, scholars regularly emphasize social contexts. There are some similarities in gender patterns repeating themselves across time and space, but also numerous differences concerning the way gender was both performed and perceived (Sørensen 2000). Thus, intersectional perspectives are key to understanding the importance and the variations of gender constructions for societal reproduction.

Medieval society expected men and women to take on different roles, perform them in different ways, and take up different responsibilities. But these roles, performances and responsibilities were changeable over the course of the life cycle: from the cradle to the grave (Gilchrist 2012).

Male behaviour was the norm to which female characteristics were related. Learned femininity appears to be more important among societal elites, where elite women's movements and tasks were more constrained and their social reputations more fragile than their urban or rural counterparts (Gilchrist 1997: 169). Female behaviour, particularly elite female behaviour, was also the focus of later medieval conduct literature, suggesting that women played a significant role as bearers of a collective elite identity. Conduct literature emerged in a time when the bourgeoisie increasingly challenged the nobility and its privileges. Correct behaviour of elite women thus served for imposing boundaries between the bourgeoisie and the nobility and for promoting their different ideals (Ashley and Clark 2001). However, whether imposed or presumed, gender identity and behaviour were always negotiated in real-life circumstances, and presumably there were also competing, bottom-up ideologies. As Tovah Bender and Tanya Stabler Miller also point out in this volume, the outcomes were often a hybrid of ideologies and reality.

GENDER AT HOME AND IN SOCIETY

The home may appear as a small social unit, and has often been situated low down in historical importance on the hierarchical ladder of social units. But the home was a space that mediated between the individual and the society, and the household provided a borderland between the intimate and the surrounding community (Rees Jones 2003: xiii–xiv). The home and household can be perceived as a social arena for individual strategies and decision making as well as the routines of daily life. The household not only imposed the ideals and structures of society on an individual, but also the opposite must have been the case. That is, social relations within the household were reproduced outside the household, in society at large, not the least of which were asymmetrical gender relations (Svensson 2008: 13–14). The gendered division of labour, legal and property rights, right of inheritance, marriage ages and household structures were all produced at the intersection of home and society's ideological, economic and status regimes.[1]

Work is one of the most visibly gendered aspects of household, both in texts and archaeology. Below the aristocracy and gentry, the family was the core production unit, and gender served as a foundation for the division of labour. Some tasks were assigned to men, others to women. There were also chores that required cooperation between the sexes, although quite often men and women were in charge of different parts or sequences of the process. Social position, involvement in trade, specialized production and regional traditions all played important roles in structuring the gendered labour division.

Whereas urban and elite ways of gendering daily life shared many characteristics across Europe, regional traditions, including different production profiles, strongly influenced the gendered division of labour in rural communities. Features such as natural conditions, demography, social stratification and specialized production for a market were important in the development of different rural strategies, and for which gendered labour division often appears to have been a flexible tool. But gendered labour division was not always open to strategic negotiations, and flexibility could be overruled by social and ideological norms. Also, what may have started as a flexible tool in a production strategy might ultimately develop into an institutionalized gendered labour division (Löfgren 1982; Herlihy 1990).[2]

Ethnographically, the stereotyped differences in the gendered division of labour in pre-industrial southern and northern Europe are often emphasized in relation to concerns about maintaining private and public domains. In southern Europe, women were more restricted to the home and carried out most of their tasks within its boundaries. In contrast, women in northern Europe had larger working spaces, including chores in the home as well as in distant outlying areas.[3] However, there is reason to question if these stereotyped gender differences were in place in the Middle Ages. For instance, in the Cathar village of Montaillou in southern France, women appear to have been considerably mobile outside the domestic confines (Ladurie 1976).

The inconsistencies between the ethnographic stereotypes and medieval cases may well be the result of changes over time in gender relations. For instance, David Herlihy (1990) has demonstrated that during the Middle Ages there was social and gendered segregation; women's work was increasingly confined to the home, and segregated in relation to social position in the household. Female space shrank to the 'rooms, houses, quarters in the cities and villages, while men's activities took them farther abroad to streets, highways, fields, cities, oceans, battles and council tables' (Hanawalt and Kobialka 2000: x) (Figure 6.1).

The segregation process did not have an equally strong impact everywhere or in all social contexts, and there are many examples of a more flexible gender pattern. In northern Scandinavia it was common for women to cover large working spaces and to carry out what might appear to be traditional male chores (Löfgren 1982; Johansson 2002). An illustrative example of the differences between northern Scandinavia and southern Europe is the long-distance herding of cattle in mountain areas, including use of seasonal settlements. In Scandinavia the herders and dairy workers were women, often young, while in southern Europe they were men. In Scandinavia this was a way of expanding the household, but this practice also maintained the norm of dairy

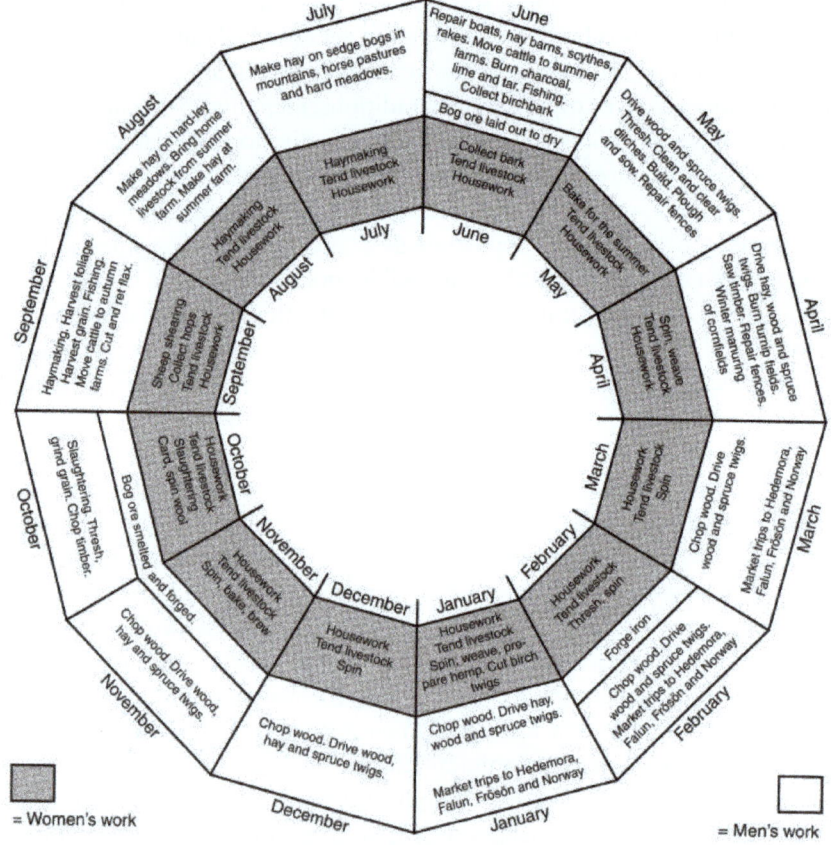

FIGURE 6.1: The forest farmer's year in Offerdal parish, Sweden, during the mid-eighteenth century. Svensson 2008, fig. 3, with references. Private photograph © Eva Svensson

work as a strictly feminine task. In contrast, in southern Europe men generally performed dairy work instead of sending women to outlying areas (Svensson 2015).

STUDYING GENDER IN MEDIEVAL HOMES

Gender should be an inherent analytical category in many contexts, and it stands out as being of particular importance when studying daily life at home. For the Middle Ages, contemporary statements on domestic gender structures are most easily accessible in elite contexts due to the relative abundance of written and pictorial sources, even if the purpose of these sources seldom was to give evidence on how gender structures played out in real life. Ethnography, on the other hand, has paid greater attention to broader segments of society, but for studies on medieval conditions has the disadvantage of distance in time. The ethnographic material bears witness to other temporal contexts than the medieval ones, even if the pre-industrial societies described by ethnographers certainly have some similarities to medieval conditions.

The main medieval archaeological material for studying gender at home is settlement sites and, in pre- and early Christian contexts, burials that may be connected with specific settlements. For medieval archaeological material there is also a bias towards elite contexts, which are often more attractive to excavate. Archaeological material also needs to be decoded for gender interpretations, often by means of analogy. In general, medieval archaeologists rely on documentary, pictorial or ethnographical studies as analogical frameworks for interpretation, even if there is a growing confidence in the archaeological record as such (Andrén 1998).

An important methodological perspective developed over the last decades for studying social structures, including gender, at settlements is the use of spatial analyses, including different versions of access analyses.[4] Access analysis starts from the theoretical position that space is a socially active medium, through which social relations are negotiated, enforced and manifested. By analysing how space was divided in a building, and which people had access to which parts of the building, a social map of the household emerges. The method is most suitable for more elaborate buildings with many rooms, corridors, doors, storeys and stairs, and has in medieval contexts mostly been applied to castles.

According to the Australian archaeologist Penelope Allison, historical archaeologists study household activities and the experience of everyday life through a multiple-source method using ethnography, written sources, buildings, the structures within the buildings, and the spatial distribution of artefacts in the buildings. On the other side of the globe, the Swedish archaeologist Stig Welinder (1992; Allison 1998: 16–18) reached the same conclusion; he also included ecofacts as important source material. Both Allison and Welinder put forward the use of artefact distribution in relation to construction of buildings for identifying different activity areas, the meaning of which could be interpreted using historical or ethnographical analogies. Concerning the European Middle Ages, this method has so far mostly been used to its fullest extent on Scandinavian sites, as will be clear from examples presented in this chapter.[5] This method emphasizes the potential of the archaeological record by highlighting the testimony of ordinary finds. It is also a way of retrieving microhistories, permitting closer encounters with people, irrespective of their status in the household and in society. Gender stands out as an important analytical category in these microstudies.

Access analysis and the multiple source method have brought spatial organization, the material world, and the importance of the home and household to gender studies. Such studies have enriched the field with new perspectives and information targeting important social strategies and practices in medieval society, but have also challenged stereotyped perceptions on gender in medieval times, as we shall see in some of the detailed analysis of gender in medieval homes presented below. Unfortunately, there are only a few published investigations, and strong geographical bias as most of them use Scandinavian materials. In order to have a broader European perspective, studies targeting spatial organization of comparable sites will be used for discussion.

GENDER IN THE HOMES OF THE ARISTOCRACY

Before the time of great castle building in the high Middle Ages, it could be difficult to tell the difference between a lord's house and a peasant's.[6] With political expansion, aristocrats often came to build their homes of mortar, brick and wood, depending on geographical and social contexts. Here we are going to look at castles – the fortified residences serving as the very symbol of medieval aristocracy – as homes. Castles have mostly been studied in contexts of power or as military technology, so perspectives on castles as homes are more uncommon, and analyses of gender and castles are even rarer. Another problem is that existing investigations target limited parts of Europe, primarily northern and north-western Europe.

In a seminal study on castles and gender, Roberta Gilchrist has pointed out that castles traditionally have been considered masculine domains. According to Gilchrist's studies of English castles, gender was spatially segregated. Women had special rooms in the castles, which were located in the higher or inner, most inaccessible parts of the castle. Another feminine sphere in the castle was the gardens. Gilchrist (1997) also comments that there was an important symbolism between women and castles – that the chaste female bodies should be protected by inaccessibility and thus hard to conquer, just like a castle. The image of female confinement to the inner spheres of the castle is contradicted by numerous examples of women actively managing the castle estates. Even in times of war, they were left in charge (Drell 2013).

A castle was also home not only to its lord and lady, but also to other groups of people. The noble families were surrounded by members of their different retinues and servants in hierarchical order. People belonging to the noble families' network, such as relatives, friends and clients, could live in aristocratic homes for longer or shorter periods of time. In the later Middle Ages, large aristocratic households were organized in an inner and an outer household: the outer household comprised the nobleman and his riding retinue, and the inner household consisted of the lady and her suit. For wealthy aristocratic families, it was common to move between their different estates, sometimes with differently organized households (Dyer 1989: 50; Woolgar 1999). The mobility and the hierarchical and fluctuating household structures meant that the sense of home was relative among the members of the household. As we will see, some profound changes occurred during the Middle Ages, which strongly affected castles as homes, and the social and gendered life within.

In western Sweden, two castles, dated about a hundred years apart, were erected on small islands on the northern shores of lake Vänern. The older of the two, Saxholmen, was built in the middle of the thirteenth century, presumably by a high-ranking nobleman on behalf of the Swedish king at a time when strong aristocratic networks in the region challenged royal power. Throughout its short life span – it was deserted *around c.* 1300 CE – the castle was held and inhabited by successive high-ranking noble families loyal to the crown. The other castle, Edsholm, was erected as bailiwick castle and centre for tax collection, most likely in the 1370s, by the marshall Erik Ketilsson Puke. A number of high-ranking bailiffs held the castle until it was burned to the ground in a peasant revolt in 1434. In spite of the functional, geographical and chronological proximity of Saxholmen and Edsholm, archaeological excavations have proved them to have been completely different as homes (Svensson 2008).

The archaeological excavations of Saxholmen and Edsholm have been quite extensive and covered both the main castle buildings and baileys, thus offering windows onto the daily life of all household members. At Saxholmen, inside the perimeter wall, there was a main stone tower with a cellar, which probably accommodated the living quarters of the lord of the castle; an adjacent timber-framed building served as the ladies' quarters; another freestanding, timber-framed building contained the hall; a log timbered house probably housed the bailiff; a handicraft building provided for bronze casting and hollow-horn crafting; and a combined watchtower, storeroom and sleeping quarters kept members of the armed retinue. Outside the perimeter wall were located a smithy, a limestone oven, remains of harbours and jetties, and a possible cowshed and stable.[7]

At Edsholm, a wall separated the main castle building, which was built in stone, from a bailey. The main castle building held the lord's family quarters and their closest retinues. It also contained a storeroom. Four of the buildings in the bailey were half-timbered with white lime-painted bricks and daub-fillings. The remaining building was oddly constructed with different building techniques, one half-timbered part and the other part dovetailed log timbered. The buildings in the bailey had different functions. The two largest houses had been the sleeping quarters and a hall with a kitchen for the garrison. A third building probably housed an officer for the garrison. There was also a handicraft house with a kiln for copper and bronze casting and manufacture of antler products, such as crossbow nuts and gaming pieces. The remaining building with the odd building technique held two different functions. The half-timbered part was used for administrative purposes, probably including bookkeeping for the collected taxes. The log timbered part was a stable for the lord's charger (Figure 6.2).

The layout of Saxholmen inside the perimeter wall was open. All buildings appear to have been easily accessible, probably with the exception of the upper floors in the tower, which would have required stairs for access. The main movements of the inhabitants' daily routines are evident through the structures and the spatial distribution of artefacts and ecofacts. Taken together, they

FIGURE 6.2: Dice, chessmen and sherds of a stoneware jug from Edsholm. Photo: Håkan Thorén, Värmlands Museum. After Svensson 2008, pl. 15. Private photograph © Eva Svensson

indicate that the different social groups and genders in the castle household mixed with few restrictions. The hall appears to have functioned as a regular meeting place for all members of the castle household, men and women, lord and servants. Only the ladies' quarters displays an embryo of spatial segregation, as artefacts related to men, such as male dress accessories and weapon details, were present only by the entrance of the building (Figure 6.3).

The situation at Edsholm, a castle about a hundred years younger, was completely different. This castle was tailored on the principle of spatial segregation based on social status and gender. The rigid division between the main castle and the bailey demonstrates that there were in fact two different homes at Edsholm. The main castle was the home of an aristocratic household, of which the excavations unfortunately have given very little information. The bailey was the home of mercenaries, artisans and a horse. From a gender perspective, it should be noted that the bailey was completely void of female artefacts, and instead the finds material bears witness to male loneliness and limited future prospects. Judging from the finds material, the mercenaries, although dressed in armour, spent their days drinking and gaming while waiting to be relieved. Another impression from the excavations was that the bailey

FIGURE 6.3: Dress accessories and jewellery from Saxholmen. Finger rings, beads, clothing bell and setting gem. Photo: Lars Thorén, Värmlands Museum. After Svensson 2008, pl. 8. Private photograph © Eva Svensson

must have been an incredibly dirty and stinking place. The mercenaries had deposited their garbage, mostly food waste, everywhere in the bailey, both inside the houses and outside. This is in strong contrast to Saxholmen, where garbage had been neatly collected and carefully disposed. To the mercenaries, the bailey at Edsholm was just a temporary home, and wading among thick layers of refuse does not appear to have been a problem. The only well-kept 'home' in the bailey was the stable for the lord's charger.

From a European perspective, Saxholmen and Edsholm were small to middle-sized castles, but they shared a common 'castle grammar' dictating how a castle should be built and which functions should be in place (Mathieu 1999). Even if castles across Europe were different in many ways and came in different sizes, to a greater or lesser extent they all followed a common spatial and functional arrangement, giving residents 'an understanding of the appropriate behaviour expected . . . which areas were accessible to his or her rank' (Johnson 2002: 69).

However, the castle grammar in Europe changed during the course of the Middle Ages towards increased spatial segregation and enclosure, as is visible in the examples of Saxholmen and Edsholm, and also towards more luxury and comfort for the elite (Svensson 2008: 329). While there are few studies focusing on gendered space in castles, the spatial segregation process as such can be illuminated by two examples from different parts of Europe. Alt-Wartburg in Switzerland and Lelekovice in the Czech Republic may serve as models of the process (Meyer 1974).

At Alt-Wartburg, a stone tower, designed both for defence and as living quarters, was built in the late twelfth century. It was three or possibly four storeys high, and built completely in stone. The entrance was in the south of the tower on the second storey. Thus the tower could only be entered via a wooden staircase that led to the main door on the second storey. There are no traces of any buildings in the probably unfortified, or lightly fortified, bailey during this early phase. In the second half of the thirteenth century, the castle was rebuilt following the principles of social stratification in the noble home through spatial segregation and enclosure. A wall dividing the main castle and a ring wall around the bailey were erected. The main entrance to the castle was also reinforced with a dry moat and a ramp. Fire layers indicate that there had been wooden buildings in the bailey, probably including a smithy and stables. In connection with the construction and refortification of the bailey, a new storey was added in the stone tower in the main castle, and the rooms were renovated for increased comfort. The old wooden staircase up to the entrance was replaced with a more imposing stone staircase, emphasizing the act of castle access (Figure 6.4).

Another, more curious, example is the castle Lelekovice in the Czech Republic (Unger 1999). In the 1340s a few provisional buildings were erected

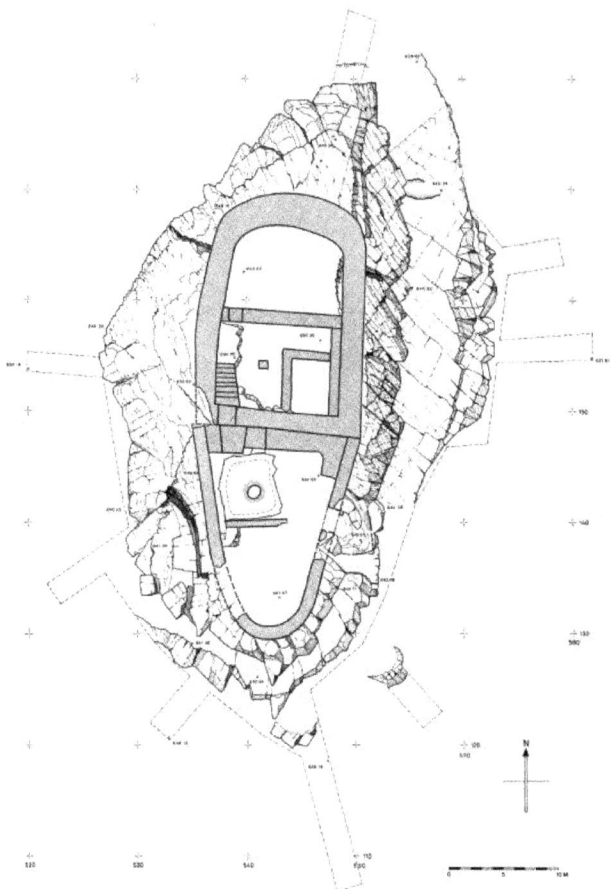

FIGURE 6.4: Alt-Wartburg, overview. After Meyer 1974, fig. 4. © Werner Meyer

on a cliff, soon replaced by a main castle building surrounded by a curtain wall, and a dry moat dug into the rock cutting the main castle off from the bailey. During the second phase, stone buildings were constructed along the curtain wall in the south-west and north-east, replacing wooden predecessors. Inside the curtain wall a new main building, a few other buildings and cellars were built. However, in the late 1370s, Lelekovice became the home of three noble families, and the castle was divided by fences into three separate castles. For almost fifteen years, Lelekovice was an unusual combination of individual castles, each of them with the obvious functions and grammar of spatial segregation in place, in addition to collective elements, such as the curtain wall and the entry through the main gate. In the 1390s Lelekovice became the seat of a single family again, and the new occupants removed the fences between the three parts of the castle (Figure 6.5).

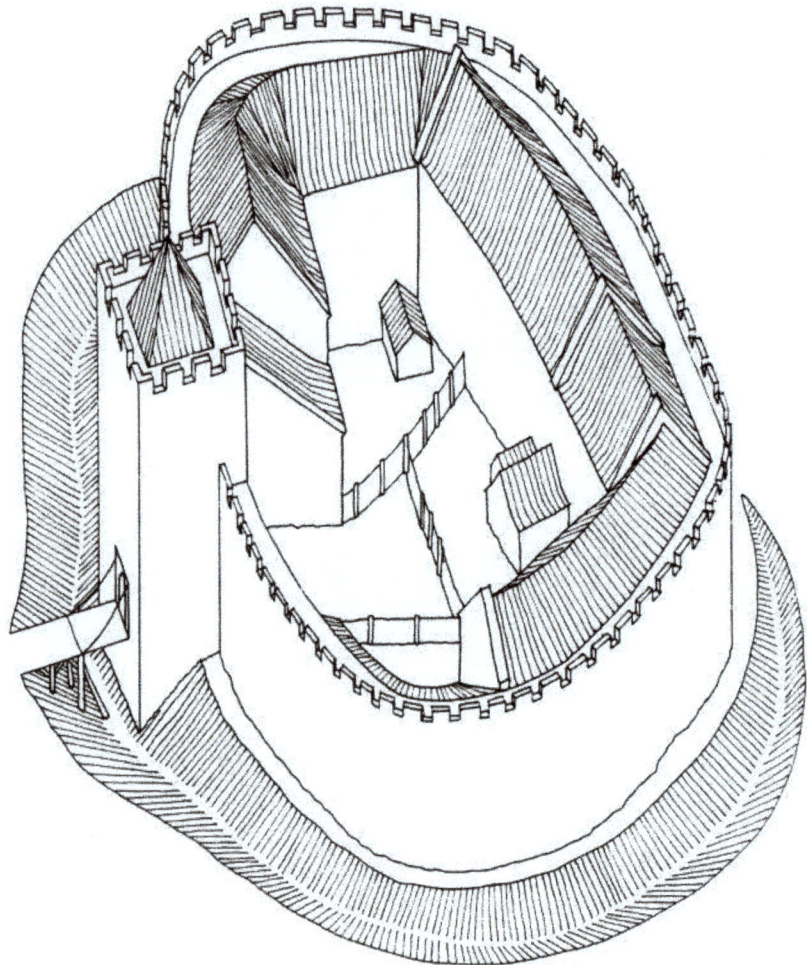

FIGURE 6.5: Reconstruction of Lelekovice, phase 2. After Unger 1999, fig. 49.
© Josef Unger

The segregated castle became a European theme in castle organization over the course of the Middle Ages, and it would be reproduced in the household structure and in the spatial organization of noble homes. However, it left a lingering notion of belonging to a communal castle household that included people of both high and low status, where courtyards and halls served as meeting places for the high and low residents. This organization accommodated outsiders not belonging to the household, such as mercenaries, housed in a castle on a fluctuating basis.

The blending of different social ranks appears to have been more common in the quarters and buildings attributed to women living in the castle. Needlework stands out as an especially uniting activity (Herlihy 1990). Sewing and embroidery was the foremost expression of the female elite, but there was also textile work of different types, such as spinning carried out within the castle by women of different social ranks. A unique encounter with feminine daily life in the castle home is offered by a spindle whorl retrieved during the excavations of the ladies' quarters at Saxholmen. The spindle whorl carried the runic inscription: 'Kristin owns me' (Old Swedish: *Kristin a mik*), with 'Kristin' most likely being Kristina Amundsdotter, one of the last ladies of the castle (Svensson 2008: 169–70 pl.11) (Figure 6.6).

FIGURE 6.6: Spindle whorl with runic inscription ('Kristin owns me') from Saxholmen. Photo: Håkan Thorén, Värmlands Museum. After Svensson 2008, pl. 11. Private photograph © Eva Svensson

The examples of the spatial segregation process in Saxholmen and Edsholm show that gendered practices and ideology changed among the aristocracy in the course of the Middle Ages. However, ideology and practice was not always the same thing, and the spatial segregation built into the castles during the course of the Middle Ages was contested by the practicalities of daily life. Still, social and gender asymmetry expressed in spatial segregation was put on display as a means for social competition, not least with the bourgeoisie and wealthy peasants striving to move up the social ladder. Spatial segregation in castles thus went hand in hand with the emerging conduct literature emphasizing dignified female manners, which brought honour upon her family and the whole aristocracy (Ashley and Clark 2001). It is important to point out that elite ideals of femininity were coupled with elite ideals of masculinity, which combined the warrior and the chevalier, as representations of the estate's political power.

GENDER IN THE HOMES OF THE THIRD ESTATE

Whereas the medieval aristocracy may be considered as exponents of emerging Europeaness, with some lingering regional qualities, peasants and rurality are deeply associated with regional attributes, such as different settlement structures and building traditions (see Mark Gardiner's chapter in this volume), despite interaction and hybridity across rural communities (Burke 2009). A European rural home could be a single farmstead, be part of a hamlet, a village, or a fortified *castrum/incastellamento* depending on where it was located. Some rural sites could also develop urban characteristics (Klápště and Jaubert 2011).

An important theme, when discussing gender in rural homes, is the stereotyped differences in the gendered division of labour between pre-industrial southern and northern Europe, and the apparent importance of private and public domains, with women in southern Europe more restricted to the private spheres of the homes than their sisters in northern Europe (Rosaldo 1974), as noted by both Tovah Bender and Tanya Stabler Miller in this volume. The dualism of private equals women, contra public equals men, is challenged not only, as discussed earlier in this chapter, by examples of women in southern Europe commonly moving outside the confines of the home, but also by the condition that the home may in fact have been a public space. For instance, in pre-industrial northern Scandinavia, the kitchen was often a public gathering point, not just for the inhabitants of the home but also for guests or strangers who happened to knock at the door (Johansson 2002: 195–6).

Alongside regional differences, rural gendered patterns also interacted with the economies and the household's social standing within the community. Rural communities were socially stratified, including wealthy peasants as well as poor labourers, and rural economies were diversified. In some areas cereal cultivation dominated, in other parts cattle breeding was more prominent. Generally there were also trade and industries included in the agrarian economies, sometimes highly specialized, imposing special demands on households and the workforce. However, as discussed earlier, seasonal settlements and transhumance offered different ways of organizing gender for similar tasks.

Regionalism is not particularly emphasized in the scholarship on early medieval towns, even if regional building traditions and ways of life played into the organization of urban functions such as trade, handicrafts, and the exercise of political power in early urban centres. Many early medieval European towns had previous histories and retained notions of Roman urbanity. As urban centres developed over the course of the Middle Ages into towns, bourgeois power structures, planning, building traditions, economies and identities also developed.[8] The new urban or bourgeois identity was embodied in the marketplace and the town hall. These developments were also related to gendered domesticity.

In a comparative study Sarah Croix (2012) has investigated work, gender and space in rural settlements in Scandinavia and France in the centuries around 1000 CE. The Scandinavian rural settlements in question were located across Scandinavia: in Iceland, northwest Norway and Denmark, which all operated under very different natural conditions. Still, the homes and the activities taking place followed a common pattern. Several tasks, such as textile production, metal working, and agrarian subsistence chores from ploughing to food processing were visible in the archaeological material collected from the settlements, and from the distribution of artefacts could often be mapped spatially.

The core of the Scandinavian home in this period was the long-house or hall, where most daily indoor life took place. The long-house was often divided into living spaces for people and cattle, which were supplemented with smaller special-purpose buildings. Although the long-house offered only a single large room for people, different functional areas can be identified within the room from structures and artefact distribution. The area around the hearth, serving as both the major heating and light source, stands out as the centre of the house, with multiple activities regularly detected. Interestingly enough, male and female work spheres were spatially integrated, both indoors and outdoors, and the above discussed presumption of an opposition between a male outdoor/public sphere and a female indoor/private sphere is not supported. Even strongly gendered activities, such as textile production, were performed in multifunctional areas, such as the area around the hearth. The observations made by Croix are supported by investigations of contemporary rural settlements in other parts of Scandinavia (Emanuelsson *et al.* 2003).

Moving over to contemporary northern and central France, which had a socially more complex rural hierarchy then Scandinavia, the gender pattern at the settlements appears to have been similar (Croix 2012). Economic activities such as agriculture, textile production and metal working were practised also on the French sites, with additional examples of baking ovens and pottery manufacture. Sometimes these handicrafts were carried out on a small scale by the homes, or – as specialized production – at a distance from the living quarters. Both male and female work took place indoors as well as outdoors, and according to written and pictorial evidence could also be extended beyond the limits of the farmstead.

In Scandinavia, many rural traits were introduced in the early and high medieval towns through migration. An urban home could be a version of a rural farm adjusted to the planned town grid, and the rural pattern of mixed-gender spaces was repeated in the towns. According to studies of the spatial organization of urban handicrafts in early medieval Bergen and Oslo, both in Norway, both male and female handicrafts such as metalworking, antler and bone handicraft, leatherwork, including shoemaking, and textile production were carried out in the homes (Rui 1993; Øye 2005a, 2005b). In Bergen, textile production, using vertical looms, appears to have been a small-scale female task, conducted in the rear parts of the tenements, while male handicrafts were performed in or adjacent to the homes.

Moving to the south-east of Europe, a different picture appears. In Byzantine towns, two main types of urban homes have been recorded in the early and high Middle Ages: the courtyard house and the linear house (Sigalos 2003). The courtyard house was predominantly located in the urban centres, whereas the linear house belonged to the outskirts of the urban topography, such as the areas close to the city walls. The two types of houses represented two different social groups in Greek towns, where the urban elite can be associated with the courtyard houses and the linear houses were homes to more humble segments of the urban population.

However different in layout and social affiliation, a similar gender praxis was at hand in both types of houses, although more elaborately expressed in the courtyard houses. In these, domestic activities related to women, such as cooking, took place in the deepest and most private parts of the building, including the courtyard, which could only be accessed through the house. Seclusion of women was somewhat differently arranged in the linear houses. Even if less elaborate, there was a spatial hierarchy built in these houses, with the rear being reserved as a female space for domestic chores. But there were mixed-gender spaces both inside and outside of the linear houses as well. For instance, due to the lack of courtyards, ovens were built in the alleys next to the houses as shared facilities. The ideal of a private versus public dichotomy and seclusion of women was thus contested by real-life practicalities, at least among the lower strata of the urban population. Another probable intrusion in the private/public ideal of the urban household's domestic life was the keeping of cattle and involvement in agrarian economy, while in the countryside it was common for women to work in the fields alongside men.

Both the courtyard houses and the linear houses in the Greek towns flourished into the high and late Middle Ages, but in the countryside a new type of settlement, the Frankish *kastra*, developed, with self-standing one- or two-storey houses of a fortified character that became a long-lasting vernacular building tradition in Byzantium (Sigalos 2003: 212–18). The single-storey house lacked visible internal divisions, whereas the two-storey houses were divided between cattle on the ground floor and people on the top floor. Most likely there was a division between a reception area and a domestic area and a hierarchy of space ranging from public to private, presumably with implications for the gendered domestic life and seclusion of women.

In other parts of the Mediterranean, the enclosed rural house, or courtyard house, appears to have been common (Bazzana 2001; Poisson 2002). In the course of the high and late Middle Ages in northern, western and central Europe, there was also a growing tendency to organize buildings in relation to a yard in an encircling manner, even though long-houses survived into modern times in some regions (Grenville 1997; Svensson 2014: 76). It has even been suggested that there was an enclosure process within late medieval houses in England, corresponding to the enclosure process in the agrarian economy (Johnson 1993).

The changes in rural domestic space came as variations on the theme of enclosing people and animals and some tasks. The standard farmstead in the Dutch village of Huis Malburg from the eleventh to thirteenth centuries comprised living quarters, farm buildings and a number of stack barns built around an open area with a well (Oudhof 2000). In the late medieval village of Bystřec in the Czech Republic, the L-shaped farmstead partly enclosing a paved courtyard with a dunghill was a dominating pattern (Belcredi 2006). Of special importance concerning rural gendered domesticity is that the altered spatial arrangements of farmhouses were accompanied by an increased use of special purpose buildings where different tasks were assigned to different buildings and places.

An insight into the gendered space in a rural settlement in the high Middle Ages is offered by the hamlet of Skramle in Sweden (Andersson and Svensson 2002). In the thirteenth-century phase, there were three farming households, each living in a single-room log house with a centrally located hearth. The houses, and two common store houses, were situated around an open area. One of the houses also had an adjacent smithy. There was another long-house for storage, shared among the households in the hamlet. Behind the houses there were three fields, one for each household. A cattle byre and a barn, commonly used by the hamlet, were located at a short distance from the settlement area. Thus, Skramle displays a somewhat odd mix of private and common, where dwelling houses and fields appear to have been the households' possessions, where cattle breeding was commonly managed. Storage appears to have been both a private and a common affair (Figure 6.7).

FIGURE 6.7: Reconstruction of farms and fields in the medieval hamlet of Skramle, around 1250–1300 AD. The buildings comprise three dwelling houses, of which one was combined with a smithy, a larger outhouse, a smaller outhouse and in the bottom left there is part of a barn and cow-house. This reconstruction was made by 'Projekt Skramle'. Photo: Bengt Holter, Bengt Andersson. After Svensson 2008, fig. 2. Private photograph © Eva Svensson

Several handicrafts were carried out in the hamlet: smithing, stone knapping, soapstone carving, brass casting, textile production, and hunting with minor skin/fur processing. Soapstone carving and hunting produced commodities for sale outside of the hamlet, whereas the other handicrafts were intended for consumption by its inhabitants. Judging from the production places, located outdoors or in a special building, there was a labour division within the hamlet concerning the male handicrafts of smithing, stone knapping and brass casting, with each household responsible for one craft. Soapstone carving may have been a common activity or reserved for the household in charge of stone knapping. Hunting also appears to have been carried out by all households, as skin-/fur-processing items were located in all the houses.

The female handicrafts of textile production and skin/fur processing were carried out in houses by the individual household, together with other domestic chores such as cooking. However, what might be seen as a female confinement to a private sphere of the houses is strongly contradicted by both the organization of cattle breeding and by the testimony of what went on in the houses apart from female handicrafts and domestic chores. Cattle breeding, in this part of the world being a female responsibility (Löfgren 1982: 10), appears to have been a joint venture for the hamlet, as there was a common cattle byre and barn. Herding took the women far away from the hearths, as cattle were grazing in the forest. The cattle path at Skramle shows that cattle passed by the hamlet and the fields out to the forest north of the settlement.

Returning to the houses, the rich and diversified finds show that houses were clearly mixed-gender zones, not only for living and eating but also for other aspects of daily life. In fact, the hearth stands out as a central element, around which the members of the household gathered repeatedly for cooking and eating, for textile production, repairing and sharpening of tools, and also for entertaining guests. With this arrangement, single-roomed houses with a centrally located hearth at Skramle remind us of the public kitchens pointed out by ethnographers (Johansson 2002: 195–6).

While the separation of male work places from the living spaces did not necessarily mean separating men from women, female seclusion is visible in the urban material from Bergen and Oslo (Rui 1993; Øye 2005a, 2005b). In the high to late Middle Ages, traces of male handicrafts disappear from the settlement areas, whereas the vestiges of female handicrafts and daily chores are still present. However, the previously important textile production appears to change character and become directed mainly to cover only the household's own needs. In considering the larger urban topography, it becomes clear that male handicrafts, such as leatherwork and shoemaking, different metalwork, antler and bone work, and also textile production for sale did not disappear, but were relocated to special buildings and workshops outside of the living areas.

The relocation of male handicrafts was part of the professionalization of handicrafts, including textile production, which was taken over by men and performed on horizontal looms instead of the older vertical looms used by women. With the professionalization of handicrafts, male work was separated from the home, and different work zones for men and women were created.

The professionalization of handicrafts and observable separation of male and female work zones in the Norwegian towns appears to have been part of a general trend in northern European towns in the late Middle Ages. Changing practices and attitudes increasingly banished women from commerce and market production (Arnade, Howell and Simons 2002: 544–5). But judging from the archaeological materials from Oslo and Bergen, small-scale economics challenged the large-scale trend towards female exclusion (Rui 1993; Øye 2005a, 2005b). Throughout the Middle Ages, women pursued small scale-textile production and other handicrafts outside production for the household. Small-scale trade items found mixed with artefacts related to domestic work in the cultural layers of settlement sites indicate that the home remained a part of the commercial sphere in the later Middle Ages. Finds also attest to women leaving home for distant workshops. According to written documents, it was common for women to work, or at least help out, in the family workshops, and sometimes to take over responsibility when widowed (Reyerson 2013: 302–4).

In contrast, the bourgeois house in northern and western Europe does not appear to have been structured for the seclusion of women, as in Greek towns, even though courtyards were common in continental urban elite homes. An access analysis of a wealthy merchant's home in Salisbury, England, showed a shallow spatial structure, mainly organizing the commercial and private spheres and not gender zones (Richardson 2003: 381–2).

ON THE FRONTIERS OF EUROPE

The early and high Middle Ages were times of population growth and settlement expansion. New settlements were created in proximity to older sites, existing settlements were enlarged, and new areas were colonized, including adventurous projects in distant places such as Iceland and Greenland. On the eastern fringes of Europe, Russians settled in the Belo Zero area in the early Middle Ages (Makarov, Zacharov and Bužilova 2001). What attracted the Russian settlers were the fur-bearing animals, which were an asset for gaining quick wealth. The colonization was quick and of considerable volume, with almost 200 archaeologically recorded dwelling sites. Included in the colonization process of Belo Zero was urbanization, with the foundation of a town and trading centre.

The excavations of settlement sites and graves demonstrate a wealthy and healthy community focusing on hunting of fur-bearing animals and trade until the thirteenth century, when trapping moved eastward. As a result, the community turned to increased agrarian subsistence. With the decline of trapping and trade, both economy and health weakened.

Of special interest here are the lavishly furnished female graves from the colonization phase, including rich sets of metal ornaments and glass beads. The grave goods included both imported and traditional Russian objects, communicating the hybrid identity of traditional ways of life mixed with extensive trading. For the colonists to achieve social status it was important to show both belonging to their original cultural sphere and success in their new ways of life. Richly adorned women, although not hunters or merchants, played an important role in the making of the social status of the new homes in newly colonized land.

GENDER AND THE HOME: A CONCLUDING DISCUSSION

This chapter has discussed medieval homes limited to castles, towns and rural settlements with respect to gender and gendered use of space. It should be remembered that we lack source material for subaltern groups as day labourers, slaves and beggars, and maybe they did not even have a real home. Another problem with studying gender in the home from an archaeological perspective is that information-rich investigations and publications are heavily geographically biased, with a strong emphasis on Scandinavian materials.

Still, there are two tendencies that appear to have been relevant for most parts of Europe. First, there was a general process of increased spatial segregation in the high and late Middle Ages within the homes and work places of different social groups or estates. The spatial segregation included both different social groups and genders, and homes and work places were increasingly constructed to increase female seclusion. Especially in elite environments, female seclusion added to aristocratic justifications of their rank in their competition with the rising bourgeoisie.

Second, while there were pronounced ideologies regarding how gender should be enacted at home in different social contexts, realities contested these ideologies. As there were many ways of dealing with reality, it is likely that there existed competing conceptions for how gendered behaviour should play out when confronted with real-life challenges. In daily life, women routinely transgressed increased spatial segregation when they worked in the fields, herded cattle, performed handicrafts, practised (small-scale) trade and defended castles. Instead of a clear dichotomy of public equals men and private equals women, there were hybrid ways of gendering life.

CHAPTER SEVEN

Hospitality and the Home

JENNIFER KOLPACOFF DEANE

INTRODUCTION

The medieval legend of St Julian, patron saint of hospitality, at first glance seems a remarkably alarming tale. As recounted in *The Golden Legend*, Jacob de Voragine's thirteenth-century hagiographical collection, the story unfolds as follows. Upon learning that he is destined to kill his own parents, the honest young Julian attempts to secure their safety by permanently leaving the family. Years afterward, when his parents unexpectedly arrive at the threshold of Julian's new home, his gracious wife offers the couple the bed in which to rest. When the devil falsely tells Julian that his wife is sleeping with another man, however, he rushes home to find a couple in his bed, whom he slaughters in a fit of rage. Horrified to realize that the victims are his own parents, he and his grief-stricken wife together dedicate their lives to the charitable care of travellers in need; their reward is a warm reception in heaven upon their deaths (de Voragine 1969).[1] It is a strange story, weaving divine and diabolical agency with the dangers of kinship and shared space. The legend also highlights the fraught potential of threshold crossings, providing an efficient cultural map of the moral stakes of extending communal belonging or 'home' to a stranger in the Middle Ages.

Hospitality is fundamentally paradoxical. The invitation to 'make oneself at home', if enacted to its most literal implications, threatens to erase the very distinction between guest and host upon which it depends.[2] To be a good host requires control of space and resources, while the role of a good guest is an exercise in privileged helplessness. In fact, the word 'hospitality' contains within its own history the precarious oppositions and intrinsic social tension propelling the system to which it refers; 'guest' and 'host' are not opposites, but instead part of a long chain of Indo-European linguistic and western cultural development (along with 'hostile', 'hostel' and even 'ghost') reflecting the uneasy proximity of enmity and friendship.[3] As we will see, medieval domestic hospitality turns upon and plays with this deceptively simple appearance of stable duality between guest and host.

Although the basic means of hospitality (food, drink, shelter and entertainment) did not in themselves shift markedly during the medieval centuries, the inclinations to and expressions of hospitable action revealed in source material clearly bear the particular striations of the era. Conceptions of community changed with remarkable speed in the centuries between $c.$ 850 and 1450, fuelled by centripetal royal-territorial ambitions, powerful localized-political tendencies, intensifying discourse of religious unity, orthodoxy and belonging, and the remarkable economic growth and concomitant increase of contact with 'strangers'. How, then, did hospitality work within the particular cultural context of medieval homes? What various models or exemplars inflected the behaviours of guests and hosts? And what does domestic hospitality reveal more broadly about medieval concerns beyond the walls of home?

TWO MODELS OF HOSPITALITY

Like Julian's story with its echoes of both Oedipus and Abraham, the larger history of medieval hospitality and the home reworks much older cultural traditions from classical and biblical models (Figure 7.1). And it will be the peculiar tension between two distinct traditions that interests us here: one the 'transformative', mirroring earlier Greco-Roman and Germanic patterns, and the second a 'revelatory' model inherited from Judaic and early Christian practice. In both traditions, the threshold represents a birth site of communal meaning, although the intent, action and outcome of hospitable encounters varied tremendously over time and place. Two early examples from this landscape will illustrate these foundations: first, the epic tale *Beowulf* explores transformative hospitality in a model that would later underpin the courtly virtue of *largesse*; and second, the sixth-century Benedictine Rule, which embodies a particularly early and influential medieval articulation of Christian hospitality, one that would resonate across the centuries within the pious quality of *caritas*. Each contributed a different but equally powerful understanding of human community, the purpose of threshold crossings, and the hidden potential of the knock at the door.

Sharing shelter, resources and vulnerability with a stranger was always beneficial for making friends and cementing alliances, yet the potent cultural energy through which hospitality creates new social bonds simultaneously carries with it destructive potential. This is the model of transformative

FIGURE 7.1: Hospitality of Abraham. *The Golden Haggadah* (Barcelona, second quarter of the fourteenth century). London, British Library Add. Ms. 27210, fol. 3. © The British Library Board.

hospitality. Guests and hosts encountering one another at the medieval threshold, whether in experience or imagination, risked the consequences of delicately calibrated social exchanges gone wrong. According to James Heffernan (2014: 14), classical hospitality literature involves three distinct types of peril: first, guest/host relations might sour through offence (real or perceived) and retaliation; second, seduction by a female host might indefinitely trap the (always male) traveller and prevent his return home; and third, eating and drinking at a shared table (communal nourishment) might become debased into violence and death. Whether a knock on the door heralded new social bonds hinged entirely on all parties' willingness to participate fully in the process. The trick was to know whom to trust, and medieval hospitality thus always bore within it a kernel of anxiety.

Perhaps the best example of transformative hospitality is the Anglo-Saxon tale *Beowulf*, written down roughly between 700 and 1000 CE, after having long circulated in an earlier oral tradition. In this early northern context, alliances are formed by exchanges: gift giving, marriage and hospitality rank among the most important; the eponymous hero thus fights and serves and reciprocally gifts his way through the warrior world of Scandinavian society. Informed by the code of the *comitatus*, an arrangement between a lord and his loyal war band, power flowed through relationship; generosity, sealed with martial prowess, was the essential mark of a successful leader. Foremost among Beowulf's preoccupations, therefore, is his reputation; loyalty, bravery and successful observance of social rules are the tools that earn and protect that esteem. The functions and purpose of hospitality within such a framework were in many ways the same as those at play in other expanding societies.

Rituals of hospitality take on a central role in the text, not only for Beowulf, but for many other characters, whose actions provide the audience with both positive and negative didactic examples. King Hrothgar and Queen Wealhtheow, for example, model Anglo-Saxon ideals of hospitality. During feasting within the great hall at Heorot, Queen Wealhtheow enacts the ideal hostess responsible for courteously serving guests in a highly gendered performance of authority; her graciousness in pouring mead and observing the requisite hierarchies of social status among the men in attendance reflects honourably upon the king's (and the kingdom's) authority. It is thus incumbent upon the king to welcome allies within Heorot's walls even as he simultaneously defends it against intrusion. When Beowulf and his men arrive to provide support against the marauding beast Grendel, they are stopped at the threshold. Only after the king identifies Beowulf as a family friend ('bid him and the Geats he has in attendance to assemble and enter . . . they are welcome in Denmark') are the men invited 'to move forward to met Hrothgar' (Heaney 2001: 27). Even so, the hospitality is not all-encompassing; the visitors must leave their shields and spears 'until the outcome of the audience is clear', and friendship has been established.

The monster Grendel, by contrast, is the consummate unwelcome guest, 'a fiend out of hell' descended from Cain who does not know how to behave or reciprocate appropriately. Envious of human society, he breaches the threshold of Heorot without invitation, gorges himself on men (a solitary meal back in his lair), and continues his attacks 'until the greatest house in the world stood empty, a deserted wallstead' (Heaney 2001: 11). In contrast to a traditional hand-shaking on first encounter, the antagonists Grendel and Beowulf are locked into a death-grip of impossible strength – one that ultimately tears off the beast's arm and hand to be left behind as a gruesome relic of the contest. Grendel is the eternal stranger, '[h]is fatal departure regretted by no-one who witnessed his trail', an outsider to the social rules of space and place who cannot be transformed into an ally through hospitality. Wreaking vengeance for her son against Beowulf, Grendel's mother is equally taboo; dragging the warrior into her lair, she represents an obscene hostess, and another example of what happens when the threshold is breached by one who will not or cannot be incorporated into the social realm. The monsters are not the only 'bad guests' in the poem, but certainly enact the most spectacular upendings of early medieval hospitality.

Within the framework of *Beowulf* sketched above, a few elements of the transformative model of hospitality are evident: the relationship between guest and host is binary and reciprocally bound; there are clear rules and expectations, whether for the king's subjects, allies, enemies, or the beasts themselves; and established political consequences follow both successful or failed observance of these rules. It is, of course, not an entirely secular model: Grendel's descent from Cain and his lament at being excluded from humanity and salvation represents a Christian theme, and the poet invokes Old Testament themes with some regularity. But it is a rather thin scriptural veneer that leaves intact the poet's underlying view of a guest as a stranger who might be transformed into an ally through the proper performance of social ritual. Within a few centuries, however, the simple relationship of host and guest would become intriguingly complicated in western Europe, as a specifically scriptural conception of hospitality began to occupy increasingly more imaginative space in the hearts and minds of medieval people.

In the revelatory model of hospitality, scriptural traditions, both Hebrew and Christian, formed the second foundational influence upon medieval guests, hosts, and the writers who harnessed threshold encounters for their various ends. In contrast to the sociopolitical ideal of hospitality dependent upon reciprocity for transforming a stranger into communal member, scriptural ideals of hospitality were rooted in a broader conception of human community – one that directly acknowledges the possibility that any knock at the door might prove revelatory as the disguised divine. Abraham's and Sarah's encounter with angels became a model for the millennia, as did the related passage in Hebrews 13:2: 'Do not neglect to show hospitality to strangers, for thereby some have entertained angels unawares.' Abraham's courtesy and cheer in welcoming the strangers brought blessings upon them, as did Sarah's (even rather reluctant) service from the kitchen. Scriptural hospitality does not *transform* a person into something else (say, a stranger into a friend); rather, it *reveals* the person's inner value and identity, whether angelic, demonic, or somewhere in between. The angels' hidden identity thus allowed them to discern the elderly couple's inner worth, with startling consequences for their people.

Hospitality would remain a vital *mitzvah* within Judaism throughout and beyond the Middle Ages; the model of the Jewish home as a place of religious devotion and the extension of communal bonds through rituals of hosting and feeding bore enduring implications for Christian conceptions. And yet, new cultural inflections came into play as well. Whereas the Hebrew scriptures envisioned hospitality as unfolding 'within the world of God's chosen people', the New Testament introduced 'a radical departure from this exclusivity as well as presenting a fundamentally new way in which anyone, Jew or Gentile, might reperform Abraham's entertainment of God' (Heffernan 2014: 64). Within the revelatory model, the extension of hospitality does not so much create or transform relationships as it confirms a pre-existing shared humanity; once the door is opened and a welcome offered, the end has been achieved regardless of a guest's subsequent behaviour.

New Testament scriptures amplified the charitable qualities of hospitality, providing powerful new images and encouragements to care for others. Of the seven corporal works of mercy called for by Jesus, for example, four involve specific acts of hospitality: feeding the hungry, quenching the thirsty, sheltering the homeless, and clothing the naked (Matthew 25:34–40) (Figure 7.2). Such practices formed the basis of later medieval charitable giving and an entire economy of spiritual exchange. In contrast to transformative hospitality, however, in which the interactions following a welcome are crucial for determining whether the process has been successful, spiritual hospitality relieves the guest of responsibility for (or influence over) the practice. The act of giving, of hosting, and of providing for those in need is here the focus, not the participants' subsequent states of mind or relationship.

Among the many scriptural encounters between host and guest, it was Jesus' invitation at the Last Supper that most transfixed the medieval Christian imagination. In his sacred act of table-welcome, he created a new understanding of community forged in both fleeting and eternal bonds by the shared visceral experience of feeding. Yet the hospitable episode is simultaneously rooted in the foreknowledge of treachery and grief that a guest, one of the collective 'We' at the table, would betray that trust. By an 'exquisitely apt etymological accident, the survival of *hostia* in the Eucharistic *host* – the consecrated bread of communion – places the figure of the betrayed host quite literally at the very center of Christian ritual' (Heffernan 2014: 71). Christ himself is keenly aware of the dangers of hospitality; indeed, he 'foresees the treachery to come and he signifies the traitor by means of a quintessentially hospitable gesture: feeding a guest', passing Judas the dipped bread (Heffernan 2014: 52). The infusion of treachery into the hospitable New Testament

FIGURE 7.2: St. Martin of Tours Dividing his Cloak with the Beggar from the Sacramentary of Warmund d'Ivrea (c. 966–1002). Ivrea, Italy, Biblioteca Capitolare, Ms. 31 Cod. LXXXVI, f. 114v. © Scala/Art Resource.

moment would prove excruciatingly pertinent to European conceptions of the thresholds as the centuries passed; in particular, central medieval Christian writers would wield charges of Hebrew betrayal to amplify differences between themselves and Jewish communities, and in so doing, justified the devastating waves of violence against their neighbours over the centuries to come.

In the following centuries, the writings of church fathers further strengthened the association between domestic hospitality and Christian charity. St Ambrose (d. 397) specifically addressed the earthly *and* heavenly benefits of serving that network, underscoring the essential itinerancy of human life: 'In this earthly abode we are all guests; here we have only a temporary dwelling place', he cautions. 'Let us be careful not to be discourteous or neglectful in receiving guests, lest we be denied entrance into the dwelling place of the saints at the end of our life' (Oden 2007: 125). Rather than concluding on that aspirational note, however, Ambrose returns to the personal and prosaic: 'While we are in this body, there often arises the necessity of traveling . . . If everyone decided not to receive guests, where would those who are traveling find rest? Then we would have to abandon human habitations and seek out the dens of the wild beasts' (Oden 2007: 120). While selfish denial of others means withdrawal and isolation – a cave of one's own creation – ideal Christian hospitality is expansive, charitably responsive to the needs of others.

If *Beowulf* embodies the transformative type of early medieval hospitality, the sixth-century Benedictine Rule exemplifies the revelatory model. An explicit contrast to the inhospitable den of wild beasts evoked by St Ambrose, Benedictine monasteries under the Rule became reliable sites of refreshment and shelter, offering safety to all in name of Christ.[4] 'All guests who present themselves are to be welcomed like Christ', reads the Benedictine Rule, 'for He himself will say, "I was a stranger and you welcomed me" (Matt. 25:35). Proper honor must be shown to all, especially to those who share our faith and to pilgrims' (Benedict of Nursia 1998: 53)[5] (Figure 7.3). The Rule carefully articulates the ritual and responsibilities of monastic hospitality from arrival to departure: 'All humility must be shown in addressing a guest on arrival or departure. By a bow of the head or a complete prostration of the body, Christ is to be adored because he is indeed welcomed in them' (Benedict of Nursia 1998: 51). The act of humble hospitality becomes almost sacramental in its recognition of Christ within each guest. And to this extent, it is revelatory rather than transformative: it derives from an assumption of pre-existing shared belonging, and its practitioners sought to look past outer appearances to the inner divine.

Yet such intrinsic openness should not be mistaken for naïveté, for the Rule is exceedingly practical in its caution: Benedictines and other later brethren knew the stranger at the door might indeed be Christ, and acted accordingly, but they also knew full well the knock might be a demon or Satan himself come to assault the household. Monastic hospitality, therefore, incorporated an additional ritual intended to discern and deflect threat at the threshold. 'First of all they are to pray together and thus be united in peace, but prayer must always precede the kiss of peace because of the delusions of the devil' (Benedict of Nursia 1998: 52). Once satisfied that the stranger is not malicious, the Rule continues, brothers may allow him in for refreshment and edification. Even for monks, utterly unconditional hospitality was never practicable. In revelatory hospitality, therefore, the apparent binary of guest and host is actually triangulated with a third presence – either in the form of the divine or diabolical presence or in God's eternal observation of charitable acts necessary for salvation. For better or worse, medieval men and women knew that great powers lay at the threshold.

FIGURE 7.3: Pilgrim from *The Luttrell Psalter* (English, first half of the fourteenth century). London, British Library, Add. Ms. 42130, fol. 32r. © Hulton Archive / Getty Images.

Medieval hospitality in the home wove older strands into new historical fabric with a novel tension, variously combining or reprioritizing the two foundational types discussed above. As populations boomed along with agricultural production in the eleventh and twelfth centuries, so did the networks of roads and markets, fairs, villages, and also the scale of familial homes. Monastic ideals flowed into non-monastic settings and, despite reformers' best efforts, vice versa. Influenced by both social and spiritual models, domestic hospitality became a particularly vital and relevant social process in Middle Ages – the decision to open the door to strangers a necessary but dangerous act. Whether recorded in law, legend, hagiographical material, handbooks, normative texts, or bawdy stories, medieval accounts of hospitality reveal the aspirations and fears of societies in transition. If 'scenes of welcome evoke, suspend, and defy many of our most powerful binaries', then there is much to learn by exploring what happens to those binaries as they are idealized, complicated and inverted at the thresholds of medieval homes.

THRESHOLD IDEALS

Between the ninth and fifteenth centuries, hospitable ideals were further developed in law, catechism, and literature, a cumulative reading of which illuminates the cultural centrality and crucial historical necessity of providing charitable 'welcome' to strangers. The careful limning of expectations within such texts further underscores the high stakes underpinning the social sword-dance of hospitality; it also underscores the potentially serious risks taken at every turn by guest and host alike in a world increasingly concerned with rank, etiquette and communal boundaries. Both secular and canon law thus focus on regulating the relationship between host and guest, articulating the exchanges that underpinned communal trust and the precisely calibrated behaviours expected of different social groups.

Examples abound of medieval secular laws concerned with hospitality. Brehon, or early native Irish law, established many context-specific stipulations, such as compensating guests if their possessions were stolen during hospitality (Binchy 1970: 252). The eighth-century Irish legal tract, the *Críth Gablach* confirmed travellers' rights to food and shelter at the home of wealthy farmers. Provision of hospitality was woven into the Frankish Salian legal or witnessing process itself, a means of forging and proving the strength of social bonds. A routine transfer of property, for example, required temporary but hospitable shared housing among parties as a procedural requirement confirming mutual ease. Later in the law code anyone providing 'bread and shelter' to someone exiled for grave desecration or other crimes was subject to a fine (Drew 1990: 108–9, 188). And in the early medieval Iberian peninsula, hospitality and provisions were among the many tributes levied on royal tenants (Callahan 1983: 119).

As Christian concepts began to permeate western kingdoms, legal codes soon invoked scriptural ideals, outlining expectations for the treatment of pilgrims specifically within a broader framework of reciprocal sociopolitical exchange. A capitulary issued by Charlemagne in 802 aligned both models of hospitality, mandating the charitable treatment of pilgrims as a social duty: 'We order that no one in our kingdom, whether rich or poor, should dare to deny hospitality to pilgrims: that is, no one should refuse roof, hearth, and water to any pilgrims who are traveling the land on God's account, or to anyone who is journeying for love of God or for the salvation of his soul' (Carver 2012: 190). Within Carolingian halls, the hospitality of aristocratic women served the overlapping purposes of facilitating relationships with secular and religious figures alike. Bishops or other clergy were as likely to be guests within

Carolingian domiciles as were aristocratic laypeople, and thus 'no strict division separated these two forms of hospitality' (Carver 2012: 176). The provision of basic food and shelter to a stranger in need continued to be a social expectation beyond elite circles. Scriptural enjoinders to take in the stranger had by the ninth century fallen into rhythm, albeit not a perfectly syncopated one, with the political exchanges and social reciprocity necessary for kingdom building.

Friction over ideals of hospitality put into practice was a regular feature of later medieval law and literature. Some of the earliest examples appear in continental royal law, particularly regarding hospitality for royalty and accompanying retinues; royal legislation frequently idealized pious voluntary hospitality but simultaneously demanded it from subjects.[6] Forced hospitality became a controversial issue, particularly in turbulent political periods; Henry I's 1130 charter to the City of London, for example, specifically prohibited seizing lodging by force (Kerr 2002: 330). It was not until the later twelfth and thirteenth centuries that jurists began to address when or how one might legitimately refuse hospitality to a noble or royal guest.

Canon law, on the other hand, took a decidedly different approach to the rights of guests and the responsibilities of hosts. Emphasizing clerical responsibilities for *'tenere hospitalitem'*, for example, Gratian wrote in the *Decretum*: 'Hospitality is so necessary in bishops that if any are found lacking in it, the law forbids them to be ordained' (Tierney 1959: 68). Thus were regulations increasingly set forth to meet the various needs of itinerant and impoverished guests. As we will see, the particular explosion of pilgrimage travel in the twelfth through fourteenth centuries prompted a corresponding boom in contemporary reflection on such journeys and on the social meanings of the people who embarked upon them. Pilgrims bore special privileges as *miserabiles personae* (poor people), including that of hospitality; marked symbolically by clothing, scrip, staff and purse, pilgrims were to be welcomed as friendly strangers who had temporarily and voluntarily chosen their impoverished status. The common literary motif of a worthy pilgrim denied hospitality indicates that practical wariness likely weighed as heavily on medieval minds as did the spiritual injunction to welcome possible angels at the door.

Although legal texts on hospitality shared the same essential framework as other texts, different medieval genres employed threshold encounters to diverse ends. In chronicles, romances and household guides, authors of secular literature of the eleventh through fifteenth centuries dramatically expanded the scope of hospitable ideals and amplified the significance of gender and socio-economic status. Chronicles, for example, entertain readers with extreme examples of masculine hosting. In the context of Ottonian Germany, the chronicler Thietmar of Merseburg (2001: 47) praises the Duke of Poland's hospitable reception of the emperor, beginning with the claim that '[i]t would be impossible to believe or describe how the emperor was then received by him'. Some chronicles celebrate a nearly aggressive expansiveness in hosts and guests alike. 'Although all the Hyperboreans are noted for their hospitality, our Swedes are so in particular', wrote Adam of Bremen in his *Gesta hammaburgensis*. 'To deny wayfarers entertainment is to them the basest of all shameful deeds, so much so that there is strife and contention among them over who is worthy to receive a guest. They show him every courtesy for as many days as he wishes to stay, vying with one another to take him to their friends in their several houses' (Christoph 2010: 47). As Siegfried Christoph (2010: 47) notes, the text interestingly sets no time limits on hospitality ('as many days as he wishes to stay'), a risky temporal suspension of the threshold. Traditional limits were comparably extended to extremes in an account of the Prussians indicating that they think they have not been hospitable until a guest has drunk so much he vomits (Fischer 2012: 72).

Within literary traditions written for aristocratic audiences, such as romances and *lais*, however, the same medieval ideals of hospitality are presented as embodying the aspirational virtues of courtly society. As Sarah Gordon (2007: 27) puts it, 'Hospitality and the keeping of a well-maintained household are a prerequisite of courtly behavior and social status'. Whereas chronicle accounts – often penned in the service of particular rulers – are more likely to emphasize the sociopolitical value of hospitality, romances, lais, and other aristocratic literature tend to play with the tension between political and spiritual models. Through a dense web of obligation and privilege, hospitality here serves 'as a platform from which the host could exhibit largesse and thereby consolidate or enhance his reputation' (Kerr 2002: 328). Central and later medieval authors creatively developed those tensions as they explored the limits of chivalric ideals, whether in lavish display, humble modesty, or simple piety.

Scenes of welcome are fundamental to the plot of twelfth-century poet Chrétien de Troyes' 'Erec and Enide', for example, which presents exemplary models in both modest and lavish circumstances. Seeking shelter one night, young Erec encountered 'an elderly vavasour, whose dwelling was very poor' but who cheerfully offered him hospitality on the spot: '"Good sir", said he, "welcome!" If you deign to lodge with me, here are your lodgings already prepared' (Chrétien de Troyes 1991: 42). The 'well-born and noble' man and his beautiful daughter graciously provide for Erec despite their poverty, and 'they had as much as they wanted of everything they needed' (Chrétien de Troyes 1991: 43). Via this initial threshold encounter, strangers are transformed into friends and then, when Erec later marries the beautiful daughter Enide, into kin.

Chrétien uses their wedding celebration as an opportunity to present another ideal of hospitality, a more lavish form appropriate for royalty:

> No wicket or door was closed: the entrances and exits were all wide open that day; neither poor man nor rich was turned away. King Arthur was not

parsimonious; he ordered the bakers, cooks, and wine-stewards to serve bread, wine, and game in great quantity to each person – as much as he wished. No one requested anything, whatever it might be, without receiving all that he wanted.

—Chrétien de Troyes 1991: 62

In this case as well, Arthur's domestic generosity facilitates new sociopolitical bonds, not only between the married couple and their families, but also between the knights, courtiers, and citizens in attendance and the royal realm itself. Along with the new social bonds of marriage, Arthur simultaneously cements another set of communal alliance via hospitality when he seizes the opportunity to knight several men new to his service.

A similarly extravagant ideal appears in the writings of Chrétien's contemporary, Marie de France, who envisioned proper observance of hospitable ritual as a vital strand of the chivalric code. In *Lanval*, the main character demonstrates just this charitable hospitality via noble personal intention:

There was no knight in the town in sore need of shelter whom he did not summon, and serve richly and well. Lanval gave costly gifts, Lanval freed prisoners, Lanval clothed the jongleurs, Lanval performed many honorable acts. There was no one, stranger or friend, to whom he would not have given gifts.

—Marie de France 1999: 75

The sovereign authority of Arthurian rulers and knights thus depends upon careful discernment at the castle threshold, their actions rooted in distinct social expectations and the quasi-spiritual underpinnings that nurtured chivalric ideals (Figure 7.4).

Pious willingness to welcome and tend to others is a staple feature of hagiographies and vision texts as well, a theme particularly frequent in the lives of saintly women.[7] Saint Brigid of Ireland was renowned for hospitality and her care of the poor, and the eighth-century Anglo-Saxon abbess and saint, Leoba, was specifically praised in the later Middle Ages for hospitality: 'she kept open house for all without exception, and even when she was fasting gave banquets and washed the feet of her guests with her own hands, at once the guardian and the minister of the practice instituted by our Lord' (Mursell 2001: 35). The thirteenth-century St Zita of Lucca, a poor servant, simultaneously modelled domestic sanctity and the gendered power of charity by giving to the poor from her employer's wealth. Similarly inverting traditional hierarchies, Ida of Louvain (d. *c.* 1300) chastized her own father for refusing hospitality to a beggar (Bynum 1987: 121). Finally, Catherine of Siena (d. 1380) (1980: 275)

FIGURE 7.4: Kings and queens feasting, while servants below the table serve them with two large pitchers from *Omne Bonum* (London, 1360–1375). London, British Library Royal Ms. 6 E VI, fol. 259v. © British Library Board/Robana/Art Resource.

records God's direction to 'never stop knocking at the door of my Truth', to which she responds 'your burning charity neither can nor should hold back from opening to those who knock with perseverance'. In her theologically challenging view, the divine cannot choose to be inhospitable because He is defined by mercy. Whether in text or reality, hospitality offered potent channels of action to later medieval women.

The text of the English rule for anchorites, the *Ancrene Wisse*, invokes the mystical 'house' of St Julian itself as a salvific threshold:

> For other pilgrims go with much toil to seek the bones of a single saint, such as St. James or St. Giles; but these pilgrims, who go toward heaven, they go

to be made saints themselves, and to find God Himself . . . surely they find St. Julian's inn, which wayfarers search for so eagerly.

—Savage 1991: 176–7

At 'St. Julian's inn', therefore, the worth of honest seekers is recognized as they enter and are transformed into members of the community of saints. Despite the evident contextual differences, the process is comparable to the courtly exchanges explored by Chrétien in King Arthur's hall; at Camelot, the worth of chivalric men is recognized at threshold crossing, after which they are formally welcomed into the community of knights.

Medieval household records, guides, and popular poetry share the same fundamental ideas of hospitality as those explored above, yet the directives are pitched differently according to social status. For example, the household rules written by Bishop Robert Grosseteste (d. 1253) for the Countess of Lincoln emphasized sociopolitical elements underpinned by a Christian foundation; on the reception of guests, he advises her to 'Command strictly that all your guests, secular and religious, be quickly, courteously, and with good cheer . . . and by all be courteously addressed and in the same way lodged and served'. Yet thirteenth-century noble hosts were no more egalitarian spirited than were Carolingian aristocrats centuries before. Grosseteste continues:

Make your free men and guests sit as far as possible at tables on either side . . . And you yourself always be seated at the middle of the high table that your presence as lord or lady may appear openly to all, and that you may plainly see on either side all the service and all the faults . . . . and of this be sure, that you shall be very much feared and reverenced.

—Lamond 1890: 187

Exactly that fear and reverence are suggested to noblemen in the closing lines of the second *Book of Courtesy* (published by William Caxton in 1477) 'Look thou sit – and make no strife – Where the host commands, or else his wife, Eschew the highest place to win, Save thou be bidden to sit therein' (Rickert 1966: 95). Such directives suggest that guests had indeed been known to argue, disrespect the host or hostess, or otherwise make strife at the table.

Such outlay on food, drink, and the other features of hearty hospitality were also vital for bolstering local economies. Records from great English households of the fifteenth century, for example, indicate massive gentry spending and strategizing around hospitality. Household accounts such as those of Dame Alice of Briene illustrate the routine, expense, and content of elite hospitality. Between 29 September 1412 and 28 September 1413, for example, Dame Alice hosted at least one visitor every day (Kunz 2001: 32, 140). Purchasing local agriculture, fish and meat, cheese and other produce for hospitable

FIGURE 7.5: January: The Feast of the Duke of Berry from *Les Très Riches Heures de Duc de Berry* (1416). Chantilly, France, Chantilly Ms. 65, fol. 1V. © Scala/Art Resource.

entertainment, English nobility infused large amounts of money into neighbouring villages and countryside and built important commercial relationships; records thus reveal a strong sociopolitical *and* economic interdependence via hospitality between the nobility and those who served them (Kunz 2001: 138) (Figure 7.5).

THRESHOLD COMPLICATIONS

Ideals are notoriously difficult to put into practice, however, and hospitable aspirations are no exception. Given the many behavioural expectations on all sides of a threshold encounter in the Middle Ages, the potential for conflict far outweighed the likelihood of an uneventful stay, and even a little ignorance, mischief, miscommunication, or simply an unexpected turn of events could derail the process. Law and literature both tackle the issue of complications between guests and hosts, expounding on the many possible sources of trouble. 'At every doorway, what you have to do is look around you and look out; never forget: no matter where you are you might find a foe', cautions an early Norse poem. 'The careful guest comes to a meal and sits in wary silence; with his eyes and ears wide open, every wise man keeps watch' (Terry 1969: 13–14). In particular, hospitality becomes complicated when hosts behave badly, when guests behave badly, and when the thresholds themselves – that is, the dividing line between here and there, host and guest, 'us' and 'them' – becomes unstable. As we will see, particular genres of literature, particularly chronicles, romances and fabliaux, were particularly well suited to exploit the complications of hospitality.

The historical record does contain some shocking examples of traumatic hosting, such as Ralph Glaber's chilling report during the 1033 famine that if starving travellers had 'found lodgings on the way, they would have been killed at night by those who had them in, and eaten' (Ohler 1989: 81). However, a far more routine role for bad hosts in medieval literature was as a foil or counter-example to the hero. Such tropes unsurprisingly crop up frequently in chronicle accounts, not least because such texts were generally written to present a very specific political perspective in support of one or another figure. In Ralph of Caen's *Gesta Tancredi*, for example, the twelfth-century author seizes an opportunity to cast aspersion on the deceitful Greeks. The brave Norman leader, Bohemund, he writes, 'feared the ambushes of the Greeks, since they had the habit of attacking even those whom they had earlier invited as guests, and moreover, guests who were worthy of receiving gifts' (Ralph of Caen 2005: 23). The infamous treachery of the Byzantines, those 'exasperating people', is a resounding trope in crusading literature, as is the generally inhospitable context of Outremer. Ralph drily notes in passing that 'Tancred was happier as an exile than a guest in the city [of Artah] since he did not experience any loss, attacks, or chains'.[8] A similarly poor host appears in the *Chronicle of the Czechs* by Cosmas of Prague (d. 1125) (2009: 61), who reported that 'during the midday meal, peace, faith, and the law of hospitality were broken . . . [when] Duke Boleslav was seized and deprived of his eyes, and all the rest of his men were either slaughtered, slain, or shoved in prison'. The tone is one of indignation over the faithless breaking of bonds by a despised enemy, the 'perfidious' Duke Miezko.

Within the realm of fictional knighthood, the ceaseless questing, travel, and chivalric ambition of Arthurian men made hospitable complications a wonderfully rich plot device. One good example of bad hosting is the story of Sir Gawain and the Carle of Carlisle, which plays on the gap between chivalric expectations as guests and the rough, even savage, treatment they receive at the hands of an uncouth host (Figure 7.6). The Carle (or Churl) is shaggy, unkempt, rude and

FIGURE 7.6: 'A Strange Guest' from *Sir Gawain and the Green Knight* (English, c. 1400). London, British Library, Cotton Nero A. X. fol. 90/94 v. © The British Library

crass – nearly an animal – and tries Gawain's chivalry through a series of obnoxious behaviours ranging from the annoying to the deadly (Maslanka 2008). 'Gawain's success in these tests consists of the conspicuous restraint he exercises over his own powers and prerogatives, his perfect willingness to concede the Carle's rights of property and control within his own domain, even when his fellow knights see no need to do so' (Hahn 1995: 81–2). The chivalric ideal here proves strong enough to contain even the chaos of a deranged host in his own castle.

A fascination with host debacles extended beyond courtly antiheroes to a much broader and quite gleeful audience for whom earnest *cortesie* was hardly the point. Fabliaux, or bawdy trick stories, explore with crass delight the various ways in which hospitality could reveal fault lines within both household and society. In 'The Poor Cleric', for example, an ungracious wife refuses hospitality to a hungry young student by hiding her household's abundance; her deceit (financial as well as sexual) is ultimately discovered and punished by the husband (Gordon 2007: 29). Clergy could also be bad hosts in fabliaux, offering both authors and audiences an opportunity to enjoying skewering the sanctimonious priesthood. In *The Butcher of Abbeville*, a deacon refuses hospitality to the good man: 'Go seek your shelter with the Lord! By Saint Hubert, I'll not accord a layman lodgings for the night!' The cleric's disregard for laity ultimately earns him humiliating retribution and literal fleecing at the butcher's hands (Dubin 2013: 561).

In the fabliaux, refusing of hospitality is a social breach meriting consequences – but it is not the only way to be a bad host. Since ideal hospitality presumes the physical safety and integrity of a guest, much secular literature creatively developed the theme of sexual threat to guests. In the fabliau *The Miller of Arleux*, for example, the miller is the bad host, planning with his hired hand to seduce a young girl staying in the household. Pleading to the miller's wife for help, she explains 'he's offered hospitality because he means to sleep with me if you and Jesus will not help' (Dubin 2013: 649). Moved by her distress, the miller's wife gamely takes her place in bed and takes with spirit 'what he has to give', followed by the usual comedic complications of the genre, which culminate in the public humiliation of the miller and a broad laugh at the wife's voracious sexual appetite.

Hosts bore most responsibility in medieval hospitality, but guests could and did irritate said hosts in turn. Norse verse neatly articulates the annoyance of an early guest ('To many houses I came too early, to others much too late: the beer was all gone or they hadn't brewed it'), an unwanted guest ('unwelcome guests find no feasts') or the guest who would not leave ('Don't stay forever when you visit friends, know when it's time to leave; love turns to loathing if you sit too long on someone else's bench') (Terry 1969: 18). Across genres, the trope of bad guests provided myriad opportunities for authors to test a host's patience: refusing hospitality, bringing one's own food and drink, disrupting the household or table, engaging in improper sexual activity, and making strange or burdensome demands of the host.

The proper acceptance of hospitality was a vital theme within Arthurian tales, against which characters trespassed in various ways. Erec refuses Kay's offer of lodgings, for example: 'I shall not go where you dwell. You have no knowledge of my need and I have further to proceed. Let go of me, I won't delay' (Chrétien de Troyes 2000: 117). Lancelot's refusal of a hospitable offer in *Merveilles de Rigomer* actually makes an old man cry. And while Perceval appropriately accepts hospitality from the gracious Fisher King, he nonetheless fails to ask his crippled host a courteous question about his pain; the hero is too passive and withdrawn, showing little concern for the well-being of his gracious host, and the mistake draws a curse upon the land (Chrétien de Troyes 1999). Similarly, the Faerie Queen offends King Arthur by accepting his hospitality but bringing her own provisions to Camelot. Her overly assertive act, geared more towards her own satisfaction than toward the requisite social etiquette, irks the king because power and status lie at the heart of royal hospitality; Arthur takes her rejection of his food as an insult, and their relationship is shadowed as a result (Christoph 2010: 45). In a more comedic turn, Chaucer's *Shipman's Tale* relates how a naïve merchant host is inveigled and cuckolded by a guest monk, Sir John, whom the beautiful wife has strategically manipulated.

The most famous example of an egregiously strange guest, however, is that of the Green Knight, who surprises King Arthur and guests during the Christmas festivities by suddenly arriving in the hall, uninvited and on horseback. 'Entirely emerald green', the belligerent knight observes no courteous conventions but instead rudely bellows 'who is the governor of this gaggle?' Despite a calm welcome and slightly forced invitation to hospitality from Arthur, the Green Knight refuses, instead challenging the men to a beheading game: if one of the men can cut off the Green Knight's head, he will have to submit to the same treatment a year in the future. The Knight provokes by calling their honour and bravery into question. "So here is the House of Arthur', he scoffed, 'whose virtues reverberate across vast realms. Where's the fortitude and the fearlessness you're so famous for? And the breath-taking bravery and the big-mouth bragging?' (Armitage 2007: 41). Unable to tolerate the baiting in the Great Hall any longer, Arthur's nephew Sir Gawain takes up the challenge and beheads his opponent; in response, the Green Knight picks up his own severed head and returns across the threshold as strangely as he arrived.

Here, as with most 'bad guest' tales, the visitor's behaviour at the domestic threshold does not injure the host, but also bears no transformative potential; his failure to conform to hospitable convention negates the possibility of friendship or alliance. The relationship remains static until a year later when the story continues. Venturing forth to complete his end of the challenge, Gawain once again encounters the Green Knight, although this time the strange guest has become an equally strange host, one joined by a dangerously flirtatious wife-hostess. After sparring through games, traps, and the promised axe blow to the neck, Gawain and the Green Knight come to terms with one another, their formerly hostile relationship transformed into a surprisingly lighthearted camaraderie. Revealed as the nephew of sorceress Morgan Le Fay, the Green Knight's identity serves to explain his previous strangeness as both guest and host; Gawain returns home relieved but chastened from the adventure.

The dropping away of false appearances emerges as a particularly central theme when the specifically spiritual aspect of hospitality is emphasized. Boccaccio's *Decameron* offers two illustrative examples. In 'The Highwayman and the Abbot', for example, a suspicious abbot fears and is rude to his host, a known criminal, whose hidden good nature the abbot cannot discern; the truth is revealed slowly through action wherein the abbot is converted through the healing hospitality of the highwayman from bad guest to good guest, and from a good guest to a host or patron in his own right; the story concludes with the host's transformation at the abbot's behest into a Knight Hospitaller (Boccaccio 2003: 706). Here the transformative and redemptive models seem to fuse into a didactic hospitality with the power to save.

THRESHOLD CORRUPTIONS

Complicated relationships and unstable thresholds were not, however, the worst case in late-medieval imaginations: the real terror was a relationship between host and guest corrupted by treachery, depraved in its upending of sovereignty and social order. Two examples of 'hellish hospitality' from very different contexts illustrate the destructive imaginative potential of the guest/host relationship and its roots in hospitality's fundamentally paradoxical tensions: first, inquisitors' precise unravelling of hospitality networks within 'heretical' communities in the later Middle Ages; second, Dante's stomach-churning representation of treacherous hosts' punishment in the ninth circle of hell. Both draw from the same cultural wellsprings of hospitality and, although the purpose and context and genre are quite different, both perspectives are fuelled by fears of an annihilated or irredeemably defiled social order.

Medieval domestic hospitality bore dark potential in the eyes of ecclesiastics tasked with patrolling the boundaries and spiritual integrity of Christendom. By the mid-thirteenth century, professional thinkers such as theologians, canon lawyers and inquisitors were already deeply invested in the project of countering 'heresy' in all its apparently multiplying forms. For inquisitors such as Bernard Gui, Peter Zwicker and Nicholas Eymerich, heretical communities were by definition purposefully excluding themselves from the body of the church and divine grace; therefore the virtue of hospitality was here rendered pernicious, applied as it was to thresholds of wickedness. From the inquisitorial point of view, the definition of 'heretic' was clear, as was its equation with an individual who has placed him or herself *by choice* outside of the pre-existing community; thus the decision to host a heretic was necessarily a choice to side against orthodoxy.

The canons of the Fourth Lateran Council (1215) included the condemnation of 'receivers, defenders, and supporters' of heresy, and questions about social contact and interaction in the home are a marked feature of later medieval inquisitorial process.[9] Bernard Gui (d. 1331) instructed colleagues questioning 'Manicheans' or 'Cathars' as follows: 'First the person to be examined must be asked if he has anywhere seen or met one or more heretics . . . also whether he has any acquaintance with them, when, how, and through whose introduction.'

If a suspect responded in the affirmative, the questions continued: 'Whether he has received any such heretics into his house, and who they were; who brought them; how long they stayed; who came to see them; who took them away and where they went' (Gui 2006: 43). Physical movement, travel, social contact and familial networks all began to occupy a more central role within inquisitorial frameworks over the course of the thirteenth century, as did concern about the physical spaces in which suspected heretics gathered.

For Occitan 'Cathars' in the early decades of the fourteenth century, for example, 'houses constituted the axle of the system' – much as domestic spaces had in fact served the early church (Bruschi 2009: 69). Accused men and women confessed to having hosted associates, in a number of different circumstances and for a number of reasons. In 1308, a widow named Blanche of Ferrus apparently reported to inquisitors that she provided hospitality to the so-called Good Men in her home, 'where they slept, ate and drank' (Sparks 2014: 113). Domestic hospitality bore a similarly important meaning for southern French beguines in the early fourteenth century, German Waldensians of the later fourteenth, and English Lollards of the fifteenth. Once inquisitorial pressure increased on such living churches and the travelling preachers or masters who sustained them, the bonds of secretive hospitality became ever more important.

Although the variously termed 'heretics' understood their hospitable actions as wholesome expressions of community, inquisitors – invested in the notion of aggressive evil – denied them any positive meaning. Presumed traitors both to the faith and the broader body of Christendom, those found guilty of hosting heretics could be consigned to the stake. Conviction also routinely included the permanent destruction of such houses and the thresholds defining them. Inquisitorial records thus reveal fears of pernicious hospitality in which the 'right' ideals were enacted by and for the 'wrong' people.

An equally dangerous scenario could unfold when the 'right' people performed hospitality 'wrong', perverting the deeply established social and spiritual ideals of hospitality and thereby weakening western Christian order. Perhaps the most vivid example comes from the turbulent world of thirteenth-century Italian city states, and its most famous text, *The Divine Comedy*. In this imaginative map of spiritual-geographical journey, Dante schematically placed historical figures in the precise topographies of hell, purgatory, or heaven, allowing each to speak in turn of the consequences of earthly behaviour. While inquisitors worried that unorthodox groups would infect Christendom through their spiritual treachery, Florentines feared that unreliable leaders would weaken the republic through their political heresy. And it is to the darkest realms of hell that Dante banishes those who betrayed family, friends, or guests.

Such is the account of Count Ugolino della Gherardesca and Archbishop Rugggieri degli Ubaldini, whose fate in the *Inferno* represent a total collapse of the spatial, social, and spiritual expectations of traditional hospitality. As they travel into the deepest circle of hell, the fictional Dante and his guide, Virgil, encounter the ghastly scenario of the two men jammed into a pit together, one gnawing on the back of the other's neck (Figure 6):

> ... when I beheld two frozen in one hole,
> One's head become a hood worn by the other.
> As bread in ravening hunger is devoured,
> The upper pressed his teeth down to reveal
> Where brain and nape together are united.

In response to Dante's query ('O you who show with every bestial bite your hatred for the head you are devouring ... tell me your reason'), the shade of Ugolino responds – though not before wiping his bloody lips with the hair remaining on the archbishop's skull. (Alighieri 2003: 179).[10] He tells Dante how he was tricked and imprisoned by the Archbishop Ruggieri and slowly starved to death along with his two sons and two grandsons. The ultimate bad host, Ruggieri starves his 'guests' nearly to the point of familial cannibalism: 'My children', laments Ugolino, 'who thought that I chewed my hands in hunger, came close and cried: "O father, we would suffer less if you would but consume us: you who gave us life in this sad flesh, please take it from us!"' Dante acknowledges Ugolino's own sins, but lays the greater blame on the archbishop for imposing suffering on the innocent sons. Having so violated social and physical boundaries, Ruggieri's punishment is to be similarly degraded – excruciatingly eaten by his guest for eternity.

Dante here plays repeatedly with the darkly understated adjective 'unneighbourly' to characterize the men's savage relationship. Unlike St Julian, therefore, whose violation of hospitable precepts (the murder of parent-guests) was unintentional and righted through a lifetime of pious action, Ugolino and Ruggieri have forfeited all claim to human relationship. The two traitors spend eternity in a hellish togetherness, a veritable den of beasts. According to Dante, therefore, it was not the stranger at the door who posed the greatest threat to Christian sovereignty but rather the known but treacherous one who has already breached the threshold.

CONCLUSION

Medieval people strategically used the threshold interactions of guests and hosts to work through a wide range of cultural projects, simultaneously exploring the various rules governing the reception of strangers, and considering the many perils of failing to act correctly. For the developing societies of Europe between *c.* 850 and 1450, domestic hospitality became a uniquely productive site where all social problems – ranging across individual, familial, communal and territorial – could be conceptualized. St Julian's own story, containing as it does telling traces of earlier Greek, Germanic and Christian influences, is characteristically medieval in its blend of ideals, complications and nightmare scenarios. Martyred emotionally, if not physically, by the unpredictable burdens of hosting others, Julian served as both inspiration and warning to the increasingly dynamic populations of the medieval West.

CHAPTER EIGHT

Religion and the Home: Jewish and Christian Experiences

ELISHEVA BAUMGARTEN[1] AND KATHERINE L. FRENCH

INTRODUCTION

While both Judaism and Christianity mandated some form of public worship, a range of concerns, interests and mandates brought religious practices into the house, where they intertwined with the patterns of daily life. Both faith communities performed aspects of their religion within their homes, creating domestic religious activities and injecting religious identity into everyday practices and mundane objects within the household. Jews and Christians shared some similar concerns and practices, but within both faiths, common needs and objects could also distinguish household inhabitants' religious identities.

SOURCES FOR DOMESTIC RELIGION

The sources for Christian domestic devotion are varied; they are stronger for urban contexts than rural ones and more fulsome for the later Middle Ages. Despite some concern on the part of Christian authorities that Christianity practised in the home could be a symptom of heresy, by the late Middle Ages there were numerous instruction manuals that urged Christian householders to turn their daily lives into opportunities for devotion. Inventories and wills also become more plentiful by the fourteenth century, some of which include items with religious connotations or functions. Archaeology has also provided examples of the kinds of religious objects described in wills and inventories, suggesting something of their use by their variety, size and material.

Much like the sources for Christian households, the sources about Jews written by both Jewish and Christian authors reflect urban realities. Although Jewish families lived within rural settlements, without other Jews nearby, there are few sources that describe their lives, with the exception of reports of how they gathered in larger Jewish centres for the high holidays or their need/desire to be buried within larger communities.[2] This absence is all the more unfortunate, since one could imagine that within such settings, most religious activity took place within the house, because there were no Jewish public institutions nearby. Among the central sources for medieval Jewish daily, annual and life-cycle rituals is the growing body of custom manuals (*sifrei minhagim*), the earliest being *Mahzor Vitry*, written by Rashi's student, Simha of Vitry in the early twelfth century. Books of commandments written in France during the thirteenth century, biblical and liturgical exegesis, and halakhic responsa provide additional details about practices within and outside the home. Lastly the few ethical wills that have survived from Europe, alongside notarial documents, and records of donations to the synagogue provide some evidence of household activities. Combining prescriptive literature with recovered objects or detailed lists from inventories and wills helps to create a rich picture of Christian and Jewish domestic devotional practices.

HOUSES AND RELIGIOUS SPACES

The contents of houses embodied religious ideologies and facilitated domestic religious practices and, no less importantly, the practices themselves generated religious identity and distinction. Christians understood that Jesus had instructed his followers to blend their religious practices and domesticity when he said: 'When you pray, go into your room, close the door and pray to your Father who is unseen' (Matt. 6:5) (Deane 2013: 263). These instructions gave Christians wide latitude for incorporating religious behaviour in their homes. While for Christians, the basic unit of public worship was the parish or local chapel, where they received some or all of the sacraments, attended the weekly liturgy and celebrated the life cycle, religious venerations and behaviour were not confined to these spaces. The home also served as a place of religious practice and instruction. At the very least, Christians were supposed to pray the *Angelus* at least at midday upon hearing the church bell, a devotion that commemorated the Incarnation and which derived from the monastic hours.

Jewish communities, when they were large enough, worshipped publicly in the local synagogue, celebrating the liturgical year and human life cycle. This building also often served as the communal court and a house of study and/or school (Abrahams 1932: 29–48, 49–77, esp. 129–78; Kanargofel 2012: 37–84; Isaacs 2002). Many urban centres had more than one synagogue.[3] Alongside communal prayer in the synagogue, Jews were also expected to perform religious activities and devotions throughout the day's routine activities. Every food consumed by a Jew had a benediction associated with it, as did many other everyday activities including going to the bathroom, donning specific clothes, or seeing a natural phenomenon (Berenbaum and Skolnik 2007: 330–3). Instructions for these activities are detailed in many central Jewish sources from the Mishna through the medieval commentaries and customaries. Moreover, the 'classic' benedictions from late antiquity were repeated together with a growing body of private benedictions and prayers in the Middle Ages (Elbogen 1993: 213–28, 271–84).

Jewish daily prayer consists of three separate prayers – one in the morning, a second in the mid- to late afternoon, and a third after sunset – but most Jews who attended services did so twice a day, combining the two evening prayers together (Katz 1998). While many moral sermons and books emphasize the importance of praying at a synagogue with a quorum of ten men, individuals could also pray on their own with specific adjustments to the liturgy. Medieval moral compositions emphasize the importance of praying within the communal group, even in cases where specific people would have preferred praying on their own (Judah b. Samuel 1924: #442, 447). At the same time, a quorum of men constituted a prayer cohort and could pray together anywhere, including a private house.[4] Many sources from Germany suggest that Jewish women as well as men frequented the local synagogue daily. This practice changed over the course of the thirteenth century when women faced growing restrictions concerning their synagogue attendance (Baskin 2007; Grossman 2004: 180–7; Baumgarten 2014: 24–50). Jewish children, like Christian children, were taught the daily and Sabbath prayers as part of their education and many sources report these prayers being taught within the home.[5] For example, Dulcia of Worms is said to have taught both her daughters how to pray.[6] Daily benedictions recited over food, after going to the bathroom and when rising and going to sleep were also supposed to be a constant part of all Jews' daily practice.

Christian houses often had places specifically designated for prayer, but they also had religious imagery on wall hangings, furniture and bed linens. While some of these images may have been more decorative than inspirational, distinguishing the wall hanging that might inspire or protect a viewer from that which promoted the owner's reputation and wealth is difficult.

Christians living in castles, manor houses or well-appointed urban homes had private chapels in their dwellings. In the early sixteenth century, the wealthy London mercer, Alexander Plymley had chapels in both of his houses (TNA Prob2/487). In these households, daily services were probably the norm. Most people, however, could not afford a separate room for a chapel, nor a chaplain's salary. Financial limitations did not prevent people from setting up small shrines or devotional niches, although how widespread they were is unclear. Daniel Lord Smail (2016: 79–83) found little evidence of religious objects in the inventories of Marseille and Lucca. What evidence there was comes from relatively well-off people. The most common place for a shrine appears to be sleeping quarters, where births and deaths occurred and marriages were consummated (Morse 2007: 105; Webb 2005: 26). While birth and death were sanctified by the church, their unpredictable nature meant the clergy often arrived too late. Thus these events were as much household moments as sacramental ones and usually took place in or by a bed. A shrine and religious imagery in a bedroom thus made sense. The bedroom shrine of London widow Isabell Hart was quite elaborate. It included an altar, alter cloths and vestments, and saint images (TNA Prob2/22/168). As she lay on her deathbed, the altar was ready for a priest to say mass for her, while small portable images of the saints focused her devotion in his absence. Even if there was no formal shrine, saints often adorned the bedding, thus providing their protection while inhabitants slept. Johanna Kent had a valance over her bed with the images of SS Ambrose and Isadore (LMA DL/C/B/004/Ms09171/7: 9v–10).

In Jewish households, there was no requirement that daily prayers take place in a specific location; wherever one prayed, however, cleanliness was a basic recommendation (Abrahams 1926).[7] Nevertheless, some texts refer to an *aliyah*, an attic of sorts, and some texts emphasize the importance of praying in the highest part of the house. This follows with general instructions that required the synagogue to be the highest building in its surroundings (Rabinowitz et al. 2007: 355; Zevin 1981: 191–2). These attics may have served individuals or groups who used it as a synagogue. Archaeologists have discovered a seventeenth-century synagogue of exactly this type in Alsace (Kaplan 2016).[8] While strictly speaking, decorations were unnecessary and images forbidden, surviving medieval synagogues sport floral and geometric decorations as well as animal imagery. However, we know little of the decorations of these domestic prayer spaces. In addition to these formal prayers, Jews recited blessings as part of and in accordance with their daily activities, in the different parts of the house where they performed these actions: in bed, when eating, etc.

Over the course of the high and late Middle Ages, Christian devotion increasingly relied on material to convey spiritual concerns. Thus, Christian houses contained objects that could be construed as religious or apotropaic. Crucifixes, images of the saints in various media, and religious books were all popularly available, with the most common devotional object being prayer beads and pilgrimage badges. By the fifteenth century, Venetian merchants routinely purchases large quantities of icons from Crete, with expectations of selling them for domestic use (Cooper 2006: 192). Given the sheer number of saints, the choice of images filling a house could be highly individualistic, motivated by personal devotion or local convention. In 1471, when Lawrence Stockwood, a London salter, made his will, he tells us he had a banner in his house with John the Evangelist and St Lawrence, his name saint (TNA Prob11/6/74). Some religious concepts were also popularly rendered in domestic decor. Joan Candell of York had hangings of the Seven Works of Mercy in her house (Ward 1998: 29).

Owners often introduced household shrines with a holy water stoup. Holy water was also widely used for curing illnesses and as protection from dangerous forces. Even without a shrine, the bedroom was a logical place for a stoup, as occupants were most vulnerable when sleeping. John Hanson, a Westminster baker, had a holy water stoup of pewter in his 'chief chamber' (TNA Prob2/89). The presence of a holy water stoup also shows that for some inhabitants at least, blessing oneself as one moved about the house was part of household behaviour.

St Mary, the most popularly venerated saint, was depicted in a variety of media and in a variety of aspects. London archaeologists have found small, mass-produced statues of the Virgin Mary imported from Cologne and made of pipeclay that are only about four inches tall. Some have the remains of red pigment on them (Barber 2013: 58). These modest and affordable objects suggest the broad appeal of such devotional objects.

St John the Baptist was another popular image appearing in a variety of media. Walo of Sarton purportedly brought the head of St John back from the Fourth Crusade to Amiens in 1206 and it became a popular pilgrimage site and devotional object (Baert 2013: 120). An unnamed Southwark tailor kept an alabaster St John head his sleeping quarters (TNA Prob2/44). It was also a common image for wall hangings. John Hartyngton had a 'Saint John's cloth of purple velvet' in his hall (TNA Prob2/67). St John was commonly believed to cure epilepsy, convulsions, headaches and melancholy. As a model of behaviour, he promoted chastity, humility and justice (Baert 2013: 123; de Voraigne 1993: 134; Smith n.d.). Thus his image served a variety of purposes for householders. Its many forms and functions suggest the many ways Christians interacted with it. One could offer prayers to it on a small altar, but a concerned wife or mother might also tuck a small alabaster John's head under a pillow or hang by a bed for healing or protection. Other objects of domestic devotion were pax bredes or tablets: plaques of wood, ceramic, metal, or even ivory, usually with an *agnus dei*, a biblical metaphor for Christ. The Gospel of John describes Jesus as the lamb of God 'that taketh away the sins of the world' (John 1:29), making the *agnus dei* a popular charm against range of evil spirits (Ridder 2012: 104). Some pax bredes or tablets were very elaborate. The one that Isabel Frowik owned had an image of the *agnus dei* with pearls and a sapphire (TNA Prob11/5/113). Frowik's pax probably served a variety of protective and healing purposes as well as being an object to guide devotion. According to medieval lapidaries, sapphires reduced fevers and anxiety and pearls staunched the flow of blood (Ridder 2012: 104; Evans and Serjeantson 1933: 108). The so-called Middleham Jewel, a fifteenth-century gold locket found near Middleham Castel in Yorkshire, blends many of the same elements found in Frowik's pax. On the front of the Middleham Jewel is mounted a sapphire, the verse from John 1:29, and an image of the crucifixion. It also has healing words for curing epilepsy (Ridder 2012: 104–5) (Figure 8.1).

Holy dolls, which fell in a grey zone between toys and devotional object, were also popular. In Florence, images of infants were made of terracotta and dressed in damask clothing. Sometimes they were part of a Florentine bride's trousseau (Klapisch-Zuber 1985). These items taught and encouraged both maternal behaviour and affective piety directed at the baby Jesus.

FIGURE 8.1: Middleham Jewel (1475–1499). York, England, York Museums Trust. © Image courtesy of York Museums Trust.

More ephemeral, but very common, were pilgrimage badges and prayer beads. As mass-produced items, they were more affordable than a tablet encrusted with pearls. Giving pilgrimage badges as gifts might have associated the recipient with the beneficial pilgrimage. Medieval illustrations show people wearing them on cloaks and hats. In the Netherlands, pilgrimage badges were also buried at foundations or entrances to houses, barns and cowsheds, to protect the occupants from harm. When dipped in water, the water served as medicine (Spencer 2010: 18). Prayer beads facilitated devotion by serving as a memory aid for Christians saying the *Ave* and the *Pater Noster*. Women typically wore long strings, while men favoured shorter ones (Vossler 2011: 424). It was the most common devotional object listed in Marseille's inventories (Smail 2016: 79). Rosary or paternoster beads have been found in archaeological digs across Europe in both urban and rural contexts (Gilchrist 2012: 158). In his will, Roger Flore of Oakham, Lincolnshire left his prayer beads 'that I use my self, with the ten *Aves* of silver and a *Paternoster* over gilt' to the master of Manton 'praying him to have mind of me sometime when he says our Lady's psalter on them' (TNA Prob11/3/174). When not in use, prayer beads were hung on a girdle or by the bed. Protective devices and prayer beads were not unique to Christianity. Many Muslims and Jews also wore amulets and charms to protect the wearer against the evil eye, disease and sudden death.

Emergencies, such as the danger of a newly delivered baby dying before it was baptized, could transform ordinary household items such as ewers and basins into baptismal vessels. Once used in a sacrament, however, these items could not return to household use (Mirk 1868; Gilchrist 2013: 178). Agnes Wyngar, the widow of a London alderman, addressed these concerns with her bequest to her parish church of a basin and ewer 'to the intent that the same basin and ewer shall doo service ... for the christening of any man's child of the said parish (TNA Prob11/21/4).

Jewish homes also had many objects used for religious rituals, and others which gained significance when used for a religious purpose. However, as a minority well aware of the objects used by their Christian neighbours for their devotions, Jewish homes were defined as much by what they did not have or how they took care of their domestic space. For example, there were no crucifixes or pictures of saints on the walls, nor were there rosary beads. Basins and ewers would not be used to baptize an infant, although they were used to wash babies. Some Jewish sources discouraged using objects identified with Christianity whether for mundane, business, or medicinal purposes. One well-known source tells of a Jewish woman with a sick son, who refused the advice and the stone offered by her Christian neighbour because the stone was purportedly a holy land relic from Jesus' tomb (Judah b. Samuel 1924: #1332).[9] Little is known about specific objects Jews had at home for ritual purposes and more is known about the beliefs attributed to the objects rather than the 'Jewish' character of the objects themselves.

Cleaning the house and the placement and use of objects was central to religious identity, as is evident in the trial records of *conversas* from Iberia. The inquisition interrogations report that *conversa* women cleaned the house on Friday before the Sabbath, 'adorning their houses as for a holiday', unlike their Christian neighbours, who cleaned on Saturday. *Conversa* women were also accused of wearing specific clothes on the Jewish Sabbath (Melammed 1999: 74–83). In this way the use of specific objects, such as a broom, even though common in all houses, could identify its user's religion. In other words, many objects took on religious significance due to the circumstances and time of their use.

Candles kindled for the Sabbath are an additional oft-mentioned example. Halakhic responsa discuss possible prohibitions against the use of candles bought from non-Jews, if the purchaser knew the candles could also be used for Christian liturgical purposes. The medieval rabbinic deliberations follow debates concerning the same matter from late antiquity, but also indicate the relevance of these questions for medieval life (Kanarfogel 2015: 155–6). The candles lit for the Sabbath utilized common designs like the star-shaped lamp that allowed the lighting of many candles at once, and took on ritual significance as these lamps became symbols of Sabbath observance (Fraiman 2013: 99–102) (Figure 8.2).

Other household objects adorned the ritual Sabbath and facilitated holiday blessings.[10] Elaborately embroidered cloths were used as decorations and props for life-cycle rituals, both within and outside the house. Some items became identified as 'religious' only when being used for religious purposes. For example, at the death of an inhabitant, windows were covered and water spilled out of vessels within the house, giving these mundane items religious meaning at the moment of death (Shimshon b. Tzadok 1858: #447; Stahl 2007: 193–4; Shoham-Steiner 2013). Clothing associated with specific rituals, be they menstrual purity, penance, or certain holidays, also became expressions of devotion (Baumgarten 2014: 58, 71, 190–1; b. Judah 2014).[11] Cloth and candle holders were the kinds of items included on lists of donations to synagogues.

Medieval Jews, like their Christian neighbours, used amulets and protective scrolls. Some had a long history reaching back to the Bible, such as phylacteries or the mezuzah, posted on the doorway (Cohn 2008: 145–70).[12] Scholars have argued that as a rule, medieval Jewish homes probably did not have mezuzot on their doorposts in the period leading up to the fourteenth century. After the Black Death, mezuzot became more widely used. In contrast to private homes, synagogues and other communal buildings did have a mezuzah. This may be the result of the need for protection that became imperative during times when epidemics were widespread. Living arrangements within most medieval urban centres may have also been a factor, as Jews and Christians shared courtyards and living spaces and Jews may have been less likely to mark the shared spaces with a mezuzah (Horowitz 1986).

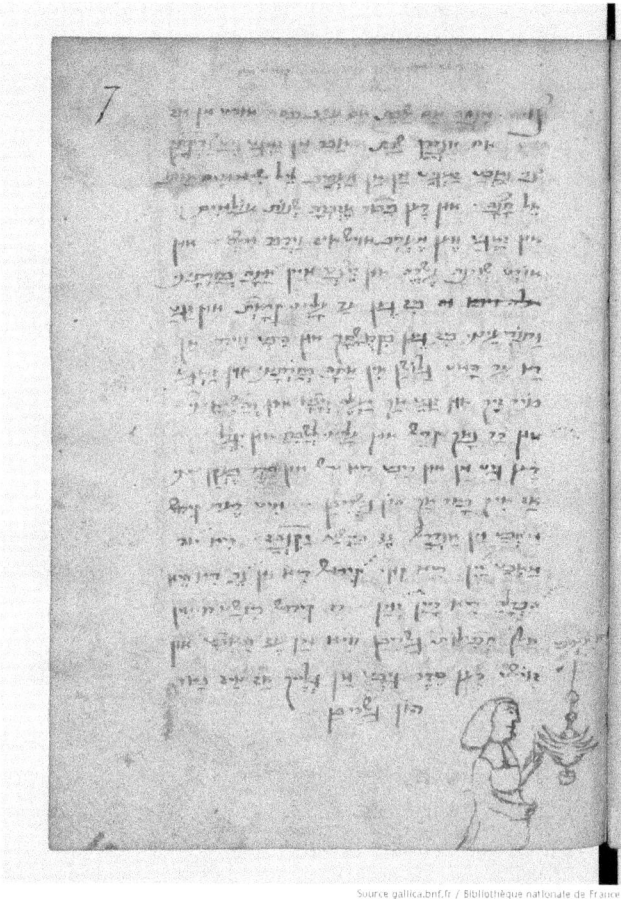

FIGURE 8.2: Lighting Sabbath Lamp (c. 1503, North Italian). Paris Paris, Bibliothèque nationale de France Ms. héb. 586, fol. 6r. © Bibliothèque nationale de France.

The most frequently used amulets or talismans were rolls of paper inscribed with Hebrew writings that were used for everyday protection (Harari 2010, 2011; Bohak 2008). These were similar in shape and sometimes in content to those used by medieval Christians and Muslims. They were Jewish because they were inscribed with Hebrew words and biblical verses. One amulet against thieves is a Hebrew translation of a Latin formula used for the same purpose with an omission of the Virgin Mary (Bohak 2006). Most of these materials have not survived but are mentioned in passing in stories, commentaries or manuscripts that include the formulae written on the amulets (Bodleian Library Mich 9: Amulets).

Both Jews and Christians valued, possessed and adapted religious books for domestic use. By the late Middle Ages, religious books became more common in urban Christian households, where literacy was higher than in rural ones. Religious books included prayer books, collections of saints' lives, and Christian instruction manuals. Probably the most popular Christian text was the so-called Book of Hours, a highly variable compendium of prayers in either Latin or the vernacular to be said throughout the day (Duffy 2006: 5–9). Whether deluxe or modest, owners of these books adapted and modified them to reflect personal and familial interests and handed them down for generations. The books focused a web of patronage and intercession, with the saints and God at the pinnacle (Reinburg 2014: 236–41). The growing use of prayer books and instructional manuals was part of a larger religious movement, the *vita activa*, the active life; designed to validate a Christian life lived in the world as opposed to the monastery. For practitioners, work and domestic life became increasingly imbued with religious concerns (Corbellini and Hoogvliet 2013: 524). The Italian Franciscan Cherubino da Spoleto wrote *The Rule for Married Life* for the Italian merchant Giacomo Bogianni. Cherubino recommended family reading as a way of building family piety (Corbellini and Hoogvliet 2013: 526). The pattern of finger smudges on Netherlandish books of hours suggests that reading in bed was by no means only a modern habit. These marks of use suggest that readers often fell asleep before finishing their devotions (Rudy 2010: 5).

In some areas and at some points in time, possession of vernacular religious books, especially the Bible, was a sign of heresy. The inquisitor Bernard Gui believed that Cathar texts and the New Testament in the vernacular indicated adherence to Catharism (Biller 1994: 66). Indeed followers of both Catharism and the Lollardy often connected to co-religionists by sharing books and group readings. According to one deposition, male and female Cathars of various ranks, including the Lords of Labécède in southern France, would gather at a knight's house to listen to the *perfecti* preach and others read (Biller 1994: 75). Similarly in the fifteenth century, Alice Rowley, one of the leaders of the Lollards in Coventry, England, owned, lent and borrowed numerous books including 'De vite Thobie', 'A book of the Gospels', and a book of Pauline Epistles. She and other Lollards in the group hid their books in a room in Rowley's house known as the 'chapel chamber' (McSheffrey 1995: 34–5). Vernacular books did not belong only to heretics, however. Jehan Danvaing, a tanner in Tournai, had a Bible in French, which caused little concern for those probating his will (Corbellini and Hoogvliet 2013: 530).

Books were among the most basic religious objects in medieval Jewish households. Malachi Beit-Arié has documented the large number of books self-produced by medieval Jews and argued that Jews produced more books per capita for personal use than any community of Christians.[13] These were prayer books, Pentateuchs with commentaries, as well as books containing ritual instructions. While medieval Jewish households may have also owned books in the vernacular, they have not survived.

The vast majority of Jewish men as well as a significant number of Jewish women could read enough Hebrew to follow the prayers. While all Jews, men and women, were probably instructed to memorize the basic daily prayers in their childhood, the large quantity of prayer books that have survived for holidays indicate literacy, as these liturgies were long and complex and were not said often enough to be memorized (Kanarfogel 2010; Einbinder 2002: 62). Liturgical additions to the traditional prayer service in the form of *piyyutim* – special poems recited at different points in the liturgy and on special occasions – also demonstrate basic biblical literacy and familiarity with biblical stories as well as specific verses (Soloveitchik 2015).

Books were consulted and used for prayer and study both in the house and in public spaces. Beit-Arié has documented the rise in production of everyday prayer books in the thirteenth century, many of which were given to women when they married, and one can assume these were used at home as well as in synagogue.[14] Israel Ta-Shma and Judah Galinsky argue that instructional literature flourished during the thirteenth century, especially handbooks that taught specific religious functionaries their duties. For example, a family of circumcisers from Worms produced the first-known circumcisers' manual (Ta Shma 1996). Lists of commandments for daily recitation and study were also popular, as evidenced by the multiple copies of the *Sefer Mitzvot Katan* by Isaac of Corbeil (d. 1288) produced for this purpose. While it is possible this recitation was performed collectively at the end of the prayer services in the synagogues, as per the author's instructions, it is also likely that this action was repeated at home as well.

Books of instructions were read for two distinct yet related religious purposes: instruction, and as part of worship (Galinsky 2016). Jonah of Gerona, a Spanish rabbi who studied in northern France during the thirteenth century, returned home and composed his *Iggeret HaYir'ah*. Interestingly, he divided his text between men and women and included many everyday domestic activities as ways of expressing devotion to God. This is especially evident in the section concerning women. Among the women's duties Jonah presents is offering his book to their husbands every evening, so that the men will meditate on the text (Jonah of Gerondi 1990: #68). Similarly Solomon b. Isaac, a fourteenth-century Provençal Jew, emphasizes in his testament that each of his sons

> . . . shall have in his house a chair on which a volume or two of the Talmud or any other talmudical work shall rest, so that he can always open a book when he comes home. Let him read what he can, making it a duty to read in any book he likes at least four lines before taking his meal. Again that he shall not omit to read every week the Pentateuchal lesson twice in the Hebrew text and once in the Aramaic version.
>
> —Abrahams 1926: 228

Isaac of Corbeil goes on to specify that he wrote his book for women as well as for men (Isaac of Corbeil 1979: 2; Galinsky 2015).

Books were also valuable objects, often noted in wills or the subject of legal arbitrations between financial adversaries. Their value was the result both of the cost of their production and of their use and its spiritual implications (Riegler and Baskin 2008). One of the topics discussed most frequently in medieval sources is what behaviour was forbidden or permitted in the vicinity of books. Could sexual relations take place in a room with a book? Could a man read a book with a naked woman near him? Could books be placed on a dirty table?[15] Questions like this reveal the extent to which books were found within the Jewish house.

One last matter related to books and religion within the house has to do with non-Jewish books. Christian books, liturgies, tractates and medical treatises were found in Jewish houses since their value made them collateral for loans. Some extreme moralists make it clear that they were not to be read by Jews; other sources are silent on the matter, or hint that Jews did read Christian literature (Judah b. Samuel 1924: #259, 668, 1348, 1350).[16] These discussions are further evidence of the religious importance attached to books as objects and to their use and function within the house and beyond.

EATING

Of all the daily activities, eating was the most imbued with religious significance. What and how one ate created religious identity. As the instructions for Giacomo Bogianni made clear, eating could be transformed into an occasion for religious instruction or contemplation. Christian law and practice required that Christians abstain from meat on Fridays and during Lent. Those who provisioned or cooked for Christian households thus played an important role in maintaining domestic religious practices. Fasting beyond these minimal requirements, as practised by both Catherine of Siena and Margery Kempe, further integrated daily life and piety.

Another way Christians connected eating with piety was in the decoration of eating utensils and dishware. In Britain, the metal bosses in the bottoms of wooden drinking bowls called mazers typically had an image (Figure 8.3). These images tended towards the religious, with saints being particularly common. The London widow Margaret Russell had one with St James (LMA DL/C/B/004/Ms9171/7: 121–24). Spoon ends also received decorations; spoons with the Virgin Mary, called 'maidenhead spoons', and apostle spoons were very popular. Elizabeth Speke of Colshill, Somerset had collected all twelve apostles by the time she died (Weaver 1903: 195). When a household member used an apostle spoon, it connected the household meal with the Last Supper and Eucharistic piety. The brightly glazed pottery from the Mediterranean

FIGURE 8.3: Mazer with the inscription *"Potvm et nos benedicat agyos"* ("May the Holy One Bless the Drink and Us"), c. 1490, AF.3119, London, British Museum. © The British Museum.

provided another surface for decoration. Some of what survives, both the inexpensive and the highly prized, had religious motives, saint images, or simple crosses (Lafuente 2014: 82).

While meals might not be a religious event, they were an opportunity to remember Christ's sacrifice and the blessings God had given the household. The material culture of eating shows how Christians could turn this daily activity into some form of pious ritual. The objects at a meal might not qualify as religious, but they brought the saints and their protection to the meal and promoted thankfulness, humility and Christian charity in users.

Eating, drinking and fasting among Jews, as among Christians, was charged with religious meaning (Friedenreich 2011; Resnick 2011) (Figure 8.4). Much of the preparation of food and its consumption took place within the house and in medieval Europe; non-Jews partook in these activities as part of a domestic cooperation between Jewish heads of household (male and female) and their Christian hired or indentured help (Katz 1989; Baumgarten 2004: 133–44). Food preparation took place according to the laws of *kashrut* and specific utensils and methods were employed.[17] During the medieval period, rabbis paid increasing attention to the separation of meat and milk and in some cases different dishes are used for each type of food (Judah b. Samuel 1924: #1657). This plentitude of objects is part of the booming urban economies of the high Middle Ages.

FIGURE 8.4: Jewish Family Meal (fifteenth century). Paris, Paris, Bibliothèque nationale de France, Ms. héb. 1333, fol. 20b © Bibliothèque nationale de France.

Jews also ate special foods on different holidays. In some cases, this was the result of biblical law, as on Passover when Jews ate no leavening. In other cases, local traditions shaped diet, such as the ingredients of Sabbath foods and the ways they were cooked. The Sabbath also warranted special food, as cooking had to be done before the onset of the Sabbath. Central to these meals was bread and wine, each regulated by Jewish law. Wine could not be produced by a non-Jew without the involvement of Jews (Soloveitchik 2008). Bread too had to be made either by the Jews alone or as part of a cooperation between Jews and non-Jews. In many European cities bread was produced by members of different Christian orders and was made in a central oven, Jews 'participated' by throwing kindling into the oven. Especially pious Jews ate only bread baked by Jews, which some considered inferior in taste and colour to the 'Christian' bread. There is evidence that most Jews refrained from eating bread baked by non-Jews during the days between Rosh HaShanah and Yom Kippur. This was seen as an important pious attribute (Strauss 1979; Woolf 2008). These laws originated in the Talmud and medieval authorities further developed them. While it is impossible to estimate how stringently they were observed, there is evidence that they were generally observed and penitentials note the seriousness with which infringement was addressed (Eleazar b. Judah 2014 #10 30–3, #11 34–5).

Silver cups were part of Sabbath and holiday rituals. Passover celebrations called for special plates with covers. Little evidence of these objects has survived but illuminated manuscripts feature some of them[18] (Figure 8.5). In addition, discussions of objects Jews held as pawns, whether clothing or tableware, indicate that Jews often used the objects they held as collateral (Shatzmiller 2013: 22–44). We do not know whether these objects had depictions of saints on them, but the willingness to use pawned goods is evidence that the ritualization of foods and drinks went beyond the objects themselves. To some extent one can perhaps say that if a Jew was eating with a ritual blessing, this was a form of domestic religious practice determined by the way the food was prepared and the subject doing the eating, even though eating from an object owned by non-Jews, and possibly adorned for non-Jewish purposes. The etiquette of eating, modestly and neatly, was also seen as proper religious devotion. For example, Eleazer b. Samuel of Mainz, a fourteenth-century Jew, stated in his will:

> Now, my sons and daughters, eat and drink only what is necessary, as our good parents did, refraining from heavy meals . . . the regular adoption of such economy in food, leads to economy in expenditure generally . . . accustom yourselves and your wives, your sons and your daughters to wear nice clean clothes that God and man may love and honor you. In this direction do not exercise too strict a parsimony. But on no account adopt foreign fashions in dress.
>
> —Abrahams 1926: 212

LIFE-CYCLE RITUALS

The church wished the sacraments to be performed in a church, but often it did not happen. Christian marriage did not require a priest, and it could be made anywhere; a house was frequently the location. Étienne Derot claimed he had married Laurence Chippon at her godmother's house somewhere in Paris (Donahue 2007: 366). In Italy, marriage, especially among the well-to-do, was not an event, but a protracted process that could take years to accomplish.

FIGURE 8.5: Birthing Girdle, fifteenth century, Takayama ms 56. Yale University, New Haven, CT, Beineke Library. © Yale University Beineke

There were negotiations over the betrothal and dowry; these agreements had to be registered with a notary, then the exchange of vows, the bride's move to her husband's family's home, and the consummation of the marriage. Many of these stages took place in a house (Klapisch-Zuber 1985). For some, these events were a combination of religious event and legal arrangement, but some marriages were created in the heat of passion and without witnesses. While the participants might not have been thinking of the sacramental aspects of what was transpiring, the church nevertheless still considered it as such.

Medieval Jewish marriages took place in the synagogue courtyard, but the preparations and the processions accompanying bride and groom to and from the synagogue started and ended at home (Eleazar b. Judah 1960: #353; Shammes 1992). In this way, the house, the communal institutions, as well as the public space, were all part of the ritual process. Indeed, the acts of leaving one house and entering another were crucial moments in this celebration. Early modern sources stress the act of welcoming participants into the house on these occasions, with the parents of the bride and/or groom standing by the door and ushering in the guests (Shammes 1992). In addition to the ritual itself, household objects that would be used in the house, such as a prayer book, were given as part of the bride's trousseau; a 'shroud' was also given to the bride and groom at marriage, which they were expected to keep throughout their lives and use at specific times, for example by women when going to the synagogue after birth and by men on the high holidays (Baumgarten 2004: 101–5). Men also received a tallit (prayer shawl) at the time of marriage and used it for daily prayers thereafter.[19] A plate was broken as part of the betrothal (Deutsch 2012: 12 n.36).

Medieval mothers of all religions gave birth at home, usually in the care of midwives, neighbours and family members. With the potential for complications and limited medical knowledge, fertility concerns and childbirth required amulets and other religious devices to help the process along. The Italian physician Anthonius Guainerius recommended when (Christian) women went into labour that 'it is good that the legend of blessed Margaret be read, that she have relics of the saints on her, and that you carry out briefly some familiar ceremonies in order to please your patient' (Larson 2003: 94).

For Christian women, one of the most common birth aids was a birthing girdle, an amulet that predates Christianity (French 2016: 133). Several medieval examples are parchment scrolls inscribed with prayers, charms, and instructions for a successful delivery. One from France also invokes St Margaret, while several from England call upon the early Christian martyrs SS Quiricus and Julitta, a martyred mother and son (Larson 2003: 94; Gwara and Morse 2012: 39)[20] (Figure 8.6). Another common fertility and childbirth device was prayer beads of semi-precious stones. Medieval lapidaries claimed many stones were 'good for a woman who conceives & makes a woman to child' (Evans and

FIGURE 8.6: Early-Modern Depiction of a Birthing Chamber and Rituals. Hollekreisch, *Minhagbuch*, Nürnburg cod. 7058, fol. 43b–44b, from 1589. © Germanisches Naional Museum.

Serjeantson 1933: 117). Most popular was coral, which among its many beneficial properties 'makes fruit multiply' (Evans and Serjeantson 1933: 79). Jet and amber eased childbirth pains, and jasper helped expel the afterbirth (Albertus Magnus 1967: 93, 121; Evans and Serjeantson 1933: 32; Rowland 1981: 139). The amber and jet beads that London widow Margaret Brokecastre left her daughter Katherine would have thus addressed many fertility and childbirth issues (French 2016: 136; Gilchrist 2012: 143).

For families with enough means, special bed linens with appropriate decorations might also be purchased to adorn the birthing space and protect the mother and infant. Margaret Shelley of Hunsdon, Herefordshire had a 'cradle cloth with an image of our lady' (French 2012: 131).

Unless there was an emergency, babies were processed from the home to the church for their baptism. The procession was an opportunity to show off the healthy baby (ideally a boy). Families often wrapped the baby in special cloth to enhance the proceedings, and family, friends and patrons carried the necessary items for the baptism, such as a basin and ewer for the godparents to wash their hands (French 2007: 50). Mothers remained at home in bed for a period of confinement that lasted from four to six weeks while family and friends helped with the household chores. Churching, or the ritual of purification, ended the mother's confinement. Another procession ushered the new mother from her house to the church, where she received her blessing from the priest. When she returned home, she resumed her household duties (French 2007: 61–5).

These amulets and girdles used by Christian women had Jewish equivalents. Containing words in Hebrew, embroidered by Jewish women and used by them while reciting Hebrew or vernacular sayings, they were widespread (Baumgarten 2000). As with Christian women, the birthing chamber also received special attention before a baby was born because of the danger attributed to birth. Some early modern texts describe bedrooms at childbirth, explaining that midwives and other communal functionaries brought a Torah to the house and placed it outside the birthing chamber for the birth (Baumgarten 2004: 92–105). During the birthing process and in the weeks following it, the house was the focal point of communal and familial gatherings (Figure 8.7).

After birth, friends of the family would gather in the house and prepare candles for the circumcision ceremony. A vigil was held around the baby's bed the night before the circumcision and there is evidence for a variety of ceremonies that took place while chanting special verses and blessings (Baumgarten 2004: 93–9).[21] With the birth of a boy, the circumcision ceremony took place in the synagogue during the high Middle Ages. However, fifteenth- and sixteenth-century sources suggest that some circumcisions took place at home. In any case, even those ceremonies that took place in the synagogue began with a procession leading participants from the house, much like in the case of marriage (Gershom the Cicumcisor 1891: 64). Whether a boy or girl was born, during the weeks after birth the mother was entertained within the house, gradually allowing wider circles of community members into the house. During these same weeks, an older woman would draw a circle around her bed every evening, reciting a Yiddish poem in which protection was requested for the mother and baby (Baumgarten 2008).

At the end of the lying-in period, a naming ceremony for boys and for girls took place within the house. This ritual, known as the *Hollekreish*, provided the infant with a non-Jewish name and was performed by children who gathered around the cradle. Scholars have suggested that this ritual had pagan origins and perhaps in this case one can see the reticence of the community to hold this ritual outside the house in the synagogue (Baumgarten 2004: 96–8).

Dying a good death was important to Christians, and many went to great extents to ensure this happened. This undoubtedly also helps explain the popularity of bedroom shrines and religious objects by beds. In his memoir, Florentine merchant Giovanni Morelli described his son's death in 1406. He had been unable to secure his last confession, an omission that troubled Morelli a year after the child's death. Morelli does tell us that on his deathbed, the boy clutched a 'tavola' or tablet of the Virgin (Cooper 2006: 194). Isabell Hart's bedroom shrine, described earlier, also had a tablet, which she too could hold while dying. A year after his son's death, Morelli undertook a series of meditations directed at various images in the room: the Crucifixion, the Virgin, and John the Evangelist. During these prayers to grant his son retroactively a good death, Morelli wore only a shift and halter around his neck, a traditional sign of penance (Cooper 2006: 194–5).

Death was not private. For most Christians, the hope was that their local or personal priest would arrive to receive their last confession, administer extreme unction, and if they had not yet written their last will and testament, then the priest could do that too. Family members, neighbours and friends hovered around the bed praying on beads, or tablets. Once dead, the corpse needed to be prepared for burial, a task that usually fell to women. Typically the priest sprinkled the body with holy water, and the women then washed the body and wrapped it in a shroud. The household then stood vigil with the body, until the funeral procession and burial. In 1434, Margaret Ashcombe, a widow of London, asked for 'two tapers to stand at my head while my body resteth in my house of dwelling' (Daniell 1997: 42).

Medieval Jewish death also included confession and last testaments compiled and performed at home. An account from Provence known as *Evel Rabbati*, written by Jacob b. Solomon the Physician in 1383, describes the death of three of his children, Israel, Sarah and his beloved daughter Esther, in a plague. Esther's deathbed confession is described at length (Einbinder 2009: 112–37; Barkai 2001). Ethical wills also provide further documentation of the process of death as well as of conduct within the house at large. For example, Eleazar of Mainz, mentioned above, instructs his children and specifically his daughters:

> They ought to be always at home and not gadding about. They should not stand at the door, watching whatever passes. I ask, I command that the daughters of my house be never without work to do, for idleness leads first to boredom, then to sin. But let them spin or cook, or sew.

He also provides detailed instructions about how he wants to be cared for at death and buried (Abrahams 1926: 217–8).

Besides the personal rituals and the donations of objects, Jewish homes announced death to those on the streets by covering the windows. Moreover, in accordance with Jewish ritual law, those in mourning did not venture outdoors for the seven days after burial, with the exception of the Sabbath. Prayer services took place in the home and the mourners recited the Kaddish prayers within the quorum that gathered. During the months that followed the death, these mourners were expected to recite the Kaddish as part of the public prayers, in the synagogue, exhibiting their mourning in the public ritual sphere.[22]

CONCLUSION

For both Jews and Christians, domestic piety and its accompanying rituals existed on a continuum with public worship in the parish church or synagogue. Some rituals, such as circumcision or baptism, could start in the home and finish in public. Others, such as those surrounding eating, were confined to the house, but referred to concerns and beliefs articulated publicly. While some houses had religious adornment to facilitate piety, they were not always necessary, and thus can reflect familial and personal choice rather than religious mandates. No less important than public and private distinctions are the ways Jews and Christians distinguished between and identified with their own religion when performing activities that were common to both religions.

This process of creating religious identities through everyday domestic practices calls for even broader comparisons, within Europe and beyond. The examination of regions in which more than two religions coexisted – for example, in parts of Spain where Jews, Muslims and Christians lived side by side, or in North Africa where Jews and Christians lived under a Muslim majority – will allow for further insight into the process of identity formation and distinction alongside shared practices and religious rituals. Entering the house and not remaining only in the public sphere allows for further elaboration and complication of the way these identities were formed and lived.

NOTES

Introduction

1. See also St Jerome's Letters to Eustochium and Demetrias http://www.newadvent.org/fathers/3001022.htm and http://www.newadvent.org/fathers/3001130.htm (accessed 15 October 2017; John Cassian as quoted in Ellen Muehlberger, *Angels in Late Ancient Christianity* (Oxford: Oxford University Press, 2013), 14.
2. See for example Deborah Simonton, *A History of European Women's Work: 1700 to the Present* (London: Routledge, 1998); Joanna Bourke, 'Housewifery in Working-Class England, 1860–1914', *Past and Present*, 143 (1994): 167–97; Amanda Vickery, 'Golden Age to Separate Spheres? A Review of the Categories and Chronology of English Women's History', *Historical Journal*, 36 (1993): 383–414.
3. See for example Felicity Riddy, 'Looking Closely: Authority and Intimacy in the Late Medieval Urban Home', in *Gendering the Master Narrative: Women and Power in the Middle Ages*, ed. Mary C. Erler and Maryanne Kowaleski (Ithaca, NY: Cornell University Press, 2003), 214–15; Shannon McSheffrey, 'Place, Space, and Situation: Public and Private in the Making of Marriage in Late-Medieval London', *Speculum*, 79 (4) (2004): 960–2.

Chapter 1

1. Also see plates 45 and 46 for other examples of similar houses, and page 217 of the same volume for Wilson's discussion of the architectural features of houses in the tapestry.
2. On the infrequent appearance of women in the tapestry, see Madeline Caviness, 'Anglo-Saxon Women, Norman Knights and a "Third Sex" in the Bayeux Embroidery', in *The Bayeux Tapestry: New Interpretations*, ed. Martin Foys *et al.* (Woodbridge, UK: Boydell Press, 2009), 85–118.

3. Felicity Riddy notes that in Middle English, '"House" is the building, "home" is the focus of feelings associated with where you belong and who you are most attached to'. Felicity Riddy, 'Authority and Intimacy in the Late Medieval Urban Home', in *Gendering the Master Narrative: Women and Power in the Middle Ages*, ed. Mary C. Erler and Maryanne Kowaleski (Ithaca: Cornell University Press, 2003), 219.
4. See for example Luke 18. 28–30, where Jesus tells his disciples that those who leave their homes and their kin to follow him will gain spiritual rewards in the next life.
5. The most vocal proponent of this point of view in recent years is perhaps Felicity Riddy. See for example her 'Authority and Intimacy in the Late Medieval Urban Home'.
6. Giorgio Riello, for instance, reminds us that inventories are 'forms of representation that are influenced by social and legal conventions'. Giorgio Riello, '"Things Seen and Unseen": The Material Culture of Early Modern Inventories and their Representation of Domestic Interiors', in *Early Modern Things: Objects and their Histories*, ed. Paula Findlen (New York: Routledge, 2012), 127. See also Goldberg, 'The Fashioning of Bourgeois Domesticity', 124.
7. See Charles du Cange *et al.*, *Glossarium mediae et infimae latinitatis*, éd. augm., Niort: L. Favre (1883–1887), t. 5, col. 030a. *Lar* was uncommon in many areas of the medieval West. In modern Portugese and Spanish the term is still used to refer to a household or residence. My thanks to Miriam Shadis and Alexandra Guerson for clarifying this use of the term in medieval and modern Portuguese contexts.
8. See Christine Klapisch-Zuber (with Michel Demonet), '"*Ad unum panem et unum vinum*': The Rural Tuscan Family at the Beginning of the Fifteenth Century', in *Women, Family, and Ritual in the Fifteenth Century* (Chicago: University of Chicago Press, 1985), 36–67.
9. Esp. 427–8. See also Sara Butler, *Divorce in Medieval England: From One to Two Persons in Law* (New York: Routledge, 2013), 10–11.
10. For instance, there was increasing concern about the irregular marital relationships of clergy and their female companions among Italian ecclesiastics after the twelfth century. Cossar, *Clerical Households*.
11. Marilyn Oliva has written about the significance of domestic materials within female monasteries during the Middle Ages, showing how the culture and objects associated with domesticity informed women's religious practices. Oliva, 'Nuns at Home: The Domesticity of Sacred Space', in *Medieval Domesticity*, 146–7.
12. Note the contrast between the Italian term *casa* and earlier uses of *domus* to mean house, but not household. Christiane Klapisch-Zuber, 'The "Cruel Mother"', in *Women, Family, and Ritual*, 117.
13. P. J. P. Goldberg, 'Space and Gender in the Late Medieval English House', *Viator*, 42 (2) (2011): 206, points out how some scholarly analysis 'mirrors contemporary normative ideology'.
14. Sara Rees Jones suggests that instead of gendered divisions in medieval houses, perhaps more division between 'safe and dangerous' areas of houses: 'Women's Influence on the Design of Urban Homes', in *Gendering the Master Narrative*, 193.
15. For one prominent example of such an argument, see Barbara Hanawalt, *The Ties that Bound*, 33–5.

16. On the genesis of this argument in English scholarship, see Grenville, *Medieval Housing*, 123–33, with a specific and trenchant critique of Barbara Hanawalt's conclusions on page 133.
17. Compare Hanawalt, *The Ties that Bound*, 34 with John Hines, 'No Place Like Home? The Anglo-Saxon Social Landscape from Within and Without', in *Anglo-Saxon England and the Continent*, ed. Hans Sauer and Jo Story (Tempe: University of Arizona Press, 2011), 39.
18. See for example Anthony Emery, 'Late-Medieval Houses as Expressions of Social Status', *Historical Research*, 78 (200) (2005): 141.
19. Amanda Richardson, 'Gender and Space in English Royal Palaces', 156, notes that the halls in royal residences were used as dormitories for servants. Anthony Emery argues that halls were sleeping spaces in the earliest centuries of the medieval era: 'Late-medieval Houses', 141. On the early functions of halls in Anglo-Saxon England see John Hines, 'No Place Like Home?', 26.
20. This was likely a comment on how much work the girl was used to doing; Alessandra was concerned to find a wife for her son who would be used to housework.
21. On spiritual life in the Roman *cubiculum*, see Kristina Sessa, 'Christianity and the *cubiculum*: Spiritual Politics and Domestic Space in Late Antique Rome', *Journal of Early Christian Studies*, 15 (2) (2007): 171–204. On prayer in the *cubiculum* in the early Middle Ages, see Julia H. M. Smith, 'Material Christianity in the Early Medieval Household', *Studies in Church History*, 50 (2014): 23–46.
22. Giovanni Boccaccio's stories treat the bedchamber in this way, as a site for sexual and other intimacies and a place where women could entrap foolish and sexually unsophisticated men. Boccaccio, *The Decameron*.
23. See Katherine French, Kathryn Smith and Sarah Stanbury, '"An Honest Bed": The Scene of Life and Death in Late Medieval England', in *Fragments: Interdisciplinary Approaches to the Study of Ancient and Medieval Pasts*, 5 (2016): 61–95. Also see Kristiansen, 'Proper Living: Exploring Domestic Ideals in Medieval Denmark', 158.
24. The statutes of Rezzo, in Liguria, punish anyone who washed laundry 'or did any other disgusting thing' in the fountains of the city. *Liber iurium ecclesiae, comunitatis, statutorum Recii*, Fonti per la Storia della Liguria XIV, ed. Sandra Macchiavello (Genova: Assessorato della Cultura, 2000), 71.
25. On laundresses selling sex in Paris, see Sharon Farmer, *Surviving Poverty in Medieval Paris: Gender, Ideology, and the Daily Lives of the Poor* (Ithaca: Cornell University Press, 2002), 138–9. On the association between prostitution and latrines, see Martha Bayless, *Sin and Filth in Medieval Culture: The Devil in the Latrine* (London: Routledge, 2012).
26. For an example from late medieval Valencia, see Blumenthal, *Enemies and Familiars*, 94–5.

Chapter 2

1. Although Philippe Aries' 1962 argument that premodern parents did not recognize childhood as a stage or form close emotional connections with their children is still influential, it has been soundly rejected by historians. For a succinct summary of this

debate, see Nicholas Orme, *Medieval Children* (New Haven: Yale University Press, 2003), 5–6.
2. For earlier pieces arguing for two regional patterns, see J. Hajnal, 'European Marriage Patterns in Perspective', in *Population in History: Essays in Historical Demography*, ed. D. V. Glass and David E. C. Eversley (London: E. Arnold, 1965), 103; R. M. Smith, 'The People of Tuscany and Their Families in the Fifteenth Century: Medieval or Mediterranean?', *Journal of Family History*, 6 (1) (1981): 111–12. For one example of more recent scholarship stressing variation, see McSheffrey, *Marriage*, 17.
3. These and all calculations are based on my own work with the catasto data unless stated otherwise. Herlihy and Klapisch-Zuber calculate that approximately 18 per cent of all urban households in Tuscany consisted of one individual while only 10 per cent of those in the Tuscan countryside did. Herlihy and Klapisch-Zuber, *Tuscans and Their Families*, Fig. 10.1.
4. On the late medieval shift in charitable giving to favour the deserving poor, see John Henderson, *Piety and Charity in Late Medieval Florence* (Oxford: Clarendon Press, 1994), 384.

Chapter 3

1. Figures based on Vittorio Fronza, 'Edilizia in Materiali Deperibili nell'alto medioevo Italiano: Metodologie e casi de studio per un'agenda della ricerca', *Post-Classical Archaeologies*, 1 (2011): Fig. 12; Paul Arthur, 'Edilizia Residenziale di età Medievale nell'Italia Meridionale: Alcune Evidenze Archeologiche', in *Edilizia Residenziale tra IX–X Secolo: Storia e Archeologia*, ed. Paola Galetti (Florence: Edizioni All'Insegna del Giglio, 2010), 18–21.

Chapter 4

1. I would like to thank Robin Fleming, Shannon McSheffrey, Helmut Puff and Kate Kelsey Staples for their help and advice.
2. For an Anglo-Saxon version see *Beowulf: A New Verse Translation*, trans. Seamus Heaney (NY: Norton, 2000), 169 (l. 2389).
3. For more on specialization of tools see Mark Gardiner, 'Implements and Utensils in *Gerefa* and the Organization of Seigneurial Farmsteads in the High Middle Ages', *Medieval Archaeology*, 50 (2006): 260–7.
4. Translation my own.

Chapter 5

1. The text has been modernized by Katherine French.
2. Especially Chapter 5.
3. For the argument that slavery died out, see Marc Bloch, 'How and Why Ancient Slavery Came to an End', in *Slavery and Serfdom in the Middle Ages: Selected Essays*, trans. William R. Beer (Berkeley: University of California Press, 1975), 1–31.

Chapter 6

1. For information on various gender conditions in medieval Europe, see Judith M. Bennett and Ruth M. Karras, *The Oxford Handbook of Women and Gender in Medieval Europe* (Oxford: Oxford University Press, 2013).
2. Cf. K. Schmidt Sabo, 'Genusrelationer i byar under medeltid. Med exempel från södra Skandinavien och England', in *Vem behöver en by? Kyrkheddinge, struktur och strategi under tusen år*, ed. K. Schmidt Sabo, Riksantikvarieämbetet arkeologiska undersökningar, skrifter (Lund: Riksantikvarieämbetet, 2005), 38.
3. E.g. M. Z. Rosaldo, 'Women, Culture and Society. Theoretical Overview', in *Woman, Culture and Society*, ed. M. Z. Rosaldo and L. Lamphere (Stanford: Stanford University Press, 1974), 17–42; L. Roubin, 'Male Space and Female Space Within the Provencal Community', in *Rural Society in France: Selections from the Annales*, ed. R. Forster and O. Ranum (Baltimore and London: Johns Hopkins University Press, 1977), 152–80. For discussion on private and public space in relation to gender see e.g. H. Moore, *Space, Text and Gender* (Cambridge: Cambridge University Press, 1986); S. R. Jones, 'Public and Private Space and Gender in Medieval Europe', in *The Oxford Handbook of Women and Gender in Medieval Europe*, 246–61.
4. Most studies using access analysis depart from the seminal study by W. Hillier and J. Hanson, *The Social Logic of Space* (Cambridge: Cambridge University Press, 1984).
5. See also R. Fellner, 'Intrasite Spatial Analysis of the Early Medieval Hamlet of Develier-Courtételle, Switzerland', *Medieval Archaeology*, 57 (2013): 183–97; C. Schmid, 'The Investigation of Domestic Space in Archaeology – Beyond Architecture', in *Dwellings, Identities and Homes: European Housing Culture from the Viking Age to the Renaissance*, ed. M. S. Kristiansen and K. Giles (Højberg: Jutland Archaeological Society, 2014), 53–67.
6. E.g. M. Colardelle and E. Verdel ''L'habitat immergé de Colletière à Charavines (Isère): Village ou chateau? Un example des difficultés de l'interpretation archéologique', *Château Gaillard: Studien zur mittelalterlichen Wehrbau- und Siedlungsforschung: European castle studies: études de castellologie européenne*, XIV (1990): 77–93.
7. Judging from the character of the houses and the artefact and ecofact materials, the castle was operated only during the summer half of the year. Only a bailiff with family stayed all year round at the castle.
8. E.g. J. Schofield and H. Steuer, 'Urban Settlement', in *The Archaeology of Medieval Europe*, Vol. 1, 111–53.

Chapter 7

1. A more recent edition by Ryan appeared in 2012, although without reference to the devil's interference in the story. *The Golden Legend: Readings on the Saints* (Princeton: Princeton University Press, 2012).
2. A theme explored at length by Jacques Derrida, *Of Hospitality* (Stanford: Stanford University Press, 2000).

3. See linguist Anatoly Lieberman's post on the origins of guest and host at *The Oxford Etymologist* http://blog.oup.com/2013/02/guest-host-word-origin-etymology/.
4. As I write this, I am partaking of the same Benedictine hospitality at St. John's Abbey guesthouse, in Collegeville, Minnesota. Fifteen hundred years later, the text and the tradition it initiated still holds firm.
5. See also 'The Reception of Guests', 51.
6. For example, the *gistum, albergamentum* and *droite de gite*. Rights of hospitality could be transferred as 'Brescia in the later twelfth century acquired two-thirds of the Counts of Lomello's lordship at Buzzolano, including rights of hospitality, and a whole complex of attached seigneurial dues.' D. P. Waley and T. Dean, *The Italian City-Republics* (Abingdon: Routledge, 2010), 70.
7. Caroline Walker Bynum's classic *Holy Feast, Holy Fast: The Religious Significance of Food to Medieval Women* (Berkeley: University of California Press, 1988) generated a massive subsequent literature on gender, nourishment and spirituality in the Middle Ages.
8. The intersection of hospitality and crusading activity is a particularly interesting site, given the explicit fusion of spiritual and political ideals, and the dynamic (and rapidly shifting) constellation of local perspectives on hosts, strangers, guests and hostilities.
9. Quoted and discussed in C. Sparks, *Heresy, Inquisition, and Life Cycle in Medieval Languedoc* (Woodbridge: York Medieval Press, 2014), 111.
10. Dante, *Inferno*, Canto XXXII (lines 133–4), 179; Canto XXXIII (1–3, 179).

Chapter 8

1. Elizheva Baumgarten's portoin of this article was supported by funding from the European Research Council (ERC) under the Union's Horizon 2020 research and innovation programme, grant agreement No. 681507, 'Beyond the Elite: Jewish Daily Life in Medieval Europe'.
2. For a brief overview of Jewish demography in medieval Europe see K. R. Stow, *Alienated Minority. The Jews of Medieval Latin Europe* (Cambridge, MA: Harvard University Press, 1992), 6–8; R. Chazan, *The Jews of Medieval Western Christendom* (Cambridge: Cambridge University Press, 2007), 124–6.
3. The volumes of *Germania Judaica* I and II (Tübingen: J. C. B. Mohr, 1963 and 1968) and Henri Gross *Gallia Judaica*, ed. S. Schwarzfuchs (Paris: Peeters, 2011) list the known communal institutions in every documented community.
4. *Sefer Hasidim* (hereafter *SHP*) #510 mentions synagogue in a private home but also suggests that most were in public buildings. See also *SHP* #535–43, 862, 1353.
5. I. G. Marcus, *Rituals of Childhood. Jewish Acculturation in Medieval Europe* (New Haven: Yale University Press, 1996); E. Kanarfogel, *Jewish Education and Society in the High Middle Ages* (Detroit: Wayne State University Press, 1992), 19–32 both overlook the question of how these basics were learned. I suggest it was done at home as commentaries on the Talmud refer to the teaching of prayers as a domestic chore which women often performed, see Rashi, BT Brakhot 20a, s.v. 'Ketanim' and Tosafot, BT Brakhot 20a, s.v. 'Ketanim peturin mekriyat shma'; Abraham b.

Ephraim, *Kitzur Sefer Mitzvot Gadol*, ed. Yohoshua Horowitz (Jerusalem: Mekize Nirdamim, 2005), #7.

6. About Dulcia see A. M. Haberman, *Sefer Gezerot Ashkenaz veTzarfat* (Jerusalem: Sifrei Tarshish, 1945), 167–8. For a discussion of women's education see J. R. Baskin, 'Some Parallels in the Education of Medieval Jewish and Christian Women', *Jewish History*, 5 (2) (1991): 41–52; Grossman, *Pious and Rebellious*, 162–5.
7. See also Isaac of Corbeil, *Sefer amudei golah hanikra Semak* (Capost, 1880, repr. Jerusalem, 1979), #8.
8. I thank Debra Kaplan for sharing her paper with me.
9. This example has been frequently discussed; see E. Baumgarten, 'A Separate People'? Some Directions for Comparative Research on Medieval Women', *Journal of Medieval History*, 34 (2) (2008): 9. For a Christian perspective see J. H. M. Smith, 'Portable Christianity: Relics in the Medieval West (c. 700–1200)', *Proceedings of the British Academy*, 181 (2012): 143–5.
10. These are evident in manuscript illuminations and also noted in sources. Abrahams, *Jewish Life*, 156–64; J. Shatzmiller, *Cultural Exchange* (Princeton: Princeton University Press, 2013), 18–20, 25–37; Kanarfogel, 'Image of Christians', 156–7.
11. According to clothing (*begadim*) in the index.
12. For mezuzot see E. R. Horowitz, 'The Way We Were: Jewish Life in the Middle Ages', *Jewish History*, 1 (1986): 77–9.
13. Malachi Beit-Arié has authored an analysis of Hebrew codicology currently available only online, *Hebrew Codicology: Historical and Comparative Typology of Hebrew Medieval Codices based on the Documentation of the Extant Dated Manuscripts from a Quantitative Approach*. See Chapter 2. http://web.nli.org.il/sites/NLI/Hebrew/collections/manuscripts/hebrewcodicology/Pages/default2.aspx.
14. I thank Malachi Beit-Arié for sharing his finding with me. See also M. Riegler and J. R. Baskin, '"May the Writer be Strong": Medieval Hebrew Manuscripts Copied by and for Women', *Nashim*, 16 (2008): 16–23.
15. SHP repeatedly tackles this subject. See 1633a, 442, 447.
16. And compare Tosafot, BT s.v. 'Vekol sheken beshitrei hedyotot', BT Shabbat 116b.
17. These laws developed from late antiquity. The study of their medieval modifications is still a desideratum. See R. Bonfil, 'Cultural and Religious Traditions in Ninth Century French Jewry', *Binah*, 3 (1994): 1–17; and more recently H. Soloveitchik, 'Agobard of Lyons, Megillat Ahima'ats and the Babylonian Orientation of Early Ashkenaz', *Collected Essays*, vol. 2, 5–22.
18. See for example the illumination of the Seder, BNF, MS héb.Paris, 1333, fol. 20b.
19. Eric Zimmer spoke on this topic at the World Congress in Jerusalem, 2013. My thanks to him for sharing a draft with me.
20. See also Gilchrist, *Medieval Life*, 140–1.
21. This ritual is described in Simhah of Vitry, *Mahzor Vitry*, ed. S. Horowitz (Nürnburg: Itzkawski Press, 1898), #507. Early modern sources recount it in great detail. See Deutsch, *Judaism in Christian Eyes*, 148–60.
22. The Kaddish recited by mourners was a novelty in medieval Ashkenaz. D. I. Shyovitz, '"You Have Saved Me from the Judgment of Gehenna": The Origins of the Mourner's Kaddish in Medieval Ashkenaz', *AJS Review*, 39 (1) (2015): 49–73.

BIBLIOGRAPHY

Primary sources

Archives

Bergamo, Biblioteca Civica. 'Angelo Mai'. Pergamene della Misericordia Maggiore, #420, 14 February 1316.
London, The National Archives (TNA). Prob2; Prob11
London, The Metropolitan Archives (LMA). DL/C/B/004/Ms9171.
Munich, Bayerische Staatsbibliothek, Clm 4435.
Oslo, Museum of Cultural History, Oseberg Exhibition [https://www.khm.uio.no/english/visit-us/viking-ship-museum/exhibitions/oseberg/ (accessed 20 July 2016)].
Oxford, Bodleian Library, Mich. 9 (1531): Amulets.
Vienna, MAK, H1705/1935.

Published primary sources

Abelard, Peter, and Heloise (2003), *The Letters of Abelard and Heloise*, ed. M. T. Clanchy, trans. B. Radice, New York: Penguin Books.
Abraham b. Ephraim (2005), *Kitzur Sefer Mitzvot Gadol*, ed. Y. Horowitz, Jerusalem: Mekize Nirdamim.
Abrahams, I., ed. (1926), *Hebrew Ethical Wills*, vol. 2, Philadelphia: Jewish Publication Society.
Alberti, Leon Battista (1969), *The Family in Renaissance Florence*, trans. R. N. Watkins, Columbia: University of South Carolina Press.
Albertus Magnus (1967), *Book of Minerals*, trans. Dorothy Wyckoff, Oxford: Oxford University Press.
Alighieri, Dante (1994), *The Inferno of Dante: A New Verse Translation*, trans. R. Pinsky and N. Pinsky, New York: Farrar, Straus and Giroux.
Amt, E., ed. (2013), *Women's Lives in Medieval Europe: A Sourcebook*, New York/London: Routledge.
Armitage, S., ed. and trans. (2007), *Sir Gawain and the Green Knight: A New Verse Translation*, New York: W.W. Norton.

Benedict of Nursia (1998), *The Rule of St. Benedict*, ed. and trans. T. Fry, New York: Vintage Books.
Boccaccio, Giovanni (1972), *The Decameron*, trans. G. H. McWilliam, New York: Penguin Books.
Bornstein, D., ed. and trans. (2000), *Life and Death in a Venetian Convent: the Chronicle and Necrology of Corpus Domini, 1395–1436*, Chicago: University of Chicago Press.
Catherine of Siena (1980), *The Dialogue*, ed. S. Noffke, New York: Paulist Press.
Cosmas of Prague (2009), *The Chronicle of the Czechs*, ed. and trans. Lisa Wolverton, Washington, DC: The Catholic University of America Press.
Chrétien de Troyes (1991), 'Erec and Enide', in W. Kibler and C. W. Carroll (eds), *Arthurian Romances*. New York: Penguin Books.
Chrétien de Troyes (2000), *Erec and Enide*, trans. R. H. Cline, Athens: University of Georgia Press.
Congdon, E., trans. (2009), 'Milk Parents, 1395', in K. Jansen, J. Drell, and F. Andrews (eds), *Medieval Italy: Texts in Translation*, 443–4, Philadelphia: University of Pennsylvania Press.
Cosmas of Prague (2008), *Chronicle of the Czechs*, trans. L. Wolverton, DC: Catholic University of America Press.
Datini, Margherita (2012), *Letters to Francesco Datini (1360–1423)*, trans. C. J. and A. Pagliaro, Toronto: Centre for Reformation and Renaissance Studies.
Dhuoda (1998), *Liber Manualis: Handbook for Her Warrior Son*, ed. and trans. M. Thiébaux, Cambridge: Cambridge University Press.
Dobson, R. B., ed. (1983), 'The Rebels in London According to the "Anonimalle Chronicle"', in *The Peasants' Revolt of 1381*, 2nd ed., 155–68, London: Macmillan.
Drew, K. F., ed. and trans. (1990), *The Laws of the Salian Franks*, Philadelphia: University of Pennsylvania Press.
Dubin, Nathaniel E., ed. (2013), *The Fabliaux*, New York: W.W. Norton.
Einhard (1998), *Charlemagne's Courtier: The Complete Einhard*, ed. and trans. P. E. Dutton, Toronto, Ontario: University of Toronto Press.
Eleazar b. Judah (1960), *Sefer Rokeah*, Jerusalem: S. Weinfled.
Eleazar b. Judah (2014), *Teshuvot Rabbenu Eleazar meWormeisa haRokeah*, ed. J. Y. Stahl, Jerusalem: Stah.
Evans, J. and M. S. Serjeanton, eds. (1933), *English Mediaeval Lapidaries*, Early English Text Society, vol. 190, London: Oxford University Press.
Furnivall, F. J., ed. (1868), 'How the Wise Man Taught his Son', in *The Babees Book*, 48–53, Early English Text Society, original series, vol. 32.
Galbert of Bruges (1982), *The Murder of Charles the Good*, ed. and trans. J. B. Ross, Toronto: University of Toronto Press.
de Garlande, John (1981), *Dictionarius*, ed. and trans. B. B. Rubin, Lawrence, KS: Coronado Press.
Geary, P., ed. (2016), *Readings in Medieval History*, Toronto: University of Toronto Press.
Greco, G. L. and C. M. Rose, eds. (2009), *The Good Wife's Guide (Le Ménagier de Paris): A Medieval Household Book*, Ithaca, NY: Cornell University Press.
Gui, Bernard (2006), *The Inquisitor's Guide: A Medieval Manual on Heretics*, ed. and trans. J. Shirley, Garden City, NJ: Ravenhall Books.
Hahn, T., ed. and trans. (1995), *Sir Gawain: Eleven Romances and Tales*, Kalamazoo: Western Michigan University.
Heaney, S., trans. (2001), *Beowulf: A New Verse Translation*, New York: Farrar, Straus and Giroux.

Hector, L. C. and B. F. Harvey, eds. (1982), *The Westminster Chronicle*, Oxford: Oxford University Press.
Hildegard of Bingen (1998), *The Letters of Hildegard of Bingen*, vol. 1, ed. and trans. R. K. Ehrman and J. L. Baird, New York: Oxford University Press.
Isaac of Corbeil (1880/1979), *Sefer Amudei Golah haNikra Semak*. Capost:, repr. Jerusalem.
Jerome, *Letters* http://www.newadvent.org/fathers/3001.htm.
de Joinville, Jean (2008), 'The Life of St Louis', in *Chronicles of the Crusades*, trans. Caroline Smith, 137–336. New York: Penguin.
Jonah of Gerondi (1990), *Iggeret HaTeshuvah*, Bnei Brak: Sifsei Chachamim.
Judah, b. Samuel (1924), *Sefer Hasidim*, ed. J. Wistenetzky, Frankfurt: Mekize Nirdamim.
Kempe, Margery (2015), *The Book of Margery Kempe*, trans. A. Bale, Oxford: Oxford University Press.
Kempe, Margery (2000), *The Book of Margery Kempe*, trans. B. Windeatt, New York: Penguin Classics.
Kristjansdottir, B. S., ed. (2008), *The Saga of the People of Laxardal and Bolli Bollason's Tale*, trans. K. Kunz, London: Penguin Classics.
Lamond, Elizabeth, ed. (1890), *Walter of Henley's Husbandry, Together with an Anonymous Husbandry, Seneschaucie, and Robert Grosseteste's Rules*, New York: Longmans.
La Tour Landry, Geoffroy de (1868), *The Book of the Knight of La Tour-Dandry*, ed. T. Wright, London: Kegan Paul, Trench, Trübner.
Liuzza, R. M., trans. (2000), *Beowulf*, Peterborough: Broadview.
Macchiavello, S., ed. (2000), *Liber Iurium Ecclesiae, Comunitatis, Statutorum Recii. Fonti per la Storia della Liguria XIV*, Genova: Assessorato della Cultura.
Machiavelli, Niccolò (1981), *Mandragola*, trans. M.J. Flaumenhaft, Prospect Heights, IL: Waveland Press Inc.
Marie de France (1999), *The Lais of Maried de France*, ed. and trans. Glyn Burgess, New York: Penguin.
McSheffrey, S., ed. and trans. (1999), *Love and Marriage in Late Medieval London*, Kalamazoo, MI: Medieval Institute Publications.
Murray, J., ed. (2001), *Love, Marriage, and Family in the Middle Ages: A Reader*, Toronto: Broadview Press.
Oden, Thomas, ed. (2007), *The Good Works Reader*. Grand Rapids, MI: William B. Erdmans Publishing.
Ralph of Caen (2005), *The 'Gesta Tancredi' of Ralph of Caen: A History of the Normans on the First Crusade*, ed. B. Bacharach and D. Bacharach, Burlington, VT: Ashgate.
Rickert, E., ed. (1966), 'Book of Courtesy', in *The Babees' Book: Medieval Manners for the Young, Done into Modern English from Dr. Furnivall's Texts*, 79–121, New York: Cooper Square Publishers.
Rowland, B., trans. (1981), *Medieval Women's Guide to Health: The First English Gynecological Handbook*, Kent State University Press.
Saccomani, A. Rossi, ed. (2000), *Le Carte dei Lebbrosi a Verona tra XII e XIII Secolo*, Padova: Antenore.
Savage, Anne, ed. (1991), *Anchoritic Spirituality: Ancrene Wisse and Associated Works*, New York: Paulist Press.
Schammes, Jousep (Juspa) (1992), *Wormser Minhagbuch*, ed. S. Hamburger *et al.*, Jerusalem: Machon Yerushalayim.
Shimshon b. Tzadok (1858), *SeferTashbetz Katan*, Lemberg.

Shuffleton, G., ed. (2008), '"How the Good Wife Taught Her Daughter", from: Codex Ashmole 61: A Compilation of Popular Middle English Verse', in *Robbins Library Digital Projects*, http://d.lib.rochester.edu/teams/text/shuffelton-codex-ashmole-61-how-the-good-wife-taught-her-daughter.
Simhah of Vitry (1898), *Mahzor Vitry*, ed. S. Horowitz, Nürnburg, Itzkawski Press.
Stahl, Jacob Yisrael, ed. (2007) *Sefer ha-kushiyot*. Jerusalem: Stahl.
Strozzi, Alessandra (1997), *Selected Letters of Alessandra Strozzi*, ed. and trans. H. Gregory, Berkeley: University of California Press.
Talbot, C. H., ed. and trans. (1987), *Life of Christina of Markyate*, reprint, Toronto: University of Toronto Press.
Terry, P., ed. and trans. (1969), *Poems of the Vikings: The Elder Edda*, Indianapolis, IN: Bobbs-Merrill.
Thietmar of Merseburg (2001), *Ottonian Germany: The Chronicon of Thietmar of Merseburg*, ed. D. A. Warner, Manchester: Manchester University Press.
Thomas of Walsingham (1874), *Chronicon Angliae*, ed. E. M. Thompson, London: Rolls Series.
Thorndike, L. ed. (1944), *University Records and Life in the Middle Ages*, New York: Columbia University Press.
von Jeroschen, Nicolaus (2010), *The Chronicle of Prussia: a History of the Teutonic Knights in Prussia, 1190–1331*, ed. and trans. M. Fisher, Burlington, VT: Ashgate.
de Voragine, Jacobus (1969), *The Golden Legend*, ed. and trans. W. G. Ryan, New York: Arno Press.
de Voragine, Jacobus (1993), *The Golden Legend*, ed. and trans. W. G. Ryan, Princeton University Press.
Wilson, David M., ed. (2004), *The Bayeux Tapestry*. London: Thames and Hudson.
Weaver, F. W., ed. (1903), *Somerset Medieval Wills*, vol. 2. Somerset Record Society, vol. 19. Taunton: Somerset Record Society.
Wright, David, trans. (1957), *Beowulf*. Baltimore, MD: Penguin Classics.
Wright, T. and J. O. Haliwell, eds. (1841–3), *Reliquiae Antiquae. Scraps From Ancient Manuscripts, Illustrating Chiefly Early English Literature and the English Language*, 2 vols., London: William Pickering.

Secondary sources

Abrahams, I. (1932), *Jewish Life in the Middle Ages*, London: Edward Goldston.
Allison, P. M. (1998), 'The Household in Historical Archaeology', *Australasian Historical Archaeology*, 16: 16–29.
Amenós, L. (2015), 'Inventory of Arab Objects Documented in Catalan Medieval Houses', in F. Sabaté (ed.), *Medieval Urban Identity*, 24–67, Newcastle upon Tyne: Cambridge Scholars Publishing.
Amundsen, C., J. Henriksen, E. Myrvill, B. Olsen, and P. Urbanczyk (2003), 'Crossing Borders: Multi-Room Houses and Inter-Ethnic Contexts in Europe's Extreme North', *Fennoscandia Archaeologica*, 20: 79–100.
Andersson, S. and E. Svensson, eds. (2002), *Skramle: The True Story of a Deserted Medieval Farmstead*, Stockholm: Almkvist & Wiksell International.
Andrén, A. (1998), *Between Artifacts and Texts: Historical Archaeology in Global Perspective*, New York: Plenum Press.
Antipov I. and D. Yakovlev (2015), 'The Faceted Palace in Novgorod the Great as part of the Archbishop's Residence', in A. Andrzejewski (ed.), *Castella Maris Baltici XIII: Castle as Residence*, 107–15, Łódź: Institute of Archaeology, University of Łódź.

Appel, K. K. (2012), 'Portrayals of Women with Books: Female (Il)literacy in Medieval Jewish Culture', in T. Martin (ed.), *Reassessing the Roles of Women as "Makers" of Medieval Art and Architecture*, 525–63, Leiden and Boston: Brill.

Archer, J. (1995), 'Working Women in Thirteenth-Century Paris', PhD diss., University of Arizona, Tuscon, USA.

Arnade, P., M. Howell, and W. Simons (2002), 'Fertile Spaces: The Productivity of Urban Space in Northern Europe', *Journal of Interdisciplinary History*, 32 (4): 515–48.

Arthur, P. (2010), 'Edilizia Residenziale di età Medievale nell'Italia Meridionale: Alcune Evidenze Archeologiche', in P. Galetti (ed.), *Edilizia Residenziale tra IX–X Secolo: Storia e Archeologia*, 17–44, Florence: Edizioni All'Insegna del Giglio.

Ashley, K., and R. L. A. Clark, eds. (2001), *Medieval Conduct*. Minneapolis & London: University of Minnesota Press.

Baert, B. (2013), 'The Johannesschüssel as Andachtsbilt: The Gaze the Medium and the Senses', in B. Baert, A. Traninger, and C. Santing (eds.), *Disembodied Heads in Medieval and Early Modern Culture*, 117–60, Leiden: Brill.

Baker, P. S. (2013), *Honour, Exchange and Violence in Beowulf*, Boydell and Brewer.

Barber, B., C. Thomas, and B. Wilson (2013), *Religion in Medieval London: Archaeology and Belief*, London: Museum of London Archaeology.

Barkai, R. (2001), 'A Medieval Hebrew Text on the Death of Children', in M. Eliav-Feldom and Y. Hen (eds.), *Women, Children and the Elderly*, 67–84, Jerusalem: Merkaz Shazar.

Barthélemy, D. and P. Contamine (1988), 'The Use of Private Space', in G. Duby (ed.), *A History of Private Life: Revelation of the Medieval World*, 395–505, Cambridge, MA: Harvard University Press.

Bartlett, R. (1993), *The Making of Europe: Conquest, Colonization and Cultural Change 950–1350*, Harmondsworth: Penguin Press.

Baskin, J. R. (2007), 'Male Piety, Female Bodies: Men, Women and Ritual Immersion in Medieval Ashkenaz', *Jewish Law Association Studies*, 17: 11–30.

Baskin, J. R. (1991), 'Some Parallels in the Education of Medieval Jewish and Christian Women', *Jewish History*, 5 (2): 41–52.

Batt, M. (2008), 'La Maison Paysanne du Moyen-Age en Bretagne: Apport de l'Archéologie et Comparaisons avec le Sud-Ouest de l'Angleterre et le Pays de Galles', in N.-Y. Tonnerre (ed.), *La Maison Paysanne en Bretagne*, 68–77, Quimper: Coop-Breizh.

Baumgarten, E. (2008), '"A Separate People?" Some Directions for Comparative Research on Medieval Women'. *Journal of Medieval History* 34 (2): 212–28.

Baumgarten, E. (2000), 'Thus Say the Wise Midwives', *Zion* 75 (1): 67–74.

Baumgarten, E. (2008), 'Women's Rituals: The Sabbath of the Parturient in its Early Modern Cultural Context', in G. Bacon et al. (eds.), *Studies on the History of the Jews of Ashkenaz: Festschrift in Honor of Professor Eric Zimmer*, 11–28, Bar Ilan University Press: Ramat Gan.

Baumgarten, E. (2004), *Mothers and Children: Jewish Family Life in Medieval Europe*, Princeton: Princeton University Press.

Baumgarten, E. (2014), *Practicing Piety in Medieval Ashkenaz: Men, Women and Every Day Religious Observance*, Philadelphia: University of Pennsylvania Press.

Bayless, M. (2012), *Sin and Filth in Medieval Culture: The Devil in the Latrine*, London: Routledge.

Bazzana, A. (2002), 'La maison rurale dans la péninsule ibérique: un atelier d'ethno-archéologie', in Jan Klápště (ed.), *Ruralia IV: 8–13 September 2001, Bad*

Bederkesa, Lower Saxony, Germany, The Rural House: From the Migration Period to the Oldest Still Standing Buildings, 216–31, Prague: Institute of Archaeology.

Bazzana, A. (2006), 'Espace Privé/Espace Public: Maisons, Ruelles et Jardins dans l'Habitat Andalou', in D. Alexandre-Bidon, F. Piponnier, and J.-M. Poisson (eds.), *Cadre de Vie et Manières d'Habiter (XIIe–XVIe Siècles)*, 293–306, Caen: CRAHM.

Bazzana, A. and N. Trauth (1997), 'L'Île de Saltés (Huelva): La ville Islamique, ventre d'une métallurgie de concentration au moyen âge', *Comptes Rendus des Séances de l'Académie des Inscriptions et Belles-Lettres*, 141 (1): 47–74.

Beattie, C. (2000), 'The Problem of Women's Work Identities in Post Black Death England', in J. Bothwell, P. J. P. Goldberg, and W. M. Ormrod (eds.), *The Problem of Labour in Fourteenth-Century England*, 1–19, Woodbridge: York Medieval Press.

Beit-Arié, M. (n.d.), *Hebrew Codicology: Historical and Comparative Typology of Hebrew Medieval Codices based on the Documentation of the Extant Dated Manuscripts from a Quantitative Approach*. http://web.nli.org.il/sites/NLI/Hebrew/collections/manuscripts/hebrewcodicology/Pages/default2.aspx

Belcredi, L. (2006), *Bystřec. O založení, životě a zániku středověké vsi*, Brno: Akademie ved České republiky Brno.

Belhoste, J.-F. (2000), 'Paris, grand centre drapier au Moyen Âge', *Mémoires de la Fédération des Sociétés historiques et archéologiques de Paris et de l'Île-de-France*, 51: 31–48.

Bell, R. (1999), *How to Do It: Guides to Good Living for Renaissance Italians*, Chicago: University of Chicago Press.

Bennett, J. M. (1996), *Ale, Beer, and Brewsters: Women's Work in a Changing World, 1300–1600*, New York: Oxford University Press.

Bennett, J. M. (2007), *History Matters: Patriarchy and the Challenge of Feminism*, Philadelphia: University of Pennsylvania Press.

Berenbaum, M. and F. Skolnik, eds. (2007), *Encyclopaedia Judaica*, 2nd ed. Detroit: Macmillan Reference USA.

Bianchi, G. (2012), 'Building, Inhabiting and "Perceiving" Private Houses in Early Medieval Italy', *Arqueología de la Arquitectura*, 9: 195–212.

Biller, P. (1994), 'The Cathars of Languedoc and Written Materials', in Peter Biller and Anne Hudson (eds.), *Heresy and Literacy, 1000–1530*, 61–82, Cambridge: Cambridge University Press.

Biow, D. (2006), *The Culture of Cleanliness in Renaissance Italy*, Ithaca, NY: Cornell University Press.

Bitel, L. (1990), *Isles of the Saints: Monastic Settlement and Christian Community in Early Ireland*, Ithaca, NY: Cornell University Press.

Bloch, M. (1975), 'How and Why Ancient Slavery Came to an End', in William R. Beer (trans.), *Slavery and Serfdom in the Middle Ages: Selected Essays*, 1–31, Berkeley: University of California Press.

Blumenthal, D. (2009), *Enemies and Familiars: Slavery and Mastery in Fifteenth-Century Valencia*, Ithaca, NY: Cornell University Press.

Bohak, G. (2008), *Ancient Jewish Magic: A History*, New York: Cambridge University Press.

Bohak, G. (2006), 'Catching a Thief: The Jewish Trials of a Christian Ordeal', *Jewish Studies Quarterly*, 13 (4): 344–62.

Bonfil, R. (1994), 'Cultural and Religious Traditions in Ninth Century French Jewry', *Binah*, 3: 1–17.

Borisov, B. D. (1999), "A Study of the Mediaeval House from the 11th–12th Centuries in South-Eastern Bulgaria". *Archaeologia Bulgarica* 3 (2): 83–92.

Boswell, J. (1989), *Kindness of Strangers*, New York: Pantheon.

Bourdieu, P. (1977), *Outline of a Theory of Practice*, trans. Richard Nice, Cambridge: Cambridge University Press.

Bourke, J. (1994), 'Housewifery in Working-Class England, 1860–1914', *Past and Present*, 143: 167–97.

Bouwmeester, J. (2014), 'The Development of Dutch Townhouses, 700–1300', in M. S. Kristiansen and K. Giles (eds.), *Dwelling, Identities and Homes: European Housing Culture from the Viking Ages to the Renaissance*, 243–53, Højbjerg: Jutland Archaeological Society.

Bove, B. (2014), *Dominer la ville: Prévôts des marchands et échevins parisiens de 1260 à 1350*, Paris: Editions du CTHS.

Boyd, R. (2015), 'Where are the Longhouses? Reviewing Ireland's Viking Age Buildings', in H. Clarke and R. Johnson (eds.), *The Vikings in Ireland and Beyond: Before and the After the Battle of Clontarf*, 325–45, Dublin: Four Courts Press.

Bruce-Mitford, R. (1997), *Mawgan Porth: a Settlement of the late Saxon Period on the North Cornish Coast: Excavations 1949–52, 1954, and 1974*, London: English Heritage.

Bruckner, M. T. (1980), *Narrative Invention in Twelfth-Century French Romance: The Convention of Hospitality, 1160–1200*. Lexington, KY: French Forum Publications.

Bruschi, C. (2009), *The Wandering Heretics of Languedoc*, Cambridge: Cambridge University Press.

Buko, A. (2010), 'Edilizia Residenziale in Europa Centro-Settentrionale (secoli IX–X)', in P. Galetti (ed.), *Edilizia Residenziale tra IX–X Secolo: Storia e Archeologia*, 199–221. Florence: Edizioni All'Insegna del Giglio.

Burr, D. (2001), *The Spiritual Franciscans: From Protest to Persecution in the Century after Saint Francis*, University Park: Pennsylvania State University Press.

Butler, J. (1993), *Bodies that Matter: On the Discursive Limits of "Sex"*, New York: Routledge.

Butler, S. M. (2013), *Divorce in Medieval England: From One to Two Persons in Law*, London: Routledge.

Bynum, C. W. (1987), *Holy Feast and Holy Fast: The Religious Significance of Food to Medieval Women*, Berkeley, University of California Press.

Calkins, R. G. (1995), 'Secular Objects and Their Implications in Early Netherlandish Painting', in C. G. Fisher and K. L. Scott (eds.), *Art into Life: Collected Paper from the Kresge Art Museum Medieval Symposia*, 183–208, East Lansing: Michigan State University.

Carver, M. (1979), 'Three Saxo-Norman Tenements in Durham City', *Medieval Archaeology*, 23: 1–80.

Carver, M. and J. Klápště, eds. (2011), *The Archaeology of Medieval Europe, vol. 2: Twelfth to Sixteenth Centuries*. Aarhus: Aarhus University Press.

Carver, M., J. Barrett, J. Downes, and J. Hooper (2012), 'Pictish Byre-Houses at Pitcarmick and their Landscape: Investigations 1993–5', *Proceedings of the Society of Antiquaries of Scotland*, 142: 145–99.

Catafau, A. and O. Passarrius (2007), 'La Restructuration du Peuplement aux Xe–XIe Siècles en Roussillon', *Domitia* 8: 89–120.

Caviness, M. (2009), 'Anglo-Saxon Women, Norman Knights and a "Third Sex" in the Bayeux Embroidery', in M. Foys *et al.* (eds.), *The Bayeux Tapestry: New Interpretations*, 85–118, Woodbridge: Boydell Press.

Chabot, I. (1988), 'Widowhood and Poverty in Late Medieval Florence', *Continuity and Change*, 3 (2): 291–311.
Chapelot, J. and R. Fossier (1980), *Le Village et la Maison au Moyen Age*, Paris: Hachette.
Chazan, R. (2007), *The Jews of Medieval Western Christendom*, Cambridge: Cambridge University Press.
Chojnacka, M. (2001), *Working Women of Early Modern Venice*, Baltimore: The Johns Hopkins University Press.
Chojnacki, S. (2000), 'Dowries and Kinsmen in Early Renaissance Venice', in S. Chojnacki (ed.), *Women and Men in Renaissance Venice: Twelve Essays on Patrician Society*, 132–53, Baltimore: The Johns Hopkins University Press.
Christoph, S. (2010), 'Hospitality and Status: Social Intercourse in Middle High German Arthurian Romance and Courtly Narrative', *Arthuriana*, 20 (3): 45–64.
Christophersen, A. (1990), 'Dwelling Houses, Workshops and Storehouses. Functional Aspects of the Development of Wooden Urban Buildings in Trondheim from c. AD 1000 to AD 1400', *Acta Archaeologica*, 60: 101–29.
Clark, A. ([1919] 1982), *Working Life of Women in the Seventeenth Century*, London: Routledge.
Clarke, D. (2000), 'The Shop Within? An Analysis of the Architectural Evidence for Medieval Shops', *Architectural* History, 43: 58–87.
Clarke, H., S. Pearson, M. Mate, and K. Parfitt (2010), *Sandwich: The 'Completest Medieval Town in England*, Oxford: Oxbow Books.
Cohn, S. K. (1980), *The Laboring Classes in Renaissance Florence*, New York: Academic Press.
Cohn, Y. B. (2008), *Tangled Up in Text: Tefillin and the Ancient World*, Providence: Brown Judaic Studies.
Colardelle, M. and E. Verdel (1990), 'L'habitat immergé de Colletière à Charavines (Isère): Village ou chateau? Un example des difficultués de l'interpretation archéologique', *Château Gaillard: Studien zur mittelalterlichen Wehrbau- und Siedlungsforschung: European castle studies: études de castellologie européenne*, 14:77–93.
Coleman, E. (1971), 'Medieval Marriage Characteristics: A Neglected Factor in the History of Medieval Serfdom', *The Journal of Interdisciplinary History*, 2 (2): 205–19.
Cooper, D. (2006), 'Devotion', in Marta Ajmar-Wollheim and Flora Dennis (eds), *At Home in Renaissance Italy*, 190–203, London: Victoria and Albert Museum.
Corbellini, S. and M. Hoogvliet (2013), 'Artisans and Religious Reading in Late Medieval Italy and Northern France (C. 1400–1520)', *Journal of Medieval and Early Modern Studies*, 43 (3): 521–44.
Cossar, R. (2017), *Clerical Households in Late Medieval Italy*, Cambridge, MA: Harvard University Press.
Cowan, A. (2011), 'Seeing is Believing: Urban Gossip and the Balcony in Early Modern Venice', *Gender and History*, 23 (3): 727.
Croix, S. (2012), 'Work and Space in Rural Settlements in Viking-Age Scandinavia: Gender Perspectives', PhD diss., Aarhus University, Denmark.
Croix, S. (2014), 'Houses and Households in Viking Age Scandinavia: Some Case Studies', in M. S. Kristiansen and K. Giles (eds.), *Dwellings, Identities and Homes: European Housing Culture From the Viking Age to the Renaissance*, 113–26, Højberg: Jutland Archaeological Society.
Croom, A.T. (2007), *Roman Furniture*. Stroud: Tempus.

Cvijanović, I. (2013), 'The Typology of Early Medieval Settlements in Bohemia, Poland and Russia', in Srđan Rudić (ed.), *The World of The Slavs: Studies on the East, West and South Slavs: Civitas, Oppidas, Villas and Archeological Evidence (7th to 11th Centuries AD)*, 289–344, Belgrade: The Institute of History.

Dale, M. K. (1933), 'The London Silkwomen of the Fifteenth Century', in *The Economic History Review*, 4 (4): 324–35.

Daniell, C. (1997), *Death and Burial in Medieval England, 1066–1550*, London: Routledge.

De Moor, T. and J. L. Van Zanden (2010), 'Girl Power: the European Marriage Pattern and Labour Markets in the North Sea Region in the Late Medieval and Early Modern Period', *Economic History Review*, 63:1: 1–33.

De Roover, F. E. (1950), 'Lucchese Silks', *Ciba Review*, 80: 2902–30.

Deane, J. K. (2013), 'Pious Domesticities', in Judith M. Bennett and Ruth Mazo Karras (eds.), *The Oxford Handbook of Women and Gender in Medieval Europe*, 262–78, Oxford: Oxford University Press.

Deane, J. K. (2014), 'Würzburg Beguines and the Vienne Decrees: Case Studies and Comparative Models of German Beguine History', in L. Böhringer, J. K. Deane, and H. van Engen (eds.), *Labels and Libels: Naming Beguines in Northern Medieval Europe*, 53–82, Turnhout: Brepols.

Debonne, V. (2014), 'Brick Production and Brick Building in Medieval Flanders', in T. Ratiainen, R. Bernotas, and C. Herrman (eds.), *Fresh Approaches to Brick Production and Use in the Middle Ages*, 27–38, Oxford: Archaeopress.

Deets, J. (1996), *In Small Things Forgotten: An Archaeology of Early American Life*, New York: Anchor Books.

Derrida, J. (2000), *Of Hospitality*, Stanford: Stanford University Press.

Deutsch, Y. (2012), *Judaism in Christian Eyes: Ethnographic Descriptions of Jews and Judaism in Early Modern Germany*, Oxford: Oxford University Press.

Dillard, H. (1989), *Daughters of the Reconquest: Women in Castilian Town Society, 1100–1300*, Cambridge: Cambridge University Press.

Donahue, Jr. C. (2007), *Law, Marriage, and Society in the Later Middle Ages*, Cambridge: Cambridge University Press.

Donat, P. (1980), *Haus, Hof und Dorf in Mitteleuropa vom 7. bis 12. Jahrhundert: Archäologische Beiträge zur Entwicklung und Struktur der Bäuerlichen Siedlung*, Berlin: Akademie Verlag.

Drell, J. H. (2013), 'Aristocratic Economies: Women and Family', in J. M. Bennett and R. M. Karras (eds.), *The Oxford Handbook of Women and Gender in Medieval Europe*, 327–42, Oxford: Oxford University Press.

du Cange, C., *et al.* (1883–7), *Glossarium Mediae et Infimae Latinitatis*, éd. augm., Niort: L. Favre.

Duby, G. (1988), 'Preface', in G. Duby (ed.) and A. Goldhammer (trans.), *A History of Private Life: Revelations in the Medieval World*, ix–xii, Cambridge, MA: Harvard University Press.

Duby, G., D. Barthélemy, and C. de la Roncière (1988), 'Portraits: The Aristocratic Households of Medieval France', in G. Duby (ed.) and A. Goldhammer (trans.), *A History of Private Life: Revelation of the Medieval World.*, 35–155, Cambridge, MA: Harvard University Press.

Duffy, E. (2006), *Marking the Hours: English People and their Prayers*, New Haven: Yale University Press.

Dyer, C. (1989), *Standards of Living in the Later Middle Ages: Social Change in England, c. 1200–1520*, Cambridge: Cambridge University Press.

Eames, P. (1971), 'Documentary Evidence Concerning the Character and Use of Domestic Furnishings in England in the Fourteenth and Fifteenth Centuries', *Furniture History*, 7: 41–60.

Eames, P. (1977), *Mediaeval Furniture: England, France, and the Netherlands from the Twelfth to the Fifteenth Century*, London: Furniture History.

Eames, P. (1977), 'The Making of a Hung Celour', *Furniture History*, 33: 35–42.

Edwards, N. (1997), 'Landscape and Settlement in Medieval Wales: An Introduction', in N. Edwards (ed.), *Landscape and Settlement in Medieval Wales*, 1–11, Oxford: Oxbow Books.

Einbinder, S. (2009), *No Place of Rest: Jewish Literature, Expulsion, and the Memory of Medieval France*, Philadelphia: University of Pennsylvania.

Einbinder, S. (2002), *Beautiful Death: Jewish Poetry and Martyrdom in Medieval France*, Princeton: Princeton University Press.

Elbogen, I. (1993), *Jewish Liturgy: A Comprehensive History*, trans. Raymond P. Scheindlin, Philadelphia, Jerusalem, New York: Jewish Publication Society and JTS.

Emanuelsson, M., A. Johansson, S. Nilsson, S. Pettersson and E. Svensson, eds. (2003), *Settlement, Shieling and Landscape: The Local History of a Forest Hamlet*, Stockholm: Almqvist & Wiksell International.

Emery, A. (2005), 'Late-Medieval Houses as Expressions of Social Status', *Historical Research*, 78 (200): 140–60.

Epstein, S. A. (1991), *Wage Labor and Guilds in Medieval Europe*. Chapel Hill, NC: University of North Carolina Press.

Erler, M. C. (2008), 'Home Visits: Mary, Elizabeth, Margery Kempe and the Feast of the Visitation', in M. Kowaleski and P. J. P. Goldberg (eds.), *Medieval Domesticity: Home, Housing, and Household in Medieval England*, 259–76, Cambridge: Cambridge University Press.

Farmer, S. (1998), 'Down and Out and Female in Thirteenth-Century Paris', *American Historical Review*, 103 (2): 345–72.

Farmer, S. (1999), '"It Is Not Good That [Wo]man Should Be Alone": Elite Responses to Singlewomen in Paris', in J. M. Bennett and A. M. Froide (eds.), *Singlewomen in the European Past, 1250–1800*, 82–105, Philadelphia: University of Pennsylvania Press.

Farmer, S. (2002), *Surviving Poverty in Medieval Paris: Gender, Ideology, and the Daily Lives of the Poor*, Ithaca, NY: Cornell University Press.

Farmer, S. (2010), 'Merchant Women and the Administrative Glass Ceiling in Thirteenth-Century Paris', in T. Earenfight (ed.), *Women and Wealth in Late Medieval Europe*, 89–108, New York: Palgrave Macmillan.

Farmer, S. (2014), 'Medieval Paris and the Mediterranean: The Evidence from the Silk Industry', *French Historical Studies*, 37: 383–419.

Fellner, R. (2013), 'Intrasite Spatial Analysis of the Early Medieval Hamlet of Develier-Courtételle, Switzerland', *Medieval Archaeology*, 57: 183–97.

Fleming, R. (2007), 'Acquiring, Flaunting, and Destroying Silk in Anglo-Saxon England', *Early Medieval Europe*, 15 (2): 127–58.

Fleming, R. (2010), *Britain After Rome: The Fall and Rise, 400–1070*, London: Penguin.

Fraiman, S. N. (2013), 'The Sabbath Lamp: Development of the Implements and Customs for Lighting the Sabbath lights among the Jews of Ashkenaz', PhD diss., Hebrew University, Jersalem, Israel.

Frances, C. (2005), 'Making Marriages in Early Modern England: Rethinking the Role of Family and Friends', in M. Ågren and A. L. Erickson (eds.), *The Marital Economy in Scandinavia and Britain, 1400–1900*, 39–56, Aldershot: Ashgate.

Frappier-Bigras, D. (1989), 'La *famille dans l'artisanat parisien* du XIIIe siècle', *Le moyen âge*, 95: 47–74.

French, K. L. (2007), *The Good Women of the Parish: Gender and Religion After the Black Death*, Philadelphia: University of Pennsylvania Press.

French, K. L. (2014), 'Nouveaux Arts de la table et convivialitiés sexuées (Angleterre, fin de l'epoque médiévale)', *Clio*, 40 (1): 45–67.

French, K. L. (2016), 'The Material Culture of Childbirth in Late Medieval London and its Suburbs', *Journal of Women's History*, 28 (2): 126–48.

French, K., K. Smith, and S. Stanbury (2016), '"An Honest Bed": The Scene of Life and Death in Late Medieval England', *Fragments: Interdisciplinary Approaches to the Study of Ancient and Medieval Pasts*, 5: 61–95.

Friedenreich, D. (2011), *Foreigners and Their Food: Constructing Otherness in Jewish, Christian and Islamic Law*, Berkeley: University of California Press.

Fronza, V. (2011), 'Edilizia in Materiali Deperibili nell'alto medioevo Italiano: metodologie e casi de studio per un'agenda della ricerca', *Post-Classical Archaeologies*, 1: 95–138.

Frost, R. (1915), 'The Death of the Hired Man', in *North of Boston*, 4–8, New York: Henry Holt and Company.

Galinsky, J. D. (2015), 'Between Ashkenaz (Germany) and Tsarfat (France): Two Approaches toward Popularizing Jewish Law', in E. Baumgarten and J. D. Galinsky (eds.), *Jews and Christians in Thirteenth Century France*, 78–82, New York: Palgrave Press.

Galinsky, J. D. (2016), 'Rabbis, Readers, and the Paris Book Trade: Understanding French Halakhic Literature in the Thirteenth Century', in E. Baumgarten, R. M. Karras, and K. Messler (eds.), *Entangled Histories: Knowledge, Authority, and Transmission in Thirteenth-Century Jewish Cultures*, 73–91, Philadelphia: University of Pennsylvania Press.

Gardiner, M. (2006), 'Implements and Utensils in *Gerefa* and the Organization of Seigneurial Farmsteads in the High Middle Ages', *Medieval Archaeology*, 50: 260–7.

Gardiner, M. (2008), 'Buttery and Pantry and their Antecedents: Idea and Architecture in the English Medieval House', in M. Kowaleski and P. J. P. Goldberg (eds.), *Medieval Domesticity: Home, Housing, and Household in Medieval England*, 37–65, Cambridge: Cambridge University Press.

Gardiner, M. (2011), 'Late Saxon Settlement', in *A Handbook of Anglo-Saxon Archaeology*, edited by Helena Hamerow, Sally Crawford and David Hinton, 198–217, Oxford: Oxford University Press.

Gardiner, M. (2014), 'An Archaeological Approach to the Development of the Late Medieval Peasant House', *Vernacular Architecture*, 45: 16–28.

Gardiner, M. (2015), 'Conceptions of Domestic Space in the Long Term: The Example of the English Medieval Hall', in J. Graham-Campbell, M. S. Kristiansen and E. Roesdahl (eds.), *Medieval Archaeology in Scandinavia and Beyond. History, Trends and Tomorrow*, 313–33, Aarhus: Aarhus University Press.

Garver, V. (2009), *Women and Aristocratic Culture in the Carolingian World*, Ithaca, NY: Cornell University Press.

Gautier, A. (2009), 'Hospitality in Pre-Viking Anglo-Saxon England', *Early Medieval Europe*, 17 (1): 23–44.

Geddes, J. (1982), 'The Construction of Medieval Doors', in S. McGrail (ed.), *Woodworking Techniques Before A.D. 1500*, 313–23, Oxford: BAR.

Gero, J. M. and M. W. Conkey, eds. (1991), *Engendering Archaeology: Women and Prehistory*. Oxford: Basil Blackwell.

Gerstel, S. E. J. and M. Munn (2003), 'A Late Medieval Settlement at Panakton', *Hesperia*, 72 (2): 147–234.

Giannichedda, E. (2008), 'Metal Production in Late Antiquity: from Continuity of Knowledge to Changes in Consumptio', in L. Lavan, E. Sanni, and A. Sarantis (eds.), *Technology in Transition, A.D. 300–650*, 187–209, Leiden: Brill.

Gilchrist, R. (1997), *Gender and Material Culture: The Archaeology of Religious Women*, London & New York: Routledge.

Gilchrist, R. (1999), *Gender and Archaeology: Contesting the Past*, London: Routledge.

Gilchrist, R. (2012), *Medieval Life: Archaeology and Life Course*, Woodbridge: Boydell Press.

Gilchrist, R. (2013), 'The Materiality of Medieval Heirlooms: From Biographical to Sacred Objects', in H. P. Hahn and H. Weis (eds.), *Mobility, Meaning and the Transformation of Things*, 170–82, Oxford: Oxbow Books.

Girouard, M. (1978), *Life in the English Country House: A Social and Architectural History*, New Haven: Yale University Press.

Goldberg, P. J. P. (1992), *Women, Work, and Life Cycle in a Medieval Economy: Women in York and Yorkshire c. 1300–1520*, Oxford: Oxford University Press.

Goldberg, P. J. P. (1999), 'Masters and Men in Later Medieval England', in D. M. Hadley (ed.), *Masculinity in Medieval Europe*, 56–70, New York: Routledge.

Goldberg, P. J. P. (2001), 'Household and the Organization of Labour in Late Medieval Towns: Some English Evidence', in M. Carlier and T. Soens (eds.), *The Household in Late Medieval Cities: Italy and North-Western Europe Compared*, 59–70, Leuven: Garant.

Goldberg, P. J. P. (2008), 'The Fashioning of Bourgeois Domesticity in Later Medieval England', in M. Kowaleski and P. J. P. Goldberg (eds.), *Medieval Domesticity: Home, Housing, and Household in Medieval England*, 124–44, Cambridge: Cambridge University Press

Goldberg, P. J. P. (2011), 'Space and Gender in the Later Medieval English House', *Viator*, 42 (2): 205–32.

Goldthwaite, R. (1972), 'The Florentine Palace as Domestic Architecture', *The American Historical Review*, 77 (4): 977–1012.

Goldthwaite, R. A. (2009) *The Economy of Renaissance Florence*, Baltimore: The Johns Hopkins University Press.

Gołembnik, A. (1987), 'The Archaeological Excavations on the Castle Hill in Pułtusk (Ciechanów Voiv) in the Years 1976–1985', *Archaeologia Polona*, 25–26: 157–97.

Gordon, S. (2007), *Culinary Comedy in Medieval French Literature*, West Lafayette, IN: Purdue University Press.

Grandchamp, P. G. (1999), 'Twelfth and Thirteenth-Century Domestic Architecture North of the Loire: A Summary of Recent Research', *Vernacular Architecture*, 30: 1–20.

Grenville, J. (1997), *Medieval Housing*, London: Leicester University Press.

Gross, H. and S. Schwarzfuchs, eds. (2001), *Gallia Judaica*. Paris: Peeters.

Grossman, A. (2004), *Pious and Rebellious: Jewish Women in the Middle Ages*, Waltham, MA: Brandeis University Press.

Gutiérrez Lloret, S. (2013), 'Coming Back to Grammar of the House: Social Meaning of Medieval Households', in S. Gutiérrez Lloret and I. Grau Mira (eds.), *De la Estructura Doméstica al Espacio Social: Lecturas Arqueológicas del Uso Social del Espacio*, 245–64, San Vicente del Raspeig: Publicaciones de la Universidad de Alicante.

Gwara, J. J. and M. Morse (2012), 'A Birth Girdle Printed by Wynkyn de Worde', *The Library*, 13 (1): 33–62.

Haas, L. (1998), *The Renaissance Man and His Children: Childbirth and Early Childhood in Florence, 1300–1600*, New York: Palgrave Macmillan.

Haberman, A. M. (1945), *Sefer Gezerot Ashkenaz veTzarfat*, Jerusalem: Sifrei Tarshish.

Hajnal, J. (1965), 'European Marriage Patterns in Perspective', in David V. Glass and David E.C. Eversley (eds.), *Population in History: Essays in Historical Demography*, 101–43, Chicago: Aldine Publishing Company.

Hamerow, H. (2002), *Early Medieval Settlements: The Archaeology of Rural Communities in North-West Europe, 400–900*, Oxford: Oxford University Press.

Hanawalt, B. A. (1986), *The Ties that Bound: Peasant Families in Medieval England*, Oxford: Oxford University Press.

Hanawalt, B. A. (1993), *Growing up in Medieval London: The Experience of Childhood in History*, Oxford: Oxford University Press.

Hanawalt, B. A. (1998), *'Of Good and Ill Repute': Gender and Social Control in Medieval England*, New York: Oxford University Press.

Hanawalt, B. A. (1999), 'Women and the Household Economy in the Preindustrial Period: An Assessment of Women, Work, and Family', *Journal of Women's History*, 11 (3): 10–16.

Hanawalt, B. A. (2007), *The Wealth of Wives: Women, Law, and Economy in Late Medieval London*, Oxford: Oxford University Press.

Hanawalt B. A. and M. Kobialka (2000), 'Introduction', in B. A. Hanawalt and M. Kobialka (eds.), *Medieval Practices of Space*, ix–xvii, Minneapolis: University of Minnesota Press.

Hansen, G. (2005), *Bergen c. 800–c. 1170: The Emergence of a Town*, Bergen, Fagbokflorlaget.

Hansen, S. S. (2013), 'Toftanes: A Viking Age Farmstead in the Faroe Islands', *Acta Archaeologica*, 84 (1): 1–239.

Harari, Y. (2010), *Early Jewish Magic: Research, Method, Sources*, Jerusalem: Ben-Zvi Institute.

Harari, Y. (2011), 'Jewish Magic, An Annotated Overview', *El Prezente: Studies in Sephardic Culture*, 5: *36–*60.

Harney, M., ed. (1993), *Kinship and Polity in the Poema de Mio Cid*. West Lafayette, IN: Purdue University Press.

Harris, B. J. (2002), *English Aristocratic Women, 1450–1550: Marriage and Family, Property and Careers*, Oxford: Oxford University Press.

Harris, R. (1989), 'The Grammar of Carpentry', *Vernacular Architecture*, 20: 1–8.

Hartman, M. S. (2004), *The Household and the Making of History: A Subversive View of the Western Past*, Cambridge: Cambridge University Press.

Hauglid, R. (1980), *Laftekunst: Laftehusets Opprinnelse og Eldste Historie*, Oslo: Dryer.

Heal, F. (1990), *Hospitality in Early Modern England*, New York: Oxford University Press.

Heffernan, J. (2014), *Hospitality and Treachery in Western Literature*, New Haven: Yale University Press.

Henderson, J. (1994), *Piety and Charity in Late Medieval Florence*, Oxford: Clarendon Press.

Henderson, J. (2006), *The Renaissance Hospital: Healing the Body and Healing the Soul*, New Haven: Yale University Press.

Herbin, P. and T. Oueslati (2011), *Archéologie en Nord – Pas-de-Calais. Saint-Georges-sur-l'Aa, une Occupation Spécifique Côtière du Haut Moyen Âge*, Lille: DRAC du Nord.

Herlihy, D. (1985), *Medieval Households*, Cambridge, MA: Harvard University Press.

Herlihy, D. (1990), *Opera Muliebria: Women and Work in Medieval Europe*, New York: McGraw-Hill Publishing Company.

Herlihy, D. and C. Klapisch Zuber (1985), *Tuscans and Their Families: A Study of the Florentine Catasto of 1427*, New Haven: Yale University Press.

Herold, H. (2007), 'Die Besiedlung Niederösterreichs im Frühmittelalter', in R. Zehetmayer (ed.), *Die Schlacht bei Pressburg und das frühmittelalterliche Niederösterreichin*, 77–91, St Pölton: Niederösterreichischen Institute für Landeskunde.

Hillier, B. and J. Hanson (1984), *The Social Logic of Space*, Cambridge: Cambridge University Press.

Hines, J. (2011), '"No Place Like Home"? The Anglo-Saxon Social Landscape from Within and Without', in H. Sauer and J. Story (eds.), *Anglo-Saxon England and the Continent*, 21–39, Tempe: University of Arizona Press.

Hoffman, M. (1983), 'Beds and Bedclothes in Medieval Norway', in N. B. Harte and K.G. Ponting (eds.), *Cloth and Clothing in Medieval Europe*, 351–67, London: Heinemann Educational Books.

Hope-Taylor, B. (1977), *Yeavering: An Anglo-British Centre of Early Northumbria*, London: HMSO.

Horowitz, E. R. (1986), 'The Way We Were: Jewish Life in the Middle Ages', *Jewish History*, 1 (1): 75–90.

Howe, N. (2004), *Home and Homelessness in the Medieval and Renaissance World*, Notre Dame, IN: University of Notre Dame.

Howell, M. C. (1986), *Women, Production, and Patriarchy in Late Medieval Cities*, Chicago: University of Chicago Press.

Howell, M. C. (1998), *The Marriage Exchange: Property, Social Place, and Gender in Cities of the Low Countries, 1300–1550*, Chicago: University of Chicago Press.

Howell, M. C. (2013), 'Gender in the Transition to Merchant Capitalism', in J.M. Bennet and R. M. Karras (eds.), *Oxford Handbook of Women and Gender in Medieval Europe*, 561–76, Oxford: Oxford University Press.

Hubert, É. (1990), *Espace Urbain et Habitat à Rome de Xe Siècle à la fin du XIIIe Siècle*, Rome: École Française de Rome.

Huizinga, J. (1924), *The Waning of the Middle Ages*, New York: St. Martin's Press.

Hunt, E. S. and S. Murray (1999), *A History of Business in Medieval Europe, 1200–1550*, Cambridge: Cambridge University Press.

Ingsta, A. S. (1995), 'The Interpretations of the Oseberg Finds', in O. Crumlin-Pederset and B. M. Thye (eds.), *The Ship as a Symbol in Prehistorical and Medieval Scandinavia*, 139–59, Copenhagen: National Museum Studies in Archaeology.

Isaacs, A. (2002), 'An Anthropological and Historical Study of the Role of the Synagogue in Ashkenazi Jewish Life in the Middle Ages', PhD diss., Hebrew University of Jerusalem [Hebrew].

Jaritz, G. (2006), 'Entre Espace Public et Espace Privé: le Décor de la Maison Urbaine (Europe centrale, XIV–XVe siècle)', in D. Alexandre-Bidon, F. Piponnier and J.-M. Poisson (eds.), *Cadre de Vie et Manières d'Habiter (XIIe–XVIe Siècles)*, 249–54, Caen, CRAHM.

Jochens, J. (1995), *Women in Old Norse Society*, Ithaca, NY: Cornell University Press.

Johansson, E. (2002), '"På byn mer än hemma". Manligt och kvinnligt i rörelse, rum och socialt liv', in E. Johansson (ed.), *Periferins landskap. Historiska spår och nutida blickfält i svensk glesbygd*, 181–204, Lund: Nordic Academic Press.

Johnson, M. (1993), *Housing Culture: Traditional Architecture in an English Landscape*. London: UCL Press.

Johnson, M. (2002), *Behind the Castle Gate: From Medieval to Renaissance*, London & New York: Routledge.

Johnson, M. (2013), 'What do Medieval Buildings Mean'? *History and Theory*, 52 (3): 380–99.

Jope, E. M. and R.I Threlfall (1958), 'Excavation of a Medieval Settlement at Beere, North Tawton, Devon', *Medieval Archaeology*, 2:112–40.

Kanarfogel, E. (2015), 'The Image of Christians in Medieval Ashkenazic Rabbinic Literature', in E. Baumgarten and J. D. Galinsky (eds.), *Jews and Christians in Thirteenth Century France*, 151–61, New York: Palgrave Press.

Kanarfogel, E. (1992), *Jewish Education and Society in the High Middle Ages*, Detroit: Wayne State University Press.

Kanarfogel, E. (2012), *The Intellectual History and Rabbinic Culture of Medieval Ashkenaz*, Detroit: Wayne State University Press.

Kaplan, D. (2016), 'Living Spaces, Communal Places: Early Modern Jewish Families and Religious Devotion', Unpublished talk.

Karras, R. M., (1988), *Slavery and Society in Medieval Scandinavia*, New Haven: Yale University Press.

Karras, R. M. (1996), *Common Women: Prostitution and Sexuality in Medieval England*, New York: Oxford University Press.

Karras, R. M. (2003), *Boys to Men: Formations of Masculinity in Late Medieval Europe*, Philadelphia: University of Pennsylvania Press.

Karras, R. M. (2012), *Unmarriages: Women, Men, and Sexual Unions in the Middle Ages*, Philadelphia: University of Pennsylvania Press.

Katz, J. (1989), *The "Shabbes Goy" A Study in Halakhic Flexibility*, trans. Yoel Lerner, Philadelphia: JPS.

Katz, J. (1998), 'Alterations in the Time of the Evening Service (Ma'ariv): An Example of the Interrelationship between Religious Customs and their Social Background', in J. Katz (ed.), *Divine Law in Human Hands: Case Studies in Halakhic Flexibility*, 89–103, Jerusalem: Magnes Press.

Kermode, J. (2002), *Medieval Merchants: York, Beverley and Hull in the Later Middle Ages*, Cambridge University Press.

Kerr, J. (2002), 'The Open Door: Hospitality and Honor in Twelfth/Early Thirteenth-Century England', *History*, 87 (287): 322–35.

Kerr, J. (2007), '"Welcome the Coming and Speed the Parting Guest": Hospitality in Twelfth-Century England', *Journal of Medieval History*, 33 (2): 130–46.

Kerr, J. (2007), *Monastic Hospitality: The Benedictines in England, c.1070–c.1250*, Woodbridge: Boydell.

Khoroshev A. S. and Sorokin, A. N. (1992), 'Buildings and Properties from the Lyudin End of Novgorod', in M. Brisbane (ed.), *The Archaeology of Novgorod: Recent Results from the Town and its Hinterland*, 107–59, Lincoln: Society for Medieval Archaeology.

King, C. (2009), 'The Interpretation of Urban Buildings: Power, Memory, and Appropriation in Norwich Merchants' Houses, c. 1400–1660', *World Archeology*, 41 (3).

Klapisch Zuber, C. with M. Demonet (1985), '"Ad Unum Panem et Unum Vinum": The Rural Tuscan Family at the Beginning of the Fifteenth Century', in L. G. Cochrane (trans.), *Women, Family, and Ritual in Renaissance Italy*, 36–67, Chicago: University of Chicago Press.

Klapisch Zuber, C. with M. Demonet (1985), 'Female Celibacy and Service in Florence in the Fifteenth Century', in L. G. Cochrane (trans.), *Women, Family, and Ritual in Renaissance Italy*, 155–77, Chicago: University of Chicago Press.

Klapisch Zuber, C. with M. Demonet (1985), 'The Cruel Mother: Maternity, Widowhood, and Dowry in Florence in the Fourteenth and Fifteenth Centuries', in L. G. Cochrane (trans.), *Women, Family, and Ritual in Renaissance Italy*, 178–212, Chicago: University of Chicago Press.

Klapisch Zuber, C. with M. Demonet (1985), 'Holy Dolls: Play and Piety in Florence in the Quattrocento', in L. G. Cochrane (trans.), *Women, Family, and Ritual in Renaissance Italy*, 310–29, Chicago: University of Chicago Press.

Klapisch Zuber, C. with M. Demonet (1985), 'Zacharias, or the ousted Father: Nuptial Rites in Tuscany Between Giotto and the Council of Trent', in L. G. Cochrane (trans.), *Women, Family, and Ritual in Renaissance Italy*, 178–212, Chicago: University of Chicago Press.

Klapisch Zuber, C. with M. Demonet (1985), 'Blood Parents and Milk Parents: Wet Nursing in Florence, 1300–1530', in L. G. Cochrane (trans.), *Women, Family, and Ritual in Renaissance Italy*, 132–64, Chicago: University of Chicago Press.

Klapisch Zuber, C. with M. Demonet (1986), 'Women Servants in Florence during the Fourteenth and Fifteenth Centuries', in B. A. Hanawalt (ed.), *Women and Work in Preindustrial Europe*, 56–80, Bloomington: Indiana University Press.

Klápště, J. (2006), 'Vivre dans la Maison Urbaine en Bohême aux Xie–Xve siècles', in D. Alexandre-Bidon, F. Piponnier and J.-M. Poisson (eds.), *Cadre de Vie et Manières d'Habiter (XIIe–XVIe Siècles)*, 209–20, Caen, CRAHM.

Klápště, J. (2012), *The Czech Lands in Medieval Transformation*, Leiden: Brill.

Klápště, J. (2016), *The Archaeology of Prague and the Medieval Czech Lands*, Sheffield: Equinox.

Klápště, J. and A. N. Jaubert (2011), 'Rural settlement', in J. Graham-Campbell and M. Valor (eds), *The Archaeology of Medieval Europe: vol. 1, Eighth to Twelfth Centuries AD*, Aarhus: Aarhus University Press. 76–110.

Komber, J. (2002), 'Viking Age Architecture in Space and Time', in J. Klápště (ed.), *Ruralia IV: 8–13 September 2001, Bad Bederkesa, Lower Saxony, Germany, The Rural House: From the Migration Period to the Oldest Still Standing Buildings*, 13–20, Prague: Institute of Archaeology.

Korpiola, M. (2011), 'Introduction: Regional Variations and Harmonization in Medieval Matrimonial Law', in M. Korpiola (ed.), *Regional Variations in Matrimonial Law and Custom in Europe, 1150–1600*, 1–20, Leiden: Brill.

Kourelis, K. (2003), 'Monuments of Rural Archaeology: Medieval Settlement in the Northwestern Peloponnese', PhD diss., University of Pennsylvania, Philadelphia, USA.

Kowaleski, M. (1999), 'Singlewomen in Medieval and Early Modern Europe: The Demographic Perspective', in J. M. Bennett and A. M. Froide (eds.), *Singlewomen in the European Past, 1250–1800*, 38–82, Philadelphia: University of Pennsylvania Press.

Kowaleski, M. (2014), 'Medieval People in Town and Country: New Perspectives from Demography and Bioarchaeology', *Speculum*, 89 (3): 573–600.
Kristiansen, M. S. (2014), 'Proper Living: Exploring Domestic Ideals in Medieval Denmark', in M. S. Kristiansen and K. Giles (eds.), *Dwellings, Identities, and Homes: European Housing Culture from the Viking Age to the Renaissance*, 149–62, Aarhus: Aarhus University Press.
Kuehn, T. (1994), *Law, Family, and Women: Toward a Legal Anthropology of Renaissance Florence*, Chicago: University of Chicago Press.
Kuna, M. and N. Profantová (2011), 'Prague-type Culture Houses. Aspects of Form, Function and Meaning', *Histria Antiqua*, 20 (20): 415–29.
Kunz, E. G. (2001), 'Hospitality, Conviviality, and the English Gentry: Social Networks of the Landed Elite in Late Medieval Suffolk', PhD diss., Fordham University, NewYork, USA.
L'Estrange, E. (2008), *Holy Motherhood: Gender Dynasty and Visual Culture in the Later Middle Ages*, Manchester: Manchester University Press.
Lafuente, P. (2014), 'Pottery and Tiles', in M. Valor, J. Avelino, G. Gonsálex (eds.), *The Archaeology of Medieval Spain 1100–1500*, 82, Sheffield: Equinox, Publishing.
Larson, W. R. (2003), 'Who is the Master of This Narrative? Maternal Patronage of the Cult of St. Margaret', in M. C. Erler and M. Kowelski (eds.), *Gendering the Master Narrative: Women and Power in the Middle Ages*, 94–104, Ithaca, NY: Cornell University Press.
Laumonier, L. (2015), 'Meanings of Fatherhood in Late-Medieval Montpellier: Love, Care, and the Exercise of *Patria Potestas*', *Gender and History*, 27 (3): 651–68.
Lavi, A. (2005), 'An Addendum to the Study of Smoke Cottages', *Estonian Journal of Archaeology* 9 (2): 132–55.
Le Goff, J. (1980), *Time, Work, and Culture in the Middle Ages*, trans. A. Goldhammer, Chicago: University of Chicago.
Le Roy Ladurie, E. (1976), *Montaillou: village occitan de 1294 à 1324*, Paris: Gallimard.
Le Roy Ladurie, E. (1984), *Montaillou: The World Famous Portrait of Life in a Medieval Village*, trans. B. Bray, New York: Penguin.
Lieberman, A. (2013), *The Oxford Etymologist* http://blog.oup.com/2013/02/guest-host-word-origin-etymology/.
Lightfoot, D. W. (2009), 'The Projects of Marriage: Spousal Choice, Dowries, and Domestic Service in Early Fifteenth-Century Valencia', *Viator*, 40 (1): 333–53.
Lindow, J. R. (2005), 'For Use and Display: Selected Furnishings and Domestic Goods in Fifteenth-Century Florentine Interiors', in R. J. M. Olson, P. L. Reilly, and R. Shepherd (eds.), *The Biography of the Object in Late Medieval and Renaissance Italy*, 54–66, Oxford: Blackwell.
Löfgren S. S. and S. Isaksson (2012), 'The Oldest Evidence of Painted Furniture from Sweden: The Twelfth-Century Chair at Suntak', *Journal of Archaeological Science*, 39 (6): 1665–73.
Löfgren, O. (1982), 'Kvinnfolksgöra – om arbetsdelning i bondesamhället', *Kvinnovetenskaplig tidskrift* (3): 11–40.
Lucas, A. R. (2005), 'Industrial Milling in the Ancient and Medieval Worlds: A Survey of the Evidence for Industrial Revolution in Ancient and Medieval Europe', *Technology and Culture*, 46 (1): 1–30.
Lucas, G. (2009), *Hofstaðir: Excavations of a Viking Age Feasting Hall in North-Eastern Iceland*, Reykjavík: Institute of Archaeology.

Lynn, C. (1994), 'Houses in Rural Ireland, A.D. 500–1000', *Ulster Journal of Archaeology*, 3rd series, 57: 81–94.
Lynn, C. and J. McDowell (2011), *Deer Park Farms: The Excavation of a Raised Rath in the Glenarm Valley, Co. Antrim*, Belfast: TSO.
Makarov, N. A., S. D. Zacharov, and A. P. Bužilova (2001), *Srednevekovoe rasselenie na Belom ozere*, Moskva: Jazyki russkoj kul'tury.
Marcus, I. G. (1996), *Rituals of Childhood: Jewish Acculturation in Medieval Europe*, New Haven: Yale University Press.
Martin, Daphne JR. (2002), 'Hospitality and Household: Bishop Metford's Household Accounts, October 1406–June 1407', PhD diss., Macquarie University, Sydney, Australia.
Maslanka, C. (2008), 'Knighthood in a Carl's House: Chivalry and Domesticity in *Sir Gawain and the Carl of Carlisle*', *Enarratio*, 15: 46–64.
Mathieu, J. R. (1999), 'New Methods on Old Castles: Generating New Ways of Seeing', *Medieval Archaeology*, 43: 115–42.
Mate, M. E. (1998), *Daughters, Wives and Widows after the Black Death: Women in Sussex, 1350–1535*, Woodbridge: Boydell Press.
McIntosh, M. (2005), 'Benefits and Drawbacks of *Femme Sole* status in England, 1300–1630', *Journal of British Studies*, 44 (3): 410–38.
McIntosh, M. K. (2005), *Working Women in English Society, 1300–1620*, Cambridge: Cambridge University Press.
McIntosh, M. K. (2012), *Poor Relief in England, 1350–1600*, Cambridge: Cambridge University Press.
McKee, S. (1995), "Households in Fourteenth-Century Venetian Crete', *Speculum*, 70 (1): 27–67.
McKee, S. (2008), 'Domestic Slavery in Renaissance Italy', *Slavery and Abolition*, 29 (3): 305–26.
McSheffrey, S. (1995), *Gender and Heresy: Women and Men in Lollard Communities*, Philadelphia: University of Pennsylvania Press.
McSheffrey, S. (2004), 'Place, Space and Situation: Public and Private in the Making of Marriage in Late Medieval London', *Speculum*, 79 (4): 987–8.
McSheffrey, S. (2006), *Marriage, Sex and Civic Culture in Late Medieval London*, Philadelphia: University of Pennsylvania Press.
Melammed, R. L. (1999), *Heretics or Daughters of Israel: The Crypto-Jewish Women of Castile*, Oxford and New York: Oxford University Press.
Mellor, M. (2004), 'Hanging Rooms: Fixtures, Fitting and Movable Goods in European Lifestyles', *Medieval Ceramics*, 28: 125–38.
Mercer, E. (1969), *Furniture, 700–1700*, London: Weidenfel and Nicolson.
Meyer, W. (1974), *Die Burgruine Alt-Wartburg im Kanton Aargau: Bericht über die Forschungen 1966/67*, Olten: Walter-Verlag.
Mijović, P. and M. Kovačević (1975), *Villes Fortifiées et Fortresses au Monténegro*, Belgrade, Ulcinj: Archaeological Institute of the Museum of Ulcinj.
Miller, M. (2017), 'The Political and Cultural Significance of the Bishop's Palace in Medieval Italy', in D. Rollason (ed.), *Princes of the Church: Bishops and their Palaces*, 34–54, New York: Routledge.
Miller, M. (2000), *The Bishop's Palace: Architecture and Authority in Medieval Italy*, Ithaca, NY: Cornell University Press.
Miller, T. S. (2014), *The Beguines of Medieval Paris: Gender, Patronage, and Spiritual Authority*, Philadelphia: University of Pennsylvania Press.

Miller, W. I. (2004), "Home and Homelessness in the Middle of Nowhere', in N. Howe (ed.), *Home and Homelessness in the Medieval and Renaissance World*, 125–42, Notre Dame, IN: Notre Dame University Press.

Mitchell, P. (2013), 'Ziegel als archäologische Artefakte: Technologie – Verwendung – Format – Datierung', *Beiträge zur Mittelalterarchäologie in Österreich*, 29: 63–70.

Mohr, J.C.B. (1963/1968), *Germania Judaica*, vols. I and II. Tübingen.

Molaug, P. (2001), 'Medieval house building in Oslo', in M. Gläser (ed.), *Lübecker Kolloquium zur Stadtarchäologie im Hanseraum III: Der Hausbau*, 765–82, Lübeck: Schmidt-Römhild.

Moore, H. (1986), *Space, Text and Gender*, Cambridge: Cambridge University Press.

Morgan, H. L. S. (2017), *Beds and Chambers in Late Medieval England: Readings, Representations and Realities*, Woodbridge: York Medieval Press.

Morse, M. (2007), 'Creating Sacred Space: The Religious Visual Culture of the Renaissance Venetian *Casa*', in M. Ajmar-Wollheim, F. Dennis, and A. Matchette (eds.), *Approaching the Italian Renaissance Interior: Sources, Methodologies, Debates*, 195–228, Oxford: Blackwell.

Mührenberg, D. (2001), 'The Lübeck Colloquium 1999 (Domestic Architecture – Summary', in M. Gläser (ed.), *Lübecker Kolloquium zur Stadtarchäologie im Hanseraum III: Der Hausbau*, 843–52, Lübeck: Schmidt-Römhild.

Muehlberger, E. (2013), *Angels in Late Ancient Christianity*, Oxford: Oxford University Press.

Munch, G. S., L. S. Johansen and E. Roesdahl (2003), *Borg in Lofoten: A Chieftain's Farm in North Norway*, Trondheim: Tapir Academic Press.

Munro, J. (1988), 'Textile Technology', in J. Strayer (ed.), *Dictionary of the Middle Ages*, vol. 11, 693–711, New York: Charles Scribner's Sons/MacMillan.

Mursell, G. (2001), *English Spirituality: From Earliest Times to 1700*, Louisville, KY: Westminster John Knox Press.

Musacchio, J. M. (1999), *The Art and Ritual of Childbirth in Renaissance Italy*, New Haven: Yale University Press.

Myhre, B. (1982), 'Settlements of Southwest Norway During the Roman and Migration Periods', *Offa*, 39: 197–215.

Nekoda, V. (1974), *Pfaffenschlag. Zanikla stredoveka ves u Slavonic*, Brno: Blok.

Nicholas, D. (2003), *Urban Europe, 1100–1700*, New York: Palgrave.

O'Sullivan, C. (2004), *Hospitality in Medieval Ireland, 900–1500*, Dublin: Four Courts Press.

Ohler, N. (1989), *Medieval Traveller*, Woodbridge: Boydell Press.

Oliva, M. (2008), 'Nuns at Home: The Domesticity of Sacred Space', in M. Kowaleski and P. J. P. Goldberg (eds.), *Medieval Domesticity: Home, Housing, and Household in Medieval England*, 145–61, Cambridge: Cambridge University Press.

Orihuela, A. (2007), 'The Andalusian House in Granada (Thirteenth to Sixteenth Centuries)', in G. D. Anderson and M. Rosser-Owen (eds.), *Revisting Al-Andalus: Perspectives on the Material Culture of Islamic Iberia and Beyond*, 169–91, Leiden: Brill.

Orme, N. (2003), *Medieval Children*, New Haven: Yale University Press.

Oudhof, J. W. (2000), 'Sporen en structuren', in J. W. M. Oudhof, J. Dijkstra, and A. A. A. Verhoeven (eds.), *"Huis Malburg" van spoor tot spoor; een middeleeuwse nederzetting in Kerk-Avezaath*, 45–77, Amersfoort: Rikjsdienst voor het Oudheidkundig Bodemonderzoek.

Øye, I. (2005), 'Women in Early Towns', in J. Sheehan and D. Ó Corráin (eds), *The Viking Age, Ireland and the West: Papers from the Proceedings of the Fifteenth Viking Congress, Cork, 18–27 August 2005*, 298–309, Dublin: Four Courts.

Øye, I. (2005), 'Kvinner som tradisjonsformidlere: Rom og redskaper', in R. Barndon (ed.), *Samfunn, symboler og identitet: festskrift til Gro Mandt på 70-årsdagen*, 439–54, Bergen: Arkeologisk institutt, Universitet i Bergen.

Pálóczi-Horváth, A. (2002), 'Development of the Late-Medieval House in Hungary', in J. Klápště (ed.), *Ruralia IV: 8–13 September 2001, Bad Bederkesa, Lower Saxony, Germany, The Rural House: From the Migration Period to the Oldest Still Standing Buildings*, 308–19, Prague: Institute of Archaeology.

Paner, H. (2000), '10th- to 17th-Century Architecture in Gdańsk', in M. Gläser (ed.), *Lübecker Kolloquium zur Stadtarchäologie im Hanseraum III: Der Hausbau*, 491–509, Lübeck: Schmidt-Römhild.

Pesez, J.-M. (1984), *Brucato. Histoire et Archéologie d'un Habitat Médiéval en Sicile*, Rome: École Française de Rome.

Peytremann, E. (2005), 'L'Architecture Rurale dans L'Ouest de la France (VIe–XIIe siècle', in Annie Antoine (ed.), *La Maison Rurale en Pays d'Habitat Dispersé de L'Antiquité au XXe Siècle*, 77–87, Rennes: Presse Universitaires de Rennes.

Phillips, W. D. (1985), *Slavery from Roman Times to the Early Transatlantic Trade*, Minneapolis: University of Minnesota Press.

Phillips, W. D. (2014), *Slavery in Medieval and Early Modern Iberia*, Philadelphia: University of Pennsylvania Press.

Phythian-Adams, C. (1979), *Desolation of a City: Coventry and the Urban Crisis of the Late Middle Ages*, Cambridge: Cambridge University Press.

Pickvance, C. (2012), 'Medieval Domed Chests in Kent: A Contribution to a National and International Study', *Regional Furniture*, 26: 105–47.

Pleinerová, I. (1986), 'Pokusy s výstavbou a obýváním staroslovanských domů v Březně', *Památky Archeologické*, 78: 104–76.

Pleinerová, I. (2000), *Die Altslawischen Dörfer von Březno Bei Louny*, Prague: Archeologický Ústav Akademie Věd Čr Praha.

Poisson, J-M. (2002), 'La maison rural médiévale en Sardaigne: un atelier d'ethno-archéologi', in J. Klápště (ed.), *Ruralia IV: 8–13 September 2001, Bad Bederkesa, Lower Saxony, Germany, The Rural House: From the Migration Period to the Oldest Still Standing Buildings*, 232–9, Prague: Institute of Archaeology.

Raftis, J. A. (1982), *A Small Town in Late Medieval England: Godmanchester, 1278–1400*, Toronto: PIMS.

Ramqvist, P. H. (1992), 'Building Traditions in Northern and Northeastern Europe During the Iron Age', in B. Hårddh and B. Wyszomirska-Werbert (eds.), *Contacts Across the Baltic Sea during the Late Iron Age (5th to 12th Centuries)*, 73–83, Lund: Institute of Archaeology, University of Lund.

Rawcliffe, C. (2009), 'A Marginal Occupation? The Medieval Laundress and her Work', *Gender and History*, 21 (1): 152–4.

Redknap, M. (2004), 'Viking Age Settlement in Wales and the Evidence from Llanbedrgoch', in J. Hines, A. Lane, and M. Redknap (eds.), *Land, Sea and Home*, 139–75, Leeds: Maney.

Rees Jones, S. (2003), 'Women's Influence on the Design of Urban Homes', in M. C. Erler and M. Kowaleski (eds), *Gendering the Master Narrative: Women and Power in the Middle Ages*, 190–211, Ithaca, NY: Cornell University Press.

Rees Jones, S. (2008), 'Building Domesticity in the City', in M. Kowaleski and P. J. P. Goldberg (eds.), *Medieval Domesticity: Home, Housing, and Household in Medieval England*, 66–91, Cambridge: Cambridge University Press.

Rees Jones, S. (2013), 'Public and Private Space and Gender in Medieval Europe', in J. M. Bennet and R. M. Karras (eds.), *Oxford Handbook of Women and Gender in Medieval Europe*, 246–61, Oxford: Oxford University Press.

Reeve, M. M. (2011), 'Gothic Architecture and the Civilizing Process: The Great Hall in Thirteenth-Century England', in R. Bork, A. McGehee, and W. Clark (eds.), *New Approaches to Medieval Architecture*, 93–112, London: Ashgate.

Reimers, E. (1982), 'Synspunkter på Bruk av Stavverk og Lafteverk i Middelalderen, Basert på Arkeologisk Materiale fra Bryggen i Bergen', in B. Myhre, B. Stoklund and P. Gjærder (eds.), *Vertnordisk Byggeskikk gjennom to Tusen År*, 80–97, Stavanger: Arkeologisk Museum i Stavanger.

Reinburg, V. (2014), *French Book of Hours: Making an Archive of Prayer, c. 1400–1600*, Cambridge: Cambridge University Press.

Resnick, I. (2011), 'Dietary Laws in Medieval Christian-Jewish Polemics: A Survey', *Studies in Christian-Jewish Relations*, 6 (1): 1–15.

Reyerson, K. L. (1997), 'Prostitution in Medieval Montpellier: The Ladies of Campus Polverel', *Medieval Prosopography: History and Collective Biography*, 18: 209–28.

Reyerson, K. L. (2013), 'Urban Economies', in J. M. Bennett and R. M. Karras (eds.), *The Oxford Handbook of Women and Gender in Medieval Europe*, 295–310, Oxford: Oxford University Press.

Rheidt, K. (1990), 'Byzantinische Wohnhäuser des 11. bis 14. Jahrhunderts in Pergamon', *Dumbarton Oaks Papers*, 44: 195–204.

Richardson, A. (2003), 'Corridors of Power: A Case Study in Access Analysis from Medieval England', *Antiquity*, 77 (296): 373–84.

Richardson, A. (2003), 'Gender and Space in English Royal Palaces: A Study in Access Analysis and Imagery', *Medieval Archeology*, 47 (1): 131–65.

Riddy, F. (2003), 'Looking Closely: Authority and Intimacy in the Late Medieval Urban Home', in M. C. Erler and M. Kowaleski (eds.), *Gendering the Master Narrative: Women and Power in the Middle Ages*, 212–28, Ithaca, NY: Cornell University Press.

Riddy, F. (2008), '"Burgeis" Domesticity in Late-Medieval England', in M. Kowaleski and P. J. P. Goldberg (eds.), *Medieval Domesticity: Home, Housing, and Household in Medieval England*, 14–36, Cambridge: Cambridge University Press.

Rider, C. (2012), *Magic and Religion in Medieval England*, London: Reaktion Books.

Riegler, M. and J. R. Baskin. (2008), '"May the Writer Be Strong": Medieval Hebrew Manuscripts Copied By and For Women', *Nashim*, 16: 16–23.

Riello, G. (2012), 'Things Seen and Unseen: The Material Culture of Early Modern Inventories and Their Representation of Domestic Interiors', in P. Findlen (ed.), *Early Modern Things: Objects and their Histories*, 125–50, New York: Routledge.

Ring, R. R. (1979), 'Early Medieval Peasant Household in Central Italy', *Journal of Family History*, 4 (1): 2–21.

Rinne, K. (2001), 'The Landscape of Laundry in Late Cinquecento Rome', *Studies in the Decorative Arts*, 9 (1): 34–60.

Roe, F. (1907), *Old Oak Furniture*, London: Methuen.

Roesdahl, E. (2009), 'Housing Culture – Scandinavian Perspectives', in R. Gilchrist and A. Reynolds (eds.), *Reflections: Fifty Years of Medieval Archaeology: 1957–2007*, 271–88, Leeds: Maney Publishing.

Rosaldo, M. Z. (1994), 'Women, Culture and Society: Theoretical Overview', in M. Z. Rosaldo and L. Lamphere (eds.), *Woman, Culture and Society*, 17–42, Stanford: Stanford University Press.

Rosser, G. (2005), *The Art of Solidarity in the Middle Ages: Guilds in England, 1250–1550*, Oxford: Oxford University Press.

Roubin, L. (1977), 'Male Space and Female Space within the Provençal Community', in R. Forster and O. Ranum (eds.) and E. Forster and P. M. Ranum (trans.), *Rural Society in France: Selections from the Annales, Economies, Sociétés, Civilisations*, 152–80, Baltimore: Johns Hopkins University Press.

Roux, S. (2009), *Paris in the Middle Ages*, trans. J. McNamara, Philadelphia: University of Pennsylvania Press.

Rudy, K. M. (2010), 'Dirty Books: Quantifying Patterns of Use in Medieval Manuscripts Using a Densitometer', *Journal of Historians of Netherlandish Art*, 2 (1): 1–26.

Rui, L. M. (1993), *Kjønnsrollerelasjoner: et arkeologisk materiale fra middelalder-oslo i feministisk perspektiv*, Oslo: Oslo University.

Rullkoetter, W. (1990), *The Legal Protection of Woman Among the Ancient Germans*, University of Chicago Press.

Salih, S. (2001), *Version of Virginity*, Woodbridge: D.S. Brewer.

Šalkovský, P. (2011), 'Frümittelalterliche Grubenhäuser Probleme der Terminologie, Typologie und Rekonstruktion', *Archaeologia Adriatica*, 3 (1): 273–92.

Sanders, G. D. R. (2011), 'Two *Kastra* on Melos and their Relations in the Archipelago', in P. Lock and G. D. R. Sanders (eds.), *The Archaeology of Medieval Greece*, 147–77, Oxford: Oxbow Books.

Schmid, C. (2014), The Investigation of Domestic Space in Archaeology: Beyond Architecture', in M. S. Kristiansen and K. Giles (eds.), *Dwellings, Identities and Homes: European Housing Culture from the Viking Age to the Renaissance*, 53–64, Højberg: Jutland Archaeological Society.

Sabo, K. S. (2005), 'Genusrelationer i byar under medeltid. Med exempel från södra Skandinavien och England', in K. Schmidt Sabo (ed.), *Vem behöver en by? Kyrkheddinge, struktur och strategi under tusen år*, 101–209, Lund: Riksantikvarieämbetet.

Schmidt, A., I. Devos, and B. Blondé (2015), 'Single and the City: Men and Women Alone in North-Western European Towns Since the Late Middle Ages', in I. Devos, J. De Groot, and A. Schmidt (eds.), *Single Life and the City, 1200–1900*, 1–24, New York: Palgrave.

Schmugge, L. (2012), *Marriage on Trial: Late Medieval German Couples at the Papal Court*, trans. A. A. Larson. Washington, DC: Catholic University of America Press.

Schofield, J. and H. Steuer (2007), 'Urban Settlement', in J. Graham-Campbell and M. Valor (eds.), *The Archaeology of Medieval Europe: vol. 1, Eighth to Twelfth Centuries AD*, 111–53, Aarhus: Aarhus University Press.

Schofield, J. (1994), *Medieval London Houses*, New Haven: Yale University Press.

Sessa, K. (2007), 'Christianity and the *Cubiculum*: Spiritual Politics and Domestic Space in Late Antique Rome', *Journal of Early Christian Studies*, 15 (2): 171–204.

Shahar, S. (1990), *Childhood in the Middle Ages*, London; New York: Routledge.

Shatzmiller, J. (2013), *Cultural Exchange*, Princeton: Princeton University Press.

Sheingorn, P. (2003), 'The Wise Mother: The Image of St Anne Teaching the Virgin Mary', in M. C. Erler and M. Kowaleski (eds.), *Gendering the Master Narrative: Women and Power in the Middle Ages*, 105–34, Ithaca, NY: Cornell University Press.

Shoham-Steiner, E. (2013), 'The Virgin Mary, Miriam, and Jewish Reactions to Marian Devotion in the High Middle Ages', *AJS Review*, 37 (1): 75–91.

Shyovitz, D. I. (2015), '"You Have Saved Me from the Judgment of Gehenna": The Origins of the Mourner's Kaddish in Medieval Ashkenaz', *AJS Review*, 39 (1): 49–73.

Sigalos, L. (2003), 'Housing People in Medieval Greece', *International Journal of Historical Archaeology* 7 (3): 195–221.

Simons, W. (2001), *Cities of Ladies: Beguine Communities in the Medieval Low Countries, 1200–1565*, Philadephia: University of Pennsylvania Press.

Simonton, D. (1998), *A History of European Women's Work: 1700 to the Present*, London: Routledge.

Skinner, P. (1994), 'Urban communities in Naples, 900–1050', *Papers of the British School at Rome*, 62: 279–99.

Skov, H. (2002), 'The Development of Rural House Types in the old Danish region 800–1500 AD', in J. Klápště (ed.), *Ruralia IV: 8–13 September 2001, Bad Bederkesa, Lower Saxony, Germany, The Rural House: From the Migration Period to the Oldest Still Standing Buildings*, 30–33, Prague: Institute of Archaeology.

Skre, D. (1996), 'Rural Settlement in medieval Norway, AD 400–1400', in J. Klápště (ed.), *Ruralia I: Conference Ruralia I Prague 8th–14th September 1995*, 53–71, Prague: Institute of Archaeology.

Skull C. *et al.* (2016), 'Social and Economic Complexity in Early Medieval England', *Antiquity*, 90 (354): 1594–612.

Smail, D. L. (2016), *Legal Plunder: Households and Debt Collection in Late Medieval Europe*, Cambridge, MA: Harvard University Press.

Smalley, B. (1981), *Studies in Medieval Thought and Learning From Abelard to Wyclif*, London: Bloomsbury Publishing.

Smith, J. H.M. (2012), 'Portable Christianity: Relics in the Medieval West (c. 700–1200)', *Proceedings of the British Academy*, 181: 143–67.

Smith, J. H. M. (2014), 'Material Christianity in the Early Medieval Household', *Studies in Church History*, 50: 23–46.

Smith, K. A. (forthcoming), '"A Lanterne of Lyght to the People": English Narrative Alabaster Images of John the Baptist in their Visual, Religious, and Social Contexts', in J. Brantley, S. Perkinson, and E. C. Teviotdale (eds.), *Alabaster Sculpture in Medieval England: A Reassessment*, Kalamazoo: Medieval Institute Publications.

Smith, R. M. (1981), 'The People of Tuscany and Their Families in the Fifteenth Century: Medieval or Mediterranean'? *Journal of Family History*, 6 (1): 107.

Smith, R. M. (1992), 'Geographical Diversity in the Resort to Marriage in Late Medieval Europe: Work, Reputation, and Unmarried Females in the Household Formation Systems of Northern and Southern Europe', in P. J. P. Goldberg (ed.), *Woman is a Worthy Wight: Women in English Society c. 1200–1500*, 16–59, Wolfeboro Falls, NH: Allen Sutton Publishing.

Soloveitchik, H. (2015), 'Agobard of Lyons, Megillat Ahima'ats and the Babylonian Orientation of Early Ashkenaz', in *Collected Essays*, vol. 2, 5–22, Portland, OR: Littman Library.

Soloveitchik, H. (2015), 'The Authority of the Babylonian Talmud and the Use of Biblical Verses and Aggadah in Early Ashkenaz', in *Collected Essays*, vol. 2, 70–100, Portland, OR: Littman Library.

Soloveitchik, H. (2008), *Wine in Ashkenaz in the Middle Ages, Yeyn Nesekh: A Study in the History of Halakhah*, Jerusalem: Merkaz Zalman Shazar.

Sparks, C. (2014), *Heresy, Inquisition, and Life Cycle in Medieval Languedoc*, Woodbridge: York Medieval Press.

Spencer, B. (2010), *Pilgrim Souvenirs and Secular Badges: Medieval Finds from Excavations in London*, London: Museum of London.

Spitzers, T. (2001), 'Archaeological Data on Domestic Architecture in Deventer from the 9th to the 15th Centuries', in M. Gläser (ed.), *Lübecker Kolloquium zur*

Stadtarchäologie im Hanseraum III: Der Hausbau, 197–211, Lübeck: Schmidt-Römhild.

Sponsler, C. (2001), 'Eating Lessons: Lydgate's 'Dietary' and Consumer Conduct', in K. Ashley and R. L. A. Clark (eds.), *Medieval Conduct*, 1–22, Minneapolis, University of Minnesota Press.

Stabel, P. (2014), 'Labour Time, Guild Time? Working Hours in the Cloth Industry of Medieval Flanders and Artois (Thirteenth–Fourteenth Centuries)', *The Low Countries Journal of Social and Economic History*, 11 (4): 27–54.

Stabel, P. (2015), 'Working Alone? Single Women in the Urban Economy of Late Medieval Flanders (thirteenth–early fifteenth centuries)', in I. Devos, J. De Groot, and A. Schmidt (eds.), *Single Life and the City, 1200–1900*, 27–49, New York: Palgrave.

Stow, K. R. (1992), *Alienated Minority. The Jews of Medieval Latin Europe*, Cambridge, MA: Harvard University Press.

Strauss, D. L. (1979), *Pat 'Akum in Medieval France and Germany*, New York: Bernard Revel Graduate School, Yeshiva University.

Stuard, S. M. (1992), *A State of Deference: Ragusa/Dubrovnik in the Medieval Centuries*. Philadelphia: University of Pennsylvania Press.

Stuard, S. Mr. (1995), 'Ancillary Evidence for the Decline of Medieval Slavery', *Past and Present*, 149: 3–28.

Sutherland, N. M. (1984), *Princes, Politics, and Religion, 1547–1589*, London: Bloomsbury.

Svensson, E. (2008), *The Medieval Household: Daily Life in Castles and Farmsteads, Scandinavian Examples in Their European Context*, Turnhout: Brepols.

Svensson, E. (2014), 'The Rural House: Local of "European' Style"', in M. S. Kristiansen and K. Giles (eds.), *Dwelling, Identities and Homes: European Housing Culture from the Viking Ages to the Renaissance*, 67–78, Højbjerg: Jutland Archaeological Society.

Svensson, E. (2015), 'Upland living. The Scandinavian Shielings and Their European Sisters', in I. Baug, J. Larsen and S. Samset Mygland (eds.), *Nordic Middle Ages – Artefacts, Landscapes and Society. Essays in honor of Ingvild Øye on her 70th birthday*, 289–300, Bergen: University of Bergen.

Swanson, H. (1989), *Medieval Artisans: An Urban Class in Late Medieval England*, Oxford/New York: Basil Blackwell.

Sørensen, M. L. S. (2000), *Gender Archaeology*, Cambridge: Polity Press.

Ta Shma, I. M. (1996), 'HaSifrut hahilkhatit hamikzoit beAshkenaz', in I. Ta Shma (ed.), *Ritual Custom and Reality in Franco-Germany, 1000–1350*, 94–111, Jerusalem: Magnes Press.

Takács, M. (2001), 'Der Hausbau in Ungarn vom 2. bis zum 13. Jahrhundert n. Chr. – ein Zeitalter einheitlicher Grubenhäuser'? in J. Klápště (ed.), *Ruralia IV: 8–13 September 2001, Bad Bederkesa, Lower Saxony, Germany, The Rural House: From the Migration Period to the Oldest Still Standing Buildings*, 272–90, Prague: Institute of Archaeology.

Tesch, S. (2001), 'Houses, Town Yards and Town Planning in Late Viking Age and Medieval Sigtuna, Sweden', in M. Gläser (ed.), *Lübecker Kolloquium zur Stadtarchäologie im Hanseraum III: Der Hausbau*, 723–41, Lübeck: Schmidt-Römhild.

Thorsteinsson, A. (1982), 'Færøske Huskonstruktioner fra Vikingetid til 1800-Årene', in B. Myhre, B. Stoklund and P. Gjærder (eds.), *Vertnordisk Byggeskikk gjennom to Tusen År*, 149–61, Stavanger: Arkeologisk Museum i Stavanger.

Tierney, B. (1959), *Medieval Poor Law: A Sketch of Canonical Theory and its Application in England*, Berkeley: University of California Press.
Trexler, R. C. (1998), 'A Widows' Asylum of the Renaissance: The Orbatello of Florence', in *The Women of Renaissance Florence*, 66–94, Asheville, NC: Pegasus Press.
Türkoğlu, I. (2004), 'Byzantine Houses in Western Anatolia: An Architectural Approach', *Al-Masāq: Journal of the Medieval Mediterranean*, 16 (1): 93–130.
Unger, J. (1999), *Zivot na lelekovickem hrade ve 14. stoleti. Antropologicka sociokulturni studie*. Edice Scientia, Brno: Nadace Universitas Masarykiana.
Urbańczyk, P. (1992), *Medieval Arctic Norway*, Warsaw: Semper.
Urbańczyk, P. (1999), 'North Atlantic Turf Architecture as an Example of Environmental Adaptation' *Archaeologia Polona*, 37: 119–33.
Valenzani, R. S. (2000), 'Residential Building in Early Medieval Rome', in J. H. M. Smith (ed.), *Early Medieval Rome and the Christian West*, 101–12, Leiden: Brill.
van Doesburg, J. (2014), 'Middeleeuwsehuisplattegronden in West- en Midden-Nederland', in A. G. Lange, E. M. Theunissen, J. H. C. Deeben, J. van Doesburg, J. Bouwmeester and T. de Groot (eds.), *Huisplattegronden in Nederland: Archeologische Sporen van het Huis*, 342–66, Amersfoort: Barkhuis.
Vickery, A. (1993), 'Golden Age to Separate Spheres? A Review of the Categories and Chronology of English Women's History', *Historical Journal*, 36: 383–414.
Viitanen, E.-M. (2001), 'Longhouses and Log Cabins: Changing Building Traditions in the late Iron Age and Early Medieval Period (AD 800–1300)', in J. R. Brandt and L. Karlsson (eds.), *From Huts to Houses: Transformations of Ancient Societies*, 95–100, Stockholm: Paul Aströms Förlag.
Vodola, E. (1986), *Excommunication in the Middle Ages*, Berkeley: University of California Press.
Volmar, L. and W. H. Zimmermann, eds. (2012), *Glossary of Prehistoric and Historic Timber Buildings*, Rahden: Marie Leidorf.
Vossler, C. (2011), 'Religious Life in Public and Private', in M. Carver and J. Klápště (eds.), *The Archaeology of Medieval Europe: vol. 2: Twelfth to Sixteenth Centuries*, 412–27, Jutland: Aarhus University Press.
Waley, D. P. and T. Dean (2010), *The Italian City-Republics*, Abingdon: Routledge.
Ward, J. (1998), 'Townswomen and their Households', in R. Britnell (ed.), *Daily Life in the Late Middle Ages*, 27–42, Thrupp: Sutton Publishing.
Warner, L. (1999), 'Widows, Widowers, and the Problem of "Second Marriages" in Sixteenth-Century France', in S. Cavallo and L. Warner (eds.), *Widowhood in Medieval and Early Modern Europe*, 84–107, London: Routledge.
Webb, D. (2005), 'Domestic Space and Devotion in the Middle Ages', in A. Spicer and S. Hamilton (eds.), *Defining the Holy: Sacred Space in Medieval and Early Modern Europe*, 27–48, Aldershot: Ashgate.
Webb, D. (2002), *Medieval European Pilgrimage, c.700–c.1500*, New York: Palgrave Macmillan
Whittle, J. (2013), 'Rural Economies', in J. M. Bennet and R. M. Karras (eds.), *Oxford Handbook of Women and Gender in Medieval Europe*, 311–26, Oxford: Oxford University Press.
Wiesner, M. E. (1991), '"Wandervögels" and Women: Journeymen's Concepts of Masculinity in Early Modern Germany', *Journal of Social History*, 24 (4): 767–82.
Williams, C. S. (2014), *Hospitality and the Transatlantic Imagination, 1815–1835*, New York: Palgrave Macmillan.

Woolf, J. (2008), 'The Prohibition of Gentile Bread During the Ten Days of Repentance: On the Genesis and Significance of a Custom', in G. Bacon *et al.* (eds.), *Studies on the History of the Jews of Ashkenaz: Presented to Eric Zimmer*, 83–99, Ramat Gan.

Woolgar, C. M. (1999), *The Great Household in Late-Medieval England*, New Haven: Yale University Press.

Worby, S. (2010), *Law and Kinship in Thirteenth-Century England*, Woodbridge, Suffolk, UK: Boydell and Brewer.

Wray, S. K. (2004), 'Boccaccio and the Doctors: Medicine and Compassion in the Face of the Plague', *Journal of Medieval History*, 30: 301–22.

Wright, S. (2008), 'Broken Cups, Men's Wrath, and Neighbours' Revenge: The Case of Thomas and Alice Dey of Alverthorpe (1383)', *Canadian Journal of History*, 43: 241–51.

Wyley, S. F. (2005), http://www.geocities.ws/chestsandcaskets/catalogueofextantchestsandcaskets.html#Oseberg%20(Norway) (accessed 20 July 2016).

Zevin, S. J., ed. (1981), *Talmudic Encyclopedia*, Jerusalem: Yad Harav Herzog.

CONTRIBUTORS

Elisheva Baumgarten is the Yitzchak Becker Professor of Jewish Studies and teaches in the departments of History and Jewish History at the Hebrew University of Jerusalem. Her work focuses on the social history of the Jews of medieval northern Europe. She is the author of *Mothers and Children: Jewish Family Life in Medieval Europe* (Princeton, 2004) and *Practicing Piety in Medieval Ashkenaz: Men, Women and Everyday Religious Practice* (Philadelphia, 2014) and editor of a number of books, most recently *Entangled Histories: Knowledge, Authority and Jewish Culture in the Thirteenth Century* (Philadelphia, 2017) with Ruth Mazo Karras and Katelyn Mesler.

Tovah Bender is a senior instructor of history at Florida International University in Miami. Her research focuses on Renaissance-era Florence, issues of gender and the family, demographics and pedagogy. She has published in *The Journal of Women's History*, *The Journal of Family History* and *The Once and Future Classroom*.

Roisin Cossar is a professor of history at the University of Manitoba. Her research focuses on religious culture, domestic life, gender and archives on the Italian peninsula. She is the author most recently of *Clerical Households in Late Medieval Italy* (Harvard, 2017).

Jennifer Kolpacoff Deane is a professor of history at the University of Minnesota Morris. Her research focuses on medieval religious movements and communities, the intersections of domestic and sacred space, the emergence and application of the construct of heresy, and gender. Along with numerous articles she is the author of *A History of Medieval Heresy and Inquisition* (Rowman & Littlefield, 2011) and editor of *Labels and Libels: Naming Beguines in Northern Medieval Europe* with Letha Böhringer and Hildo van Engen (Brepols, 2014.)

Katherine L. French is the J. Frederick Hoffman Professor of Medieval History at the University of Michigan. She is the author of *The People of the Parish: Community Life in a Medieval English Diocese* (2001) and *The Good Women of the Parish: Gender and Religion after the Black Death* (2008) both from the University of Pennsylvania. They analysed the ways in which community identity and gender shape the religious practices of English peasants and townspeople in the 200 years between the Black Death (1348) and the Reformation. She has also co-authored with Allyson Poska the textbook *Women and Gender in the Western Past* (Houghton Mifflin, 2001) and is the author of more than 20 articles and book chapters. Her next book *Household Goods and Good Households in Late Medieval London: Domesticity and Consumption After the Plague* will be published by the University of Pennsylvania in 2021.

Mark Gardiner is a reader in heritage at the University of Lincoln. He previously worked at Queen's University Belfast, where he was joint Head of Archaeology-Palaeoecology, and at University College London as the deputy director of the archaeological field unit. He has run excavations on medieval buildings in England, Scotland, Ireland and Norway. His current research focuses on the adoption of stone as a building material in Europe and the interpretation of the excavated remains of medieval timber structures. He is Vice-President of the Royal Archaeological Institute and of Ruralia, the European body for medieval and later rural archaeology.

Tanya Stabler Miller is an associate professor of history at University of Loyola at Chicago. Her research focuses on lay religion, gender and urban culture, with special emphasis on northern France. She is the author of *The Beguines of Medieval Paris: Gender, Patronage, and Spiritual Authority* (Philadelphia, 2014), which explores the intersections between gender, spirituality, political power and urban life in medieval Paris.

Eva Svensson is a professor in the Department of Life and Environmental Sciences at Karlstad University, Sweden. Her main research interests include long-term social and ecological approaches to forested landscapes, rural medieval archaeology, household archaeology, and subaltern environments and lifescapes in the eighteenth to twentieth centuries. She is the author of *The Medieval Household: Daily Life in Castles and Farmsteads: Scandinavian Examples in their European Context* along with numerous articles and edited collections of essays in both Swedish and English.

INDEX

Abbey of Saint-Étienne 76
Abelard, Peter 37, 41
Abraham (Biblical figure) 140, 143–4
access analysis 23–4, 121–2, 124–5,
    126–30, 136
Adam of Bremen
    Gesta hammaburgensis 150
Adela of Normandy 79–80
Admont Abbey 77
agnus dei 167–8
agriculture 93–6, 131–2
Alberti, Leon Battista 15, 36
ale, *see* brewing
Alice of Briene 153
Alienor of Poitiers
    Les Honneurs de la Cour 85–6
Alighieri, Dante
    The Divine Comedy 159, 160–1
Alt-Wartburg, Switzerland 126
Ambrose, Saint 145–6, 166
amulets 167–9, 170–1, 178–80, 181
anchorites and anchoresses 14, 152–3
Ancrene Wisse 152–3
Anne, Saint 17–18
apprentices 2, 42, 46, 92, 103–4
    abuse of 45
    and affective bonds 19, 22, 35
    guild regulations regarding 100–1, 108
    in hierarchy of household 43–5,
        109–11, 112–13, 114

Arthurian literature 35, 150–1, 153,
    155–6, 157–8

Baixas, France 56–7
baking 93, 95, 97, 132, 176–7
balcony 26, 57
Baldric of Dor, Abbot 79–80
Ball, John 117
'Ballad of the Tyrannical Husband' 95
baptism 112, 169, 180, 183
Bayeux Tapestry 8, 11–12, 13, 22, 77,
    80
bedchamber 87–8
    and devotion 79–80, 166, 167,
        181–2
    as moral microcosm 27–8
    place in house 57, 58, 61–2
beds 52, 166, 172
    and childbirth 86–7
    and devotion 165–6, 167, 169, 172,
        181–2
    early medieval 78–80
    late medieval 81–2
    linens 28, 79–80, 86–8, 165, 180
    and status 78–80, 88, 165
    as symbol of marriage 28, 36, 86
beer, *see* brewing
Beere, England 56
beguines 47, 107–9, 113, 160
Belgium 56

Belo Zero, Russia 136
benches
    early medieval 52, 55, 58, 74–5, 77, 78
    late medieval 62, 81–2, 84
    and status 75, 77, 78
Benedictine Rule 16, 140, 146
Benedict of Nursia 16
Beowulf 8, 34, 39
    furniture and furnishings 74–5, 77, 78, 81
    hospitality 140, 142–3
Bergen 50, 64, 132, 135
Bezno, Czech Republic 52
birthing girdles 178–9
Black Death 21–2, 82, 96–7, 114, 170
Boccaccio, Giovanni
    Decameron 21–2, 158–9
Book of Courtesy 153
books 2, 8, 166, 171–4, 179
    Bibles 172
    Books of Hours 172
    Pentateuch 172
    Torah 181
Borg, Norway 55
Bourdieu, Pierre 6
bow–walled houses 55–6
Brescia, Italy 57
brewing 7, 92, 105, 157
    commercialization of 106–7
    in rural homes 93–4, 95
    in urban homes 97
Březno, Czech Republic 53
Brigid of Ireland, Saint 151
Bristol 25
buffets 82, 84–5
Bulgaria 51
butchering 97
The Butcher of Abbeville 157
buttery and pantry 27, 57
byre-houses 50, 55–6, 58, 77, 131, 133
Byštrec, Czech Republic 133

Caen Castle, France 72
candles 170, 181, 182
Canterbury 26
Carn Dubh, Scotland 58
cassoni 86
Castille 40
casting, *see* metalworking

Castle Acre, England 74
castles 1, 2, 5, 7, 165, *see also* Alt–Wartburg, Caen Castle, Castle Acre, Edsholm, Lelekovice, Saxholmen
    division of space 121, 122–30
    furniture and furnishings 72–4, 76, 80, 82, 88
    hospitality 150–1, 155–6
    as male-dominated spaces 4, 8–9, 121, 122–6, 130
Cathars 159–60, 172
Catherine of Siena 37, 151–2, 174
Celje, Slovenia 68
chairs 173
    early medieval 77–8
    late medieval 81
chambermaids 44, 113–14
chapel, anchorite 14
chapel, parish 164, 169, 177, 180–1, 183
chapel, private 72, 165–6
Charlemagne 7, 44, 148
Charles of Flanders 16
Château Cornillion, France 86
Chaucer, Geoffrey
    The Shipman's Tale 158
chests and coffers
    early medieval 75–6
    late medieval 82, 85–6
childbirth 3–4, 35, 86–7, 178–81
childcare 2–3, 95–6, 106, 114
    by servants or enslaved persons 5, 112, 114
children 13, 34–41, *see also* childbirth, childcare, *see also under* labour
    and affective bonds 19, 22, 23, 35–6, 39
    educated at home 17–18, 37, 104, 165
    in hierarchy of household 2, 15, 44, 88
    mortality 34–5
chivalry 150–1, 153, 155–6
Christ 164, 167
    calls people to leave home 12, 16–17
    and hospitality 144–6
    in Margery Kempe's visions 19–21, 37
Christina of Markyate 13, 14, 27–8
churching 181
circumcision 173, 181, 183
Clarendon Palace, England 84
Clark, Alice 106

cleaning and cleanliness 28, 82
    moral aspect of 5, 28–9, 166, 170, 177
    by servants or enslaved persons 111, 112
    as women's work 92, 94, 106, 114
clergy 33, 181
    in alternative households 15, 16, 45, 46
    as aristocratic 14, 26, 71–2, 78, 148–9
    and death 166, 182
    and hospitality 148–9, 157, 159–60
clothing 28–9, 45, 62, 177, *see also*
        laundresses, silk industry, spinning,
        textile industry
    and devotion 149, 165
    as luxury items 73, 80
    production of 93, 97
Cologne 105, 106, 167
Colshill, England 174
conduct literature 13, 26, 118, 130
courtyard 68, 132–3, 136, 170
    early medieval 51, 57
    late medieval 60–1
Coventry 25, 46, 172
coverture 15
cradles 88, 180, 181
Críth Gablach 148
Croatia 51
cubiculum, see bedchamber
Czech Republic 126–8, 133, 155

Dagobert 77
da Spoleto, Cherubino
    The Rule for Married Life 172
Datini, Margherita 13, 19, 20, 21, 22–3
death and dying 34–6, 181–2
Deer Park Farms, Ireland 58
Denmark 55–6, 58–9, 67, 82–3, 131
Deventer, Netherlands 66
devotional and ritual objects 166–71,
    181–2
Dhuoda 39, 40
dining and drinking ware 27
    and devotion 174–5
    early medieval 73–4
    late medieval 88–9
Domesday Book 33
domesticated animals 51, 59, 62, 84
    in byre-houses 55, 56, 58, 64, 68–9,
        131
    cattle 55, 68–9, 95, 120–1, 130, 131,
        133, 135
    fowl 95
    horses 125, 126
    sheep 95
domestic language 18–19
Dublin 58, 73
Duby, Georges
    A History of Private Life 3–4, 6
Dulcia of Worms 165
Durham 58

Edsholm, Sweden 123–6, 130
Edward the Confessor (king of England
    r. 1042–66) 77
Edward III of England 72
Edward IV of England 72, 73
Einhard 44
Eleanor of Provence 84
Eleazar b. Samuel of Mainz 177, 182
The Elder Edda 155, 157
Elizabeth of York 87
embroidery, *see* needlework
England 15, 43
    brewing 93, 106–7
    castles 122–3
    demographics 34, 41
    division of space within houses 26, 27,
        56, 58, 67, 75
    furniture and furnishings 82–3
    hospitality 153–4
    house types 24–5, 56, 58–9, 65, 66–7,
        68–9, 133
    marriage 36, 37, 40
    meaning of home 3, 18–19
    wills and inventories from 84, 86, 88,
        166, 167, 169, 174, 182
    words for house 14, 50
enslaved persons 22–3, 36, 112, 137
    abuse of 44–5, 112
Estonia 53
Eyrbyggjasaga 79
Eymerich, Nicholas 159

families 2, 31–41, *see also* children,
        foster-kinship, marriage, widows
        and widowers
    and care of the body 18, 36–7
    continued ties 15, 39–41
    lineage 34–5, 79, 86, 88
Faroe Islands 55, 64
Finland 53, 54–5, 62

Finnmark, Norway 64
Florence 34, 36, 42
    demographics 45–6
    furniture and furnishings 86
    marriage 37, 38, 39, 40, 86, 168
food and eating 4, 45, *see also* dining and drinking ware
    cooking 51, 81
    and familial bonds 36, 88
    fasting 151, 174, 175
    and hospitality 74, 153–4
    as religious practice 88, 144, 165, 174–7
    and status 88–9
foster-kinship 35–6
Fourth Lateran Council 159
France 131–2
    division of space within houses 50–1, 65–6
    furniture and furnishings 82–5
    hospitality 148
    house types 56–7, 65
    wills and inventories from 84, 86, 88
France, Marie de
    Lanval 151
Francis of Assisi 16–17
furniture and furnishings 52, *see also* beds, benches, buffets, *cassoni*, chairs, chests and coffers, cradles, dining and drinking ware, stools, tables, thrones
    built-in 76–7
    ceramics 71, 74, 82–3, 174
    mobility of 24–5, 72–3, 75–6, 78, 81
    textiles 71–5, 78, 79–82, 84–5, 86–8, 165–6, 167, 170
    wooden 73–4

Garlande, John de 81–2, 83
Gdańsk, Poland 62
Germany 165
    demographics 34
    division of space within houses 65, 68–9
    hospitality 149–50
    marriage 39–40
    wills and inventories from 177, 182
The Golden Legend, see de Voragine, Jacob
The Good Wife's Guide 8, 36, 42, 43–4, 82–3, 113–14
Granada 61
Gratian 88
    Decretum 149

Greece 51, 59–60, 132–3, 136
Greenland 55, 64, 77, 136
Gregory of Tours
    Histories of the Franks 34
Grosseteste, Robert (Bishop) 153
Guainerius, Anthonius 179
Gui, Bernard 159–60
guilds 4, 99–101, 104–5, 109, *see also* trade associations
    female membership in 29, 106–9
Gutenberg, Johannes 7

hall 131
    in castles 72, 123–5, 128
    early medieval 53–6, 58–9
    and hospitality 74–5, 142–3, 148
    late medieval 67, 68
    and status 25–6, 68, 74–5
hearth 131, 133, 135
    as definition of home 14–15, 36
    early medieval 56, 57, 58
    late medieval 62, 67, 81, 83
Heloise 2–3, 4, 5, 6, 35, 36, 41
Henry III of England 72, 84
heresy 16, 32, 40, 159–60, 163, 172
Hildegard of Bingen 38–9
Hollekreish 181
holy dolls 168
home
    and affective bonds 12, 19–23, 118
    and social order 13, 15–23, 26–30, 118–9
    women's authority within 17–18
homelessness
    as destabilizing 16
    as ideal 16–17
hospitality 5, 74–5, 130, 139–41, 150–4, 161–2, *see also* chivalry, pilgrims and pilgrimage
    and bad behavior 141–2, 154–61
    in chronicles 149–50
    comitatus 142–3
    in fabliaux 156–7
    in hagiography 151–3
    in household guides 153–4
    and Judaism 143–4
    and legal codes 148–9
    in romances 150–1
    scriptural ideals of 143–5, 149

houses, *see also* bow-walled houses, byre-houses, castles, log houses, pit houses, timber-framed houses, three-aisled houses
    building materials of 51, 55, 56–9, 62–9, 122
    medieval terms for 11, 13–15
    permanence of 5, 24–5
    as places of labour 1–2, 4, 12–14, 91–115, 131–2, 134–5
    as places of religious practice and instruction 5–6, 17–18, 163–83
    rural 5, 8, 93–7, 130–2, 133–5
    urban 1–2, 5, 8, 65–8, 97–104, 131–3, 135–6, 165
    as moral units 2, 3, 5–6, 15, 26–30, 86, 88–9, 139
houses, division of space within 25–6, 30, 68–9
    early medieval 52–3, 55–6, 58–9
    and gender 94, 122–3, 125, 129–37
    late medieval 62, 65–6
    and labour 94, 97–9, 114–15, 130–7
households 2, 41–8
    aristocratic 88–9, 123–30
    communal 47–8
    female-headed 47–9, 108–9
    hierarchy of relationships within 15–16, 24, 30, 31–3, 43–5, 48, 109–113
    size of 41–2
How the Goodwife Taught Her Daughter 37
Huis Malburg, Netherlands 133
Hundred Years' War 7
Hunsdon, England 180
Hvítarhold, Iceland 55

Iceland 16, 55, 64, 77, 131
Icelandic sagas 34, 35–6, 79
Ida of Louvain 151
inheritance 33, 40, 104–5, 119
inventories
    devotional objects 167, 169
    furniture and furnishings 73, 80, 84, 85, 86, 88
    and labour 105
    as a source 8, 13, 72, 163–4
Ireland 59, 65, 148
Isaac of Corbeil
    Sefer Mitzvot Katan 173–4

Isadore, Saint 166
Italy 26, 33, 104
    demographics 41
    house types 24, 57
    marriage 177–9
    servants 43
    wills and inventories from 166

Jacob b. Solomon the Physician
    Evel Rabbati 182
James the Apostle, Saint 17
John I of England 72
John the Baptist, Saint 167
John the Evangelist, Saint 167, 182
Joinville, Jean de 17
Jonah of Gerona
    Iggeret HaYir'ah 173
journeymen 101, 103, 109–11, 112
Julian, Saint 139, 152–3, 161, 162
Julitta, Saint 179

kastra 59–62, 133
Kempe, Margery 13, 17, 19–21, 27, 36–7, 174
Kiev 53
kings and kingship 1–2, 4, 75, 123, *see also* Arthurian literature, *Beowulf*
    division of space 24, 26, 72
    furniture and furnishings 77, 78, 80, 84, 86–7, 107
    and hospitality 5, 140, 142–3, 148, 149, 150–1, 152
    households 43, 72–3
kitchen 124
    early medieval 57
    late medieval 59, 62, 81, 82
    as public space 130, 135
Kranj, Slovenia 68
Kvívik, Faroe Islands 55

labour, *see also* baking, butchering, brewing, laundresses, metalworking, silk industry, spinning, textile industry
    children's 92, 96–7, 101, 104, 108
    enslaved 4, 5, 112
    gendered 4, 91–7, 103–11, 113–15, 119–121, 130–7
    and industrialization 91–2, 106–7, 113
    piecework 42, 92, 103–108

regional traditions 4, 92, 111, 112, 119–121, 130–7
regulation of 4, 101, 104–5, 111
lamps 69, 170
La Tour Landry, Geoffrey de
    The Book of the Knight in the Tower 117
latrine 57, 165
laundresses 28–9, 111, 113
Lawrence, Saint 167
legal codes 5, 7, 13, 16, 18
    and families 15, 28, 31–2, 36, 39–40, 88
    and hospitality 148–9
Leiden 105, 111
Lelekovice, Czech Republic 126–8
Leoba, Saint 151
literacy 171–2, 173
liturgy
    Christian 164, 170
    Jewish 165, 173
    liturgical calendar 101
Llanbedrgoch, Wales 58
log houses 50, 53, 62–4, 123, 133
Lollards 160, 172
London 1–2, 40, 45, 165
    furniture and furnishings 86, 88, 166, 167
    house types 67
    trades 106
    wills and inventories from 84, 86, 88, 166, 167, 169, 174, 180, 182
long-houses, *see* byre-houses
Louis IX of France 17
Low Countries 82–3, 85–6, 102
Lübeck, Germany 66
Lucca 57, 166
Lydgate, John 89
Lynn, England 36–7

Margaret, Saint 179
marriage 19–22, 23, 37–40, 142, 150–1,
    see also sexual relations, widows and widowers
    age at 38, 46, 92, 111
    and apprentices 112–13
    as basis of household 2, 43–4
    divorce 36, 88
    dowries 23, 37, 40, 179
    and guilds 103–7
    legal aspects 15, 28, 31

as ritual 177, 179
unmarried persons 23, 38–9, 46, 47, 92–3, 107–9, 111
Marseille 84, 166, 169
Martin of Tours, Saint 145
Mawgan Porth, England 56
Medici, Lorenzo de 39
Ménagier, see *The Good Wife's Guide*
mercers 108–9, 165
merchants 34, 92, 93, 97, 158, 172, 181–2,
    see also Datini, Margherita; guilds; mercers; trade associations
    and devotional objects 166
    furniture and furnishings 82–3, 87
    in guilds 100, 106
    houses of 1, 4, 65–6, 136
    mercantile honor 113–15
    in trade associations 8
Merveilles de Rigomer 157
metalworking 93, 123, 124, 126, 131–5
    goldsmithing 73
    silversmithing 73
mezuzot 170
Middleham Jewel 168
Milan 57
The Miller of Arleux 157
Minino, Russia 53
monks and monasticism 3, 5, 16–17, 28, 93, 146–7, 164, 172
Montaillou, France 31–3, 40, 119
Montpellier, France 15

Naples 57
needlework 26, 129
Netherlands 55–6, 59, 169
Norway 55, 68, 82, 131–2, 135
Novgorod, Russia 53, 64–5, 66
Novogrudok, Russia 53

Oakham, England 169
Oseberg, Norway 75
Oslo 64, 132, 135
Ostró Lednicki, Poland 53
Otto III, Holy Roman Emperor 78

Paris 36, 42, 47, 81–2
    beguines 107–9
    trades 98–9, 103–4, 107–9
patria potestas, see patriarch
patriarch 15, 31–2, 33–4, 36, 44–5, 48

pax bredes 167
Pergamon, Greece 59–60
Pfaffenschlag, Czech Republic 62–3
Philip I of France 77
pilgrims and pilgrimage 17, 148, 149, 152–3, *see also* Kempe, Margery
pilgrimage badges 166, 169
Pitcarmick, Scotland 58
pit houses 51–4, 59, 62, 68
plague, *see* Black Death
Poland 51, 62
"The Poor Cleric" 157
Prague 65
prayer beads 166, 169, 179–80, 182
prostitution 29, 47–8
Pskov, Russia 53
Pułtusk, Poland 62

Quiricus, Saint 179

Ralph of Caen
 Gesta Tancredi 155
Ravenna 57
Richard II of England 1–2
Roger II of Sicily 80
Rome 57, 66
rosaries, *see* prayer beads
round houses 58
Russia 53, 59, 62, 136

St Victor (village in France) 38
Saint-Georges-sur-l'Aa, France 56
Saint-Germain-des-Prés, France 34, 41
Salisbury, England 136
Saltés, Spain 60–1
Sarah (Biblical figure) 143–4
Sarvaly, Hungary 62
Savoy Palace, England 86
sawmills 73, 81
Saxholmen, Sweden 123–6, 129–130
Scotland 58
Serbia 51
servants 17, 28, 151, 152, *see also* chambermaids, laundresses
 abuse of 44–5, 111–12
 and affective bonds 19, 22–3, 32
 Christian servants in Jewish households 175
 and division of space within houses 24, 26, 30, 82, 88, 125
 in hierarchy of household 4, 41, 42–5, 92, 111–13, 123
 and life cycle 96–7, 111
Seven Works of Mercy 144, 167
sewing, *see* needlework
sexual assault 27–8, *see also under* servants
sexual relations 3, 4, 36, 47, 166, 174, 179
 adultery 13
Sicily 29, 61–2, 80
sideboards, *see* buffets
Sigtuna, Sweden 64
silk industry 7, 99, 106, 107–9
Simha of Vitry
 Mahzor Vitry 164
Škofja Loka, Slovenia 68
Skramle, Sweden 133–5
slavery 42, 112
smithing, *see* metalworking
Solomon b. Isaac 173
Spain
 furniture and furnishings 80, 85
 hospitality 148
 house types 57, 60–1
 slavery 42
 wills and inventories from 80, 85
spinning 92, 93, 94, 95, 107, 108, 182
 spindle whorls 129
stools
 early medieval 75, 78
 late medieval 81, 84
Strozzi, Alessandra 13, 20, 22, 26, 40
Sturlunga Saga 42
Sugar, Abbot 77
Svidna, Czech Republic 62
Sweden 66, 77, 112, 120, 123–4, 133–5
Switzerland 126
synagogues 164–5, 166, 173, 182, 183
Szentkirály, Hungary 62

tables 4, 62
 early medieval 78
 and hospitality 142, 144, 152, 153, 157
 late medieval 81–2, 84
 as symbol of family 36
textile industry 55, 101–4, 105, 129, 131–2, 134–6, *see also* needlework, silk industry, spinning, *see also under* furniture and furnishings
 horizontal loom 7, 97, 98, 101–2, 135
Thietmar of Merseburg 149

Thomas of Woodstock, duke of Gloucester 88
thrones 75, 77
three-aisled houses 50, 55–6, 58
timber-framed houses 65, 67
Tolmo de Minateda, Spain 57
Tournai 172
trade associations 8, 111, see also guilds
Trondheim, Norway 50, 64
Troyes, Chrétien de 157–8
   "Erec and Enide" 150–1, 153, 157
Tudor, Margaret 87

Ukraine 51

Valencia 23, 36, 37, 39, 44, 112
Venice 17, 19, 26, 28, 40, 166
Verona 24–5
Vienna 66
Vikings 7, 58, 78–80
Virgin Mary 17–18, 167, 171, 174, 181, 182
Voragine, Jacob de
   The Golden Legend 139

Waldensians 160
Wales 58, 68–9
Walo of Sarton 167
Warendorf, Germany 55

washerwomen, see laundresses
Westminster Palace 84
widows and widowers 14, 31, 35, 38, 40, 92–3, 111, see also Strozzi, Alessandra
   guild regulations concerning 103–5, 107
   as head of household 31, 47, 104–5
   living alone 46
William the Conqueror 72
wills 180
   books 172, 174
   devotional objects 166, 167, 169
   ethical wills 177, 182
   furniture and furnishings 174
   gifts to servants 32
   as a source 8, 33, 72, 163–4
window 76–7
   covered at a death 170, 182
   glazed 68, 69
   in home workshops 98–9
   as problematic space 26
work, see labour
Worms 173

Yeavering, England 75
York, England 112–13, 167

Zita of Lucca, Saint 151
Zwicker, Peter 159